Resilient Oracle PL/SQL
Building Resilient Database Solutions for
Continuous Operation

Stephen B. Morris

Beijing · Boston · Farnham · Sebastopol · Tokyo

Resilient Oracle PL/SQL

by Stephen B. Morris

Copyright © 2023 Omey Communications Limited. All rights reserved.

Published by O'Reilly Media, Inc., 1005 Gravenstein Highway North, Sebastopol, CA 95472.

O'Reilly books may be purchased for educational, business, or sales promotional use. Online editions are also available for most titles (*http://oreilly.com*). For more information, contact our corporate/institutional sales department: 800-998-9938 or *corporate@oreilly.com*.

Acquisitions Editor: Andy Kwan
Development Editor: Angela Rufino
Production Editor: Katherine Tozer
Copyeditor: Justin Billing
Proofreader: Audrey Doyle

Indexer: Ellen Troutman-Zaig
Interior Designer: David Futato
Cover Designer: Karen Montgomery
Illustrator: Kate Dullea

May 2023: First Edition

Revision History for the First Edition
2023-05-10: First Release

See *http://oreilly.com/catalog/errata.csp?isbn=9781098134112* for release details.

The O'Reilly logo is a registered trademark of O'Reilly Media, Inc. *Resilient Oracle PL/SQL*, the cover image, and related trade dress are trademarks of O'Reilly Media, Inc.

The views expressed in this work are those of the author and do not represent the publisher's views. While the publisher and the author have used good faith efforts to ensure that the information and instructions contained in this work are accurate, the publisher and the author disclaim all responsibility for errors or omissions, including without limitation responsibility for damages resulting from the use of or reliance on this work. Use of the information and instructions contained in this work is at your own risk. If any code samples or other technology this work contains or describes is subject to open source licenses or the intellectual property rights of others, it is your responsibility to ensure that your use thereof complies with such licenses and/or rights.

978-1-098-13411-2

[LSI]

Always and ever for Siobhán.

Table of Contents

Part III. Synthesis of the PL/SQL Toolbox and Feature-Driven Development

Preface

Relational databases remain one of the most successful technologies of all time. There have been numerous challenges to relational databases over the years. For example, object-oriented databases came along in the late 1990s and were anticipated to supplant the dominant relational model. Nearly a quarter century later, relational systems are in as strong a position as ever, and there are many reasons for this continued success.

Also among the more recent newcomers are the NoSQL products, such as MongoDB. However, for a variety of reasons, relational databases continue to hold their prominent position in the IT landscape.

A solid knowledge of relational databases, such as those from Oracle, IBM, Microsoft, and others, remains a good addition to the IT skill set. The same is true for the open source relational databases, such as MySQL. Pretty much every developer job I've done has required at least some knowledge of SQL. Some jobs have also required knowledge of stored procedure languages, such as PL/SQL.

As you'll see in the book, there is often a great deal of confusion about the role of SQL and PL/SQL in the context of high-level languages, such as Java, C#, JavaScript, and so on. I discuss some of the more common antipatterns that can arise in these multi-language domains.

For a variety of reasons, there is often a strong motivation for adopting solutions based exclusively on embedded SQL and object relational mapping solutions rather than using PL/SQL. This may, in turn, result in the inadvertent use of antipatterns and consequently brittle code.

I look closely at Oracle PL/SQL with a view to helping lay the foundations for creating resilient database solutions. The need for resilient systems has never been greater in our increasingly data-driven and data-centric world.

Who This Book Is For

If you're interested in learning something about databases and PL/SQL, this book is a good place to start. It takes a first-principles approach, so not much foundational knowledge is required. The focus is on a good practice in PL/SQL, and the use of requirements analysis and metrics should be helpful to readers of all technical levels.

One particular audience that would find the book useful is employees of organizations that use a mix of languages, such as Java, JavaScript, C#, and so on. Often, such organizations also use one or more database technologies including PL/SQL. While their systems run PL/SQL every day, the developers may not use PL/SQL exclusively. In other words, PL/SQL is not the main development language.

Because the developers use PL/SQL on an infrequent basis, they may not employ optimal solutions in terms of language constructs and abstractions. The results are often disappointing and far from resilient. This can also add to growing DevOps costs with little hope of improvement. The latter may even be exacerbated with the advent of autonomous technology inside Oracle products. In other words, the move by Oracle toward autonomous mechanisms may have the unwelcome effect of placing a spotlight on poorly crafted database solutions.

I believe this book has much to offer people who are looking at PL/SQL for the first time as well as experienced PL/SQL developers. In addition to batch-style PL/SQL solutions, I also look at the knotty area of calling PL/SQL from within Java.

Requirements Orientation

Throughout the book, I try to formulate simple, broad design and coding requirements. These requirements are articulated in advance of diving into the details of implementation, which provides a blueprint for the code that follows and is a good general practice in terms of guiding the coding procedure.

Articulating good requirements is a powerful skill in software development in general and this helps with programming in any language, not just PL/SQL. As I've often stated in the past in my writing, requirements analysis and design are a necessary prerequisite to solid coding. It is an old adage that the sooner you start to code, the longer your project will take. This is as true in 2023 as it was in the old days.

Some of the requirements orientation adopted in these pages can be considered to be in the style of nonfunctional requirements. That is, the requirements are not specific to a given business problem or feature change. Rather, the resilience requirements described here are a guide to creating a solution that is resilient overall.

Toward Strategic Coding

Over the course of many years of IT work in numerous industries, it's my opinion that the bulk of modern coding tends to be tactical in nature. Many organizations have feature requirement lists that are so long they are effectively unachievable. This is quite a serious threat to the underlying business, which needs these new or modified features to fulfill its work.

A coding approach that resembles firefighting can easily become the norm, particularly where a weak process exists. This type of model is rarely sustainable and may even contribute to excessive developer turnover, which may in turn exacerbate the problem.

Adopting a more requirements-driven mindset can allow for a more strategic approach to coding. In the PL/SQL code examples, I aim to illustrate this mode of working. A key aspect of strategic coding is embracing certain nonfunctional requirements. As we'll see, examples of strategic coding include coding for observability and modifiability. Beyond these needs, the strategic coding style embraces simplicity, modularity, and other attributes.

Why is code simplicity important? To answer this question, one need look no further than the average codebase. Most codebases now incorporate at least one mainstream framework. I first started using frameworks such as Spring around 2007 and I was struck by the complexity. It's just my opinion, but I believe this framework eventually became so complex that it had to be substantially reworked as part of Spring Boot (which I've also used). However, Spring Boot attempts to hide much of the old Spring complexity. I've worked on Spring Boot projects where integration required debugging into the framework itself. This does not lend itself to simple coding and often involves a group of developers working together to try a variety of options to get the code to work. Simple, it is not.

As part of a strategic PL/SQL coding style, Parts II and III describe feature-driven development used as a means of modeling a macroscopic view of system capability. I believe that feature-driven development provides a way of getting underway with resilient coding.

Resilient Software Is a Journey, Not a Destination

Every new requirement and the associated code has an impact on the resiliency of the overall solution. It's difficult to simply request resilient software. We can't just say "Please ensure that this new feature is resilient." Why not? Well, we don't yet know what resilience is and how it applies to our code.

To begin to tackle these complex issues, the book starts by carefully describing what resilience is about. Even the largest trillion-dollar organizations are struggling to produce resilient code. The difficulty is that resilience is generally judged by the degree of success of the interaction of multiple systems of software during periods of stress on those systems. So, system X may be resilient, but if system Y is not resilient, then it's likely that the overall system $(X + Y)$ will not be resilient.

Disaster recovery cycle times for large corporate entities can now (in 2023) be in the range of 45 minutes or less. That's not a whole lot of time to get your code back up and running even in a depleted or impaired state where upstream or downstream systems are temporarily unavailable.

To ameliorate this difficulty in defining resilience, I introduce a scale of resilience. This is a simple set of rules that can be used to inform the design and coding effort. We aim to eliminate these five common antipatterns:

- Complexity
- Brittle code
- Future code maintenance cost
- Poor performance
- Poor separation of concerns

That sounds like an extravagant claim! How do we tackle these antipatterns? To do this, we need some sort of scale of resilience:

1. Ability to capture all errors and exceptions
2. Recoverability
3. Observability
4. Modifiability
5. Modularity
6. Simplicity
7. Coding conventions
8. Reusability
9. Repeatable testing
10. Avoiding common antipatterns
11. Schema evolution

So, what's in a scale of resilience?

A Scale of Resilience

I introduce a scale for numerically designating the resilience of a database solution. While being purely empirical, such a scale illustrates the difference between brittle use of PL/SQL and a more resilient approach. By improving the score for a given block of PL/SQL, the code becomes more resilient. Using the scale in an iterative fashion can help you to arrive at a powerful approach to PL/SQL refactoring.

There are other reasons for trying to make your PL/SQL solutions more resilient. For example, Oracle is increasingly introducing additional technology in order to improve the underlying resilience of its products. Examples of such resilience include (among others):

- Self-healing elements
- Autonomous database technology
- Avoiding oversubscription in CPU, network, and memory use

By embracing resilience in your PL/SQL work, you are to some extent keeping up to date with Oracle's efforts in this area. This makes your code a better citizen in systems built using these Oracle products. Your resilient code will sit more comfortably in the increasingly resilient Oracle ecosystem.

Resilient Solutions and Disaster Recovery

In our increasingly interconnected world, IT disasters are an unfortunate fact of life. Outages are commonplace. One aspect of the quality of an organization's IT is the speed with which it recovers from a disaster. An example is a data center going offline for some reason, which can cause significant loss of service to an organization. This is the macroscopic level of resilience.

Large organizations stand to lose a lot from outages. These can be financial losses and/or reputational losses. In either case, many such organizations will have disaster recovery targets, such as x minutes of allowed downtime per year. Even for very large organizations, the value of x can be surprisingly low. During a disaster recovery, getting code back up and running quickly is highly important. It's important to realize that you don't want your code negatively affecting the value of x.

For example, if your code fails to run after an outage resolution, it could be crucial to have adequate source code logging in place in order to track down the issue. This is especially so for the case when the problem is in a dependent downstream or upstream system which is outside of your direct control. If your logging provides a solid clue to the root cause of an issue, then it is entirely possible that your colleagues will thank you for this information during an outage remediation.

Every line of code can contribute positively or negatively to the overall resilience of an organization. This is the microscopic level of resilience. While this is a vast area and worthy of a book in its own right, I will look in depth at the topic of writing resilient PL/SQL and its importance in helping the overall organization produce resilient solutions.

A Diagram-Driven Narrative

I'm a strong believer in the power of diagrams as a means to clearly describe ideas and code workflows. The book leans heavily on screenshots in order to illustrate the real workings of the code described. I hope that this narrative style helps readers.

Conventions Used in This Book

The following typographical conventions are used in this book:

Italic
> Indicates new terms, URLs, email addresses, filenames, and file extensions.

`Constant width`
> Used for program listings, as well as within paragraphs to refer to program elements such as variable or function names, databases, data types, environment variables, statements, and keywords.

`Constant width bold`
> Shows commands or other text that should be typed literally by the user.

`<Constant width between brackets>`
> Shows text that should be replaced with user-supplied values or by values determined by context.

This element signifies a tip or suggestion.

This element signifies a general note.

This element indicates a warning or caution.

Using Code Examples

Supplemental material (code examples, exercises, etc.) is available for download at *https://github.com/stephenbjm/plsql-resilience*.

If you have a technical question or a problem using the code examples, please send email to *support@oreilly.com*.

This book is here to help you get your job done. In general, if example code is offered with this book, you may use it in your programs and documentation. You do not need to contact us for permission unless you're reproducing a significant portion of the code. For example, writing a program that uses several chunks of code from this book does not require permission. Selling or distributing examples from O'Reilly books does require permission. Answering a question by citing this book and quoting example code does not require permission. Incorporating a significant amount of example code from this book into your product's documentation does require permission.

We appreciate, but generally do not require, attribution. An attribution usually includes the title, author, publisher, and ISBN. For example: *"Resilient Oracle PL/SQL* by Stephen B. Morris (O'Reilly). Copyright 2023 Omey Communications Limited, 978-1-098-13411-2."

If you feel your use of code examples falls outside fair use or the permission given above, feel free to contact us at *permissions@oreilly.com*.

Legal Notices

All screenshots from Oracle products (SQL Developer, etc.) are subject to the following notice from Oracle: Copyright © Oracle and its affiliates. Used with permission. The SQL scripts used in Part III are derived from content on GitHub at *https://github.com/oracle-samples/db-sample-schemas* and are subject to the following notice from Oracle: Copyright © 2019 Oracle.

Screenshots from IntelliJ IDEA are subject to the following: Copyright © 2022 Jet-Brains s.r.o., used with permission. JetBrains IntelliJ IDEA and the IDEA logo are registered trademarks of JetBrains s.r.o.

O'Reilly Online Learning

O'REILLY® For more than 40 years, *O'Reilly Media* has provided technology and business training, knowledge, and insight to help companies succeed.

Our unique network of experts and innovators share their knowledge and expertise through books, articles, and our online learning platform. O'Reilly's online learning platform gives you on-demand access to live training courses, in-depth learning paths, interactive coding environments, and a vast collection of text and video from O'Reilly and 200+ other publishers. For more information, visit *https://oreilly.com*.

How to Contact Us

Please address comments and questions concerning this book to the publisher:

O'Reilly Media, Inc.
1005 Gravenstein Highway North
Sebastopol, CA 95472
800-889-8969 (in the United States or Canada)
707-829-7019 (international or local)
707-829-0104 (fax)
support@oreilly.com
https://www.oreilly.com/about/contact.html

We have a web page for this book, where we list errata, examples, and any additional information. You can access this page at *https://oreil.ly/resilient-oracle-pl-sql*.

For news and information about our books and courses, visit *https://oreilly.com*.

Find us on LinkedIn: *https://linkedin.com/company/oreilly-media*.

Follow us on Twitter: *https://twitter.com/oreillymedia*.

Watch us on YouTube: *https://youtube.com/oreillymedia*.

Acknowledgments

My editor, Corbin Collins, guided this project and helped me with advice on a multitude of thorny issues, such as the different handling of links between the print and electronic versions of the book. Thanks Corbin!

In the production phase, I had the pleasure of working with Kristen Brown, Katherine Tozer, and Catherine Dullea. Katie and Kate knocked my diagrams into shape with a combination of pragmatic creativity and good judgment. I learned a lot about image resolution and print size during this time! Thanks Kristen, Katie, and Kate.

I'd also like to say a big thank-you to Karen Montgomery for the beautiful front cover illustration.

Andy Kwan was my first contact with O'Reilly and has believed in this book since the very beginning.

Thanks are due particularly to Patrick Barel, who provided in-depth technical reviews for each chapter. Patrick pointed out some important coding errors and numerous technical issues. Thanks for sharing your knowledge and experience, Patrick. Michael McLaughlin (designated Oracle Ace Pro) also provided useful technical feedback. Thanks, Michael, for your reflections on the SQL Developer treatment and on the feature descriptions. Last but not least on the technical review team, I'd like to say thanks to Sayan Malakshinov. Sayan provided excellent (and very rapid) feedback and many useful additions to the book.

I'd like to express my gratitude to Mark Schreier and his team in the Oracle Trademark & Copyright Legal Group for permission to use Oracle-owned screenshots. The process of granting permission was lightning fast. Thanks are also due to Travis Anderson of the Oracle Global Communications group who put me in touch with Mark's team.

The magic of the web enabled me to make contact with Ben Brumm at the commencement of writing Part III of the book. Ben kindly gave me permission to use his excellent SQL scripts for installing the Oracle HR schema.

PART I

Creating a PL/SQL Toolbox

CHAPTER 1

Resilient Software and PL/SQL

Writing resilient code has never been more important. As of early 2023, most organizations that use substantial amounts of code and IT infrastructure are facing the ongoing need to do some or all of the following:

- Add new features.
- Fix bugs in existing features.
- Keep up to date with regulatory changes.
- Add new channels, such as mobile platforms.
- Migrate existing systems to use more modern tools, languages, and/or platforms.
- Adopt microservices.
- Improve security.
- Migrate to the cloud.
- Reduce DevOps costs.

Even organizations that only use code—without originating it—also face most of these issues. This includes businesses that use a lot of third-party IT products and infrastructure. One key difficulty for this type of organization appears when new requirements materialize, such as a third-party security update. Imagine the extent of the difficulties if a third-party payment gateway mandates a security update. This is not to mention the need for new business features in existing products and services. Other drivers of change can include regulatory updates, other service provider updates, and so on. IT is not getting easier and, unlike wine, it tends not to improve with age.

Regulatory change can be quite a challenge. For example, adding money laundering checks to ecommerce workflows can involve the insertion of callouts to multiple third-party providers even before fulfilling orders. Another part of this type of change relates to the need for insisting on specific customer data, such as a physical address, credit card owner details where the card is registered in the name of the purchaser, and so on. Falling foul of money laundering regulations can result in heavy fines.

Data protection is another area that requires vigilance. An example is the case of a dentist with a given customer who moves away. The customer then ceases to be a patient of the dentist. How long can the dentist hold the records for the now ex-patient? Well, in European countries, there are specific rules governing how long such records can be retained.

It's something of a cliché to say that the one thing modern enterprises can rely on is the need for constant change. However, it's not all doom and gloom. The adoption of resilient techniques can help improve the level of confidence that organizations have in their IT solutions.

It should be noted that resilience doesn't come about by accident or by just incorporating some new programming language or framework. One organizational aspect that appears to impede resilient solutions is that of excessive hierarchy. Imposing hard boundaries between development teams is, in my experience, inimical to the needs of resilience. Such boundaries may tend to diminish the close cooperation that is such a key part of achieving resilient development.

Resilience is a byproduct of a more considered approach to software development, doing things such as openly discussing algorithms, casual testing, anticipating exceptions, sharing knowledge, and so on. But I'm getting ahead of myself! Let's back up a little and look at the aims of this introductory chapter.

After reading this chapter, you should be able to do the following:

- Broadly understand what "resilient software" means.
- Understand the requirements for resilience: *what* versus *how*.
- Understand why PL/SQL is a good idea.
- Appreciate why using SQL for business logic is generally a bad idea.
- Know some of the disadvantages of PL/SQL.
- Gain a basic understanding of PL/SQL.
- Read existing or legacy PL/SQL code.
- Understand the need for a PL/SQL learning and development environment.
- Understand a basic scale of resilience.

Let's briefly look at what resilient software is about.

Resilient Software

The dictionary definition of resilience tends to reflect the ability of a software system to operate under stress or to absorb the impact of a problem. Maintaining stability and failing gracefully are other attributes of resilience where an acceptable service level continues to be offered to the business even when problems occur.

It should also be possible to know the state of the resilient system, e.g., what is the state—consistent or otherwise—if a long batch job fails halfway through? Having reliable information about the consistency then allows us to answer questions such as whether we should restart the batch job from the beginning or whether we should pick it up where we left off. An important part of resilience is knowing the state of play, i.e., knowing the level of progress of jobs and workflows. Additionally, if failures occur, you can find out how to get back up and running, or better yet, the software automatically restarts itself.

In a nutshell, resilient software is composed of rock-solid code that runs forever (i.e., decades). Such code is very difficult to write because it has to cope with all sorts of business requirement changes, unforeseen error conditions, and potentially unexpected input data. Add to this the need for ongoing updates in the form of security fixes and new features. Finally, don't forget that the runtime platform itself may come under strain as the workflows evolve. It takes a lot of effort to produce resilient code.

Another aspect of resilience is the need for new and legacy code to coexist in harmony. This is one of the great challenges of integration: it is essential that new code does not undermine systems and workflows that have run smoothly for many years.

Examples of Resilient Systems

Operating systems such as Linux, Windows, macOS, and so on are examples of systems that must be resilient. Much research and development effort in recent years has gone into making these operating systems more resilient than they used to be. The following are recent resilience improvements in operating systems:

- Carefully managing the transition from operating system user mode into kernel mode and vice versa
- Memory protection
- Process isolation
- Adding programming abstractions that facilitate these improvements

As you'll see later, resilient code goes to great lengths to protect both itself and the runtime environment. This is typically achieved by making judicious use of language abstractions and other constructs.

Requirements for Resilience: What Versus How

I should note that even the world's greatest developer will occasionally write code with bugs. Regarding bugs, PL/SQL is no different from any other programming language. In later chapters, I'll look more closely at ways to structure PL/SQL to allow for a more resilient end result.

In the meantime, let's establish some guiding principles or requirements. The merit of this approach is that it separates the *what* from the *how*. In other words, I will merely state *what* it is I want to achieve (i.e., resilient code) without making any demands on *how* that will occur in the implementation phase.

Differentiating between *what* and *how* helps avoid one of the most destructive of all modern software development habits: coding too soon. If you focus too much or too early on the *how*, then you miss out on an opportunity to elucidate exactly *what* you want the solution to achieve. By thinking about the *what* in this fashion, you can avoid complexity in the final offering.

Later in this chapter, you'll see an example of an antipattern—the big block of SQL. We can replace the big block of SQL with a modular and more powerful block of PL/SQL.

Clearly separating the *what* from the *how* also lays the groundwork for future additions to code. This is because you have invested effort up front in articulating *what* it is you wish to achieve with the solution. Only then is the solution coded as part of the *how* stage of development.

To set the scene for what I'll look at, the following are some broad coding requirements that can be useful in achieving resilience:

1. Ability to capture all errors and exceptions
2. Recoverability
3. Observability
4. Modifiability
5. Modularity
6. Simplicity
7. Coding conventions
8. Reusability
9. Repeatable testing
10. Avoiding common antipatterns
11. Schema evolution

Do these 11 requirements just sound like commonsense programming practice? That's exactly what they are, but they will provide a kind of mental framework for achieving resilience. We'll revisit these requirements in detail later and illustrate them with concrete PL/SQL code examples.

Process Versus Outcome

Developers (myself included) traditionally have a turbulent relationship with process issues. For example, few developers tend to actively prefer documentation to coding. Many of us see API creation as coding rather than as a form of design. Deep end-to-end testing can often appear to be a bit of a chore. Programmers like to program.

All of these process activities are, of course, pretty much driven by requirements definition, which is another process task that many developers may generally prefer to leave to others, such as business user groups.

For creating resilient solutions, it is preferable for developers to adopt a more holistic approach. In other words, developers should aim to acquire strong credentials across the process spectrum. This is not as difficult as it sounds. Developers can become excellent at defining or refining requirements because they have intimate knowledge of the workings of the code. Even better, the developer can structure code to facilitate future requirements even before such requirements have been articulated. These ideas will be further discussed in Chapter 5, where I cover feature-driven development.

Just like learning PL/SQL, it's not an onerous task to get better at process stuff. We'll see in later chapters that if you become an ace integration tester, you will often save yourself from having to revisit and repair code many months after having written it. Over time, it's not uncommon to completely forget how a given block of code works. You'll thank your younger self later for having had the foresight to write a test case (you'll see this in Chapter 4) or even just a short wiki article. The test case is often invaluable because it directly verifies whether the code being tested works correctly. A failing test can be just as useful as a successful one because a failing test may indicate that the code is being called incorrectly or that some key design assumption is not being met.

The main point here is that skillful adherence to and use of process can materially improve outcomes. The development process is your friend; it is wise to treat it well.

Let's dive into the motivation for learning and aiming to write resilient PL/SQL.

Motivation for Using PL/SQL: Don't Cut a Pizza with a Wrench

I'm a big fan of stored procedures in general and PL/SQL in particular. Stored procedure technology provides many advantages over trying to implement complex database logic in application development languages such as Java, C#, JavaScript, and so on. I'll discuss this later, but for now, just note that it's not uncommon to see developers trying to shoehorn complex database logic into high-level languages.

The type of database logic I'm referring to here is where high-level code makes a large number of table-level changes across numerous databases, such as in a large batch job. The performance of this hybrid approach may be poor because it necessitates translation between the high-level language and the database environment. Worse yet is the issue of data consistency that can arise if a batch job only partially succeeds.

There may also be issues concerning excessive database locks, which can affect other users of the database (or databases). This is not to say that the hybrid approach is always bad. The point is that there are cases where the mix of high-level languages and complex database operations may result in a solution that is not resilient.

Perhaps even worse than this is the practice of using raw SQL (in high-level code) as a place for business logic. Using SQL in this way potentially misses the opportunity to incorporate the many useful PL/SQL abstractions and can result in brittle solutions. It's a bad idea to try to cut a pizza with a wrench. It's not that the wrench won't cut the pizza; it's just not going to lead to a good end result.

Before looking a little at some of the disadvantages of these high-level language approaches, I should note that I do also like object relational mapping (ORM) technology (such as Hibernate). I've used ORM in Java and C# (and even in Python) and I've written about it extensively over the years. ORM allows for a smooth experience of database technology in languages such as Java and C#. However, there are many cases where a PL/SQL solution may simply be a better option, particularly when we want to achieve resilient solutions.

PL/SQL code runs natively in the Oracle Database inside a dedicated runtime engine. This makes PL/SQL code a first-class citizen in the Oracle Database ecosystem. In other words, there is no need to translate from a Java (or other high-level language) layer into the database dialect. PL/SQL is itself a native Oracle Database technology, which means that it is optimized for this use and is tightly coupled with the database platform.

Another reason for favoring PL/SQL is security: the code runs inside the database. This reduces the likelihood of vulnerabilities such as leaking important data into Java logfiles. Other advantages of PL/SQL include speed and efficiency. As noted previously, with PL/SQL there is no intermediate high-level language technology layer. This is one reason why PL/SQL solutions will often substantially outperform an equivalent effort in Java or C#. The Oracle Database also works hard to optimize PL/SQL code. There are many benefits to using PL/SQL.

With a view to being as balanced as possible, is it hard to learn another method (other than PL/SQL), such as Java ORM?

Learning Java ORM

One of the reference books I used when I was learning about ORM about 10 years ago is over 800 pages long. It's the seminal reference *Java Persistence with Hibernate* by Christian Bauer and Gavin King (Manning, 2007). It's a really great book, filled with expert knowledge and lots of code examples, but it takes a great deal of energy and commitment to complete.

Nowadays, a lot of the effort in getting to grips with ORM is handled by development tools, frameworks, and programming language features and supports such as Java annotations. Getting started with this enterprise-critical technology is less work than it used to be, but it's definitely not a trivial task.

Java-based ORM technology, such as Hibernate and Java Persistence API (JPA), necessarily aim at database portability and interoperability with a wide range of Java tools and technologies. This is a key difference between them and PL/SQL solutions. PL/SQL only has to work with Oracle products, which allows for a smaller footprint and an easier learning experience. Because PL/SQL is owned by Oracle, it is carefully managed across the different versions of the Oracle Database products.

Complex Data-Centric Workflows

Concerning the use of Java/C# ORM technologies, the main antipattern I'd avoid is using high-level languages to directly orchestrate complex data-driven workflows. In other words, the high-level language interacts with database objects. There's no technical reason to avoid this, but it may result in poorer performance than a hybrid approach with both high-level language(s) and PL/SQL. An example of this is a large, multidatabase, nightly batch job where data is extracted from a wide range of tables, views, and ancillary systems (such as data warehouses).

There may instead be a strong combined business and technical case for doing the bulk of this type of work in a language such as PL/SQL. Why? One reason is that a PL/SQL solution can be considered to provide good separation of concerns. This is because all of the database work is handled in code that is close to (i.e., resides within) the database. It shouldn't come as a surprise that Oracle Databases provide excellent support for PL/SQL. For example, scheduled jobs can be configured to run in isolation from other systems. Using these facilities in the database avoids the need to implement handcrafted, potentially fragile, high-level language alternatives.

Using PL/SQL skillfully can increase resilience because the heavy lifting is left inside the database. To summarize, the disadvantages of implementing extremely complex data processing batch jobs exclusively in high-level languages are:

- Complexity
- Brittle code

- Future code maintenance cost

- Poor performance

- Poor separation of concerns

- The fact that some high-level frameworks make use of database version–specific features

While most of these points are self-evident, the last one merits a mention. I've seen one case of a high-level language object mapping framework where it was only possible to get the database-centric application code to work by making use of a database driver version–specific feature.

At the time, it occurred to me that, aside from the unnecessary complexity and integration effort, the finished code was then tied to that particular version of the database driver. A change to the latter (e.g., for security reasons) might then result in breaking the application code. Mixing database infrastructure and logic in application code is not without its risks.

 The rationale for using a high-level language technology ORM product might even be more political than technical. If the database business logic resides solely inside Java code, then there may be no need to communicate with the database administrators (DBAs). For security reasons, communication might still be required, though, when deploying stored procedure code to the database.

I've seen a case like this where a developer didn't want to have to deal with DBAs and opted instead for a high-level language persistence layer solution. This approach was risky because it was not clear at the time of implementation if the solution would meet the organizational performance requirements. It is better to aim to deliver the best solution for the organization and not make technical decisions that are based on political considerations.

So, what are some of the advantages of using languages like PL/SQL? Here are a few:

- Keeping database logic in the database

- Security: PL/SQL code resides inside the database

- Performance

- Better management of database exceptions

- Better management of database business logic errors

- Encapsulation of business logic

- Reuse (e.g., PL/SQL procedures, functions, and packages)

- Separation of concerns
- Easy access to programming abstractions

I'll go through these key points in the later sections and chapters. They're just introduced here to set the context for the discussion. However, I do want to emphasize that the first point about keeping database logic inside the database is extremely important and is often overlooked.

Let's now look at why SQL is not a good choice for business logic. It's also a little like trying to cut a pizza with a wrench.

Using SQL for Complex Business Logic Is a Bad Idea

With correct use of PL/SQL, you avoid mixing your application code with SQL. This also helps you to keep away from the knotty area of trying to express complex business logic in SQL scripts. SQL is not nearly as strong as PL/SQL in the area of error/exception handling. A small incoming data change can easily cause a SQL script to suddenly fail with little or no indication of the cause.

The use of SQL for business logic can produce extremely brittle solutions. I think it's fair to view the use of SQL for business logic as something of an antipattern.

An example of this type of SQL is a multistep SQL script that attempts to merge data from a number of sources, while at the same time executing one or more complex joins and updates on other tables. This type of SQL construct can tend to grow over time as additions are made to accommodate new features and data changes. The end result can be unnecessary complexity.

As the SQL script grows over time, so too does the tendency for it to fail when, for example, someone attempts to insert rows into a table with the same primary key. This type of failed insertion may cause the whole SQL block to fail unexpectedly. In many cases, the failure is not noticed or even logged in the overall workflow.

PL/SQL helps avoid the antipattern by facilitating modular, procedural code that includes powerful exception handling.

A Cautionary Tale

I once saw a case where a large block of SQL was failing in a daily batch system (see Figure 1-1). The batch job was responsible for merging sales data from a range of source tables and views across a number of databases and other source systems. The end result was a report that was generated for use by a downstream finance team. The SQL was rather badly designed in that it was written to not expect any errors to occur.

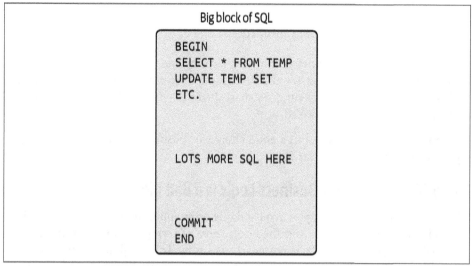

Figure 1-1. An antipattern: big block of SQL with business logic and no error handling

Notice, at the top of Figure 1-1, the insertion of a PL/SQL BEGIN statement and a corresponding END with a COMMIT. In this context, the use of PL/SQL is just a mechanism for running the contained SQL script. I'll look more closely at this as we explore the later examples, but the point is that while the example uses PL/SQL, it doesn't really take advantage of the many benefits of the language. The intention was good but the execution left a lot to be desired.

All of the code between the BEGIN and END was just plain SQL with no error or exception handling at all. Having so many inserts, updates, deletes, and joins is really an accident just waiting to happen. Initially, the developers were delighted that their code was experiencing no errors. One could even see a little of the Dunning–Kruger effect (*https://oreil.ly/RpMQB*) as they began to tempt fate by saying things like "This PL/SQL stuff is pretty simple, just add a BEGIN, COMMIT, and END and you're good to go." The only problem was that the PL/SQL code was initially running successfully each night, i.e., no inconvenient errors. This initial success would prove to be short-lived.

Over time, with new incoming data and minor modifications to the script, the overly complex SQL block failed because of an attempted duplicate key insertion. This is a common enough error condition and one that it is prudent to prepare for in your PL/SQL code. As you'll see in later chapters, it's easy enough to add this type of error handling. But in the present case, once the SQL block failed, then the whole block was automatically rolled back. Sadly, the log table update was also part of the main transaction, so it too was rolled back. The difficulty with this technique is that any clues about the source of the error are also rolled back into oblivion. This would result in a great deal of developer angst.

The overall effect was that, after the first time the error appeared, it looked like one of the following had occurred:

- The job didn't run at all.
- The job succeeded with no errors or data.
- The job was rolled back.

It was hard to know which of these had happened. It's a classic integration scenario where there is insufficient logging detail (and business workflow knowledge) to assist with any attempt at diagnosing the problem.

The job then continued to fail each night for a full week, and the issue only came to light when the downstream team began wondering why there were no sales figures for that week. In the week in question, many sales had been made and bonuses were due, but this was not known by the development team. The developers were still laboring under the misapprehension that no error had in fact occurred. After a few more days of no finance report data, the matter was escalated and it then became a development priority.

It was then quite embarrassing for the developers, who had to work late to attempt to manually cobble together the required report data. As they did not understand the business-specific data constraints and rules, this manual override approach then resulted in handcrafted changes to table data and even more errors in the final results. Worse still, some of the upstream data had changed by this time and the results were an erroneous mixture of old and new data.

Needless to say, the finance team was not impressed. Then, another downstream team from the finance group started asking for their consolidated data. It's not hard to see that tempers then started to fray, emails started to fly, and the whole sorry affair deteriorated into a blame game. All because of some poorly crafted PL/SQL and SQL script.

This type of antipattern and the resultant panicky responses to user-reported errors does tend to undermine the faith that the end users have in the overall process. It can also undermine the confidence of the developers. This is a tough road for developers trying to produce resilient solutions and it's entirely avoidable. In Part III, starting in Chapter 7, I'll develop a similar but far more resilient workflow compared to the one just described.

Embracing PL/SQL Abstractions

Rather than trying to shoehorn business logic into SQL scripts, the inclusion of some fundamental PL/SQL programming abstractions allows for more powerful and resilient code constructions. For example, adding exception handling is one way of protecting your PL/SQL code from unexpected runtime exceptions, such as the attempted duplicate key insertion from "A Cautionary Tale" on page 11.

As you'll see, well-crafted PL/SQL also facilitates observability, which helps avoid the problems just described where the critical sales data was missing. In other words, PL/SQL gives you the benefits of access to the constructs of a mature programming language. This in turn helps to move you away from such brittle SQL-based business logic and any need for handcrafted, error-prone data modifications.

Disadvantages of PL/SQL

What are some of the disadvantages of PL/SQL? All technologies have a total cost of ownership and there's no such thing as a perfect language (or, indeed, a free lunch). A few of the disadvantages of PL/SQL are as follows:

- PL/SQL is a *legacy* language.
- PL/SQL is not a *trendy* language.
- The use of PL/SQL may tie you to Oracle Database products.
- People will ask why they can't use SQL instead.
- PL/SQL is often perceived as being difficult to learn.
- Many developers don't want to learn yet another language (i.e., developer fatigue).

These disadvantages are drawn from my own experience of PL/SQL in the various development teams I've worked on. Very often, a team is extremely well versed in languages such as Java, C#, and JavaScript. Having spent years becoming proficient in their language of choice, developers can typically produce code quickly and efficiently. Consequently, developers often prefer to stay in their preferred language and not have to worry about learning a new one, such as PL/SQL. In addition, time is usually strictly limited for development work. So, it's no surprise that the bulk of developers like to remain on familiar ground.

This is understandable and it often motivates developers to search for rather creative ways of *avoiding* PL/SQL and doing things like mixing ORM and calling the PL/SQL stored procedures directly from Java or C#. This approach maintains their code in just the one language. However, if the data workflow is very complex, there may be severe performance issues with this mix-and-match approach. It's also potentially a bit of an antipattern in that the high-level code and the PL/SQL become tightly coupled to each other—changing one may unexpectedly break the other. Breakages may only be detected by end users, and this can lead to disenchantment in the user community.

Calling stored procedures from Java or some other language may also reduce the security of the database. For example, stored procedure names and other important data may inadvertently get recorded in application logfiles. Another problem is that any errors or exceptions that occur in a stored procedure invoked from a high-level language may not be handled properly. As we saw earlier, there can be serious consequences when error conditions get overlooked.

When merging high-level languages with PL/SQL, perhaps worst of all is the lack of good separation of concerns. We are, in some sense, attempting to mix oil and water.

There Is a Better Way

Learning PL/SQL is not so difficult. With a little effort and a willingness to expand your programming tool set, PL/SQL skills can be acquired with relative ease. In fact, quickly learning new programming languages is a key skill for all developers. It's also an interesting challenge and helps make for a more marketable skill set.

My advice to any developer who has a chance to learn PL/SQL is to seize the opportunity. The effort required to learn this interesting and useful language far outweighs the energy required to avoid it in favor of a more complex and potentially brittle mechanism. Your organization and its data users will thank you for creating more resilient solutions, and you'll thank yourself when your newfound PL/SQL skills turn out to be reusable in other project work.

Let's start with a few examples of PL/SQL just to see how easily the language can be learned. The code examples will be revisited later on to illustrate how to migrate them to a more resilient form. One last point in relation to looking at code examples: the ability to read code is one of the great skills in software development and integration. We'll be looking to enhance this skill as the examples unfold.

Gaining a Basic Understanding of PL/SQL

More experienced PL/SQL readers can skip this section. It's included to provide PL/SQL beginners or novices with an indication that the language can be readily understood purely on the basis of its similarity to mainstream, high-level programming languages. This content would have helped me when I first started learning PL/SQL. In the next section, you'll begin the journey of learning to read PL/SQL written by someone else.

How to Read Existing or Legacy PL/SQL Code

Let's now finally take a look at our very first piece of PL/SQL, in Example 1-1. What do you reckon this block of code is doing? I've added a few extra comments to assist the reader.

Example 1-1. Introducing PL/SQL

```
DECLARE
   x NUMBER := 100;
BEGIN
   FOR i IN 1..20 LOOP    -- A for loop similar to Java
      IF MOD(i, 2) = 0 THEN    -- if i is even
         INSERT INTO temp VALUES (i, x, 'i is even');
      ELSE
         INSERT INTO temp VALUES (i, x, 'i is odd');
      END IF;
      x := x + 100;
   END LOOP;
   COMMIT;
END;
```

The code in Example 1-1 loops from 1 to 20 and checks if the numbers are even or odd. The latter is done using the MOD function and the result is written into a table called temp. A cursory glance at the listing allows us to figure most of this out. Some confusion might also arise from these few, perhaps unfamiliar-looking lines:

- DECLARE
- IF
- END IF
- END LOOP
- COMMIT

These are just standard PL/SQL; DECLARE is used to create new variables for later use in the code. The END IF is simply a demarcation point for the opening IF statement. The END LOOP is similarly a demarcation point for the end of the LOOP operation. The COMMIT marks the end of a transaction and is required to write any updates to persistent storage (i.e., the database).

Another item in Example 1-1 that might give you pause is the use of the rather strange-looking assignment operator:

```
x := x + 100;
```

I recall showing some PL/SQL code to a Java developer a few years ago who said, "What's that weird-looking assignment?" The extra colon before the equals sign was the source of the confusion. It's interesting to see what causes cognitive dissonance. This assignment statement is functionally very similar to the equivalent operation in Java (and C), except in Java there is, of course, no colon in the assignment.

In this case, we are adding 100 to the value of x. The use of the assignment operator in PL/SQL merely reflects the origins of the language. PL/SQL was first released back in 1992 and is loosely based on Ada. PL/SQL often reminds me of the old Pascal language. For any reader interested in programming language history, PL/SQL is also quite similar to the IBM proprietary language Extended Structured Query Language (ESQL). It's quite common for the authors of different programming languages to influence each other; for example, Java has only relatively recently added support for functional programming.

So, that's the first example of PL/SQL done and dusted. The code is pretty straightforward and readable—in my opinion, it's more readable than a lot of the often convoluted constructs found in both modern Java and JavaScript.

Reading source code is one of the most important skills any developer can acquire. This is particularly true in the current era, when so much development work involves a lot of code integration in multiple languages using a range of frameworks, platforms, and libraries. It's not uncommon to labor over a programming problem for days and then find that the fix lies in adding or changing a single line of code or even just modifying some configuration data. Learning PL/SQL can help in extending your skill set and in producing resilient code. Let's look at another example.

Example 1-2 illustrates a slightly different style of writing PL/SQL, which might be more familiar to developers used to mainstream languages. Again, some comments (which start with the characters "--") are added to help in understanding it. As before, try to figure out what the code is doing before reading on.

Example 1-2. A more familiar code syntax

```
declare
  n number(10) :=1;    -- Notice the lack of spaces
begin
  while n<=10    -- Notice the lack of spaces again!
  loop
    dbms_output.put_line(n);
    n:=n+1;
  end loop;
end;
```

Some items of note in Example 1-2 are:

- The use of lowercase
- Indentation using two spaces
- The lack of spaces in the code statements
- A call to dbms_output(), which allows you to display messages to screen
- The use of end loop, which you also saw in Example 1-1

In Example 1-2, the keywords are all in lowercase. PL/SQL is not case-sensitive, so you can use uppercase or lowercase. The two-space indentation provides a nice, compact, and readable style, though you are free to use any number of spaces you like. The use of spaces is encouraged to improve readability for downstream maintainers of the PL/SQL code. So, it might be preferable to use this:

```
n number(10):= 1; -- Added an extra space
```

Similarly, I would always write the fourth line like this:

```
while n <= 10 -- Added extra spaces
```

The following use of spaces is also more readable:

```
n := n + 1; -- Added extra spaces
```

Any thoughts on what this PL/SQL code in Example 1-2 might be doing? Any idea why there is no COMMIT statement here?

To answer the first question, Example 1-2 is a simple while loop. Again, this is very similar to Java, C++, etc. The reason we have no COMMIT (or commit in lowercase) simply reflects the fact that there is no data to write to the database. In other words, the code in Example 1-2 is ephemeral; it has no persistent content.

This section again illustrates the importance of the ability and willingness to read PL/SQL code and to then try to understand it. In the next section, we'll get a little bit more ambitious and introduce a really powerful feature of PL/SQL: cursors.

 Some of the examples in this book are drawn from sample PL/SQL programs provided by Oracle (*https://oreil.ly/BBSaY*). There's lots of code at this site to assist you in your learning journey.

Cursors

Armed with the knowledge from the previous examples, let's look at Example 1-3, where you can begin to see more of the power of PL/SQL. Just to keep it interesting, I've reverted again to uppercase. Try not to be intimidated by any content you haven't seen before.

Example 1-3. More powerful PL/SQL

```
DECLARE
  CURSOR c1 is ❶
    SELECT ename, empno, sal FROM emp
      ORDER BY sal DESC;   -- start with highest paid employee
  my_ename VARCHAR2(10); ❷ ❸
  my_empno NUMBER(4);
```

```
   my_sal   NUMBER(7,2);
BEGIN
   OPEN c1;  ❹
   FOR i IN 1..5 LOOP
      FETCH c1 INTO my_ename, my_empno, my_sal;  ❺
      EXIT WHEN c1%NOTFOUND;  /* in case the number requested */
                             /* is more than the total      */
                             /* number of employees         */
      INSERT INTO temp VALUES (my_sal, my_empno, my_ename);  ❻
      COMMIT;  ❼
   END LOOP;
   CLOSE c1;  ❽
END;
```

Let's break down Example 1-3 into its component parts. Again, remember we're just practicing reading the code and trying to imagine what it's doing:

❶   A CURSOR is used: this is a PL/SQL construct for collecting blocks of table data.

❷   Some new variables are declared: my_ename, my_empno, and my_sal.

❸   The new variables and their data types are added, e.g., my_ename VARCHAR2(10).

❹   There's an OPEN on the CURSOR variable c1.

❺   There's some sort of FETCH from the CURSOR into the declared variables.

❻   There's an INSERT of the fetched data into a table called temp.

❼   There's a COMMIT of the data and a finish to the LOOP.

❽   There's a close on the CURSOR c1.

These descriptions should help you make sense of the PL/SQL in Example 1-3. It turns out that a CURSOR is simply a kind of work area composed of one or more rows returned by a SQL query. A CURSOR is a PL/SQL programming construct that points to the result of a query. Oracle supports two types of CURSORs: implicit and explicit. Let's have a quick look at these two important constructs.

Implicit CURSORs

When Oracle executes a SQL statement using SELECT, UPDATE, etc., it automatically creates an implicit CURSOR. This CURSOR is managed internally and Oracle reveals only a limited amount of information about it. For example, you can get the numbers of rows affected by the query using the following command:

```
SQL%ROWCOUNT
```

If you want to know if your query affected at least one row, you can use the following:

```
SQL%FOUND
```

If you run a query, such as SELECT * FROM <TABLE_NAME>, you can then follow it with something like this:

```
SET SERVEROUTPUT ON;
DECLARE
var_rows NUMBER := 0;
TYPE temp_type is TABLE of TEMP%ROWTYPE;
new_temp temp_type;
BEGIN
select * bulk collect into new_temp from temp;
var_rows := SQL%ROWCOUNT;
dbms_output.put_line('Number of rows affected: ' || SQL%ROWCOUNT);
END;
```

This allows you to see the numbers of rows affected by the SQL statement.

Explicit CURSORs

The other type of CURSOR is the explicit variety, which allows a lot of interaction with its lifecycle from within PL/SQL code. For example, you can do the following with an explicit CURSOR:

1. OPEN the CURSOR for use.

2. FETCH data from the CURSOR into variables.

3. CLOSE the CURSOR (an important step in cleaning up after your code has run).

Explicit cursors take care of a lot of the heavy lifting involved when accessing the database. Cursors also give you type safety. You'll see more on this later, but for the moment, the main point to note is that a knowledge of cursors and CURSOR management is a crucial part of learning PL/SQL.

Back to the CURSORs example

With that in mind about cursors, the following lines from Example 1-3 should now make a little more sense:

```
CURSOR c1 is
    SELECT ename, empno, sal FROM emp
        ORDER BY sal DESC;    -- start with the highest paid employee
```

The result of this is to create an explicit CURSOR called c1. c1 contains one or more rows that have been read from the emp table by way of the SELECT query. The last line simply orders the resultant rows. So, how do we use the CURSOR? The first thing we need to do is open the CURSOR, i.e., OPEN c1. We then loop and repeatedly transfer the current contents of the CURSOR into the three variables:

```
FOR i IN 1..5 LOOP
    FETCH c1 INTO my_ename, my_empno, my_sal;
    EXIT WHEN c1%NOTFOUND;
```

Notice the use of c1%NOTFOUND to exit the loop when all the constituent data has been processed.

The FETCH occurs for each row in the CURSOR. That is, I reuse the variables on each cycle of the containing loop. Finally, I insert the variable values into the temp table, followed by committing the changes to the database as follows:

```
INSERT INTO temp VALUES (my_sal, my_empno, my_ename);
COMMIT
```

After this, I repeat the loop for the next row in the CURSOR. When all the CURSOR data has been processed, the loop ends and I close the CURSOR.

Example 1-3 contains some powerful PL/SQL content. It's pretty concise code, and it's almost certainly better to do this type of processing in PL/SQL rather than attempting to do this type of work in SQL script. This is because PL/SQL provides good error and exception handling, which we'll see in detail in the upcoming chapters. The PL/SQL in Example 1-3 reveals a lot of the programming power and there's more to come, so stay tuned.

Understanding the Need for a PL/SQL Learning and Development Environment

As with other programming languages, PL/SQL code should be written and maintained using some sort of software tool. The tool I'll be using in the book is the venerable SQL Developer from Oracle, which has many powerful features. SQL Developer will be introduced in the next chapter as part of the description of installing a virtualized Oracle Database instance.

Before wrapping up this chapter, let's take a quick look at the proposed scale of resilience for PL/SQL code.

The Scale of Resilience

Let's now back up a little and have a look at Example 1-3 from a different perspective. Rather than just trying to understand the PL/SQL, we now want to instead try to derive some idea of the code resilience. Example 1-4 shows the same code.

Example 1-4. How resilient is this PL/SQL?

```
DECLARE
    CURSOR c1 is
```

```
      SELECT ename, empno, sal FROM emp
         ORDER BY sal DESC;   -- start with highest paid employee
   my_ename VARCHAR2(10);
   my_empno NUMBER(4);
   my_sal   NUMBER(7,2);
BEGIN
   OPEN c1;
   FOR i IN 1..5 LOOP
      FETCH c1 INTO my_ename, my_empno, my_sal;
      EXIT WHEN c1%NOTFOUND;  /* in case the number requested */
                             /* is more than the total       */
                             /* number of employees          */
      INSERT INTO temp VALUES (my_sal, my_empno, my_ename);
      COMMIT;
   END LOOP;
   CLOSE c1;
END;
```

Remember the requirements enumerated earlier in relation to resilience? Here they are again in tabular form in Table 1-1. In order for our code to be designated as being resilient, it must include elements of all of these characteristics.

This is of course just a kind of thought experiment. It's not rigorous because I'm just trying to arrive at a way of deciding whether the PL/SQL code is resilient or not. To make it a little more interesting, I've also introduced a score column in Table 1-1 with values ranging from 0 to 10, where 0 is the lowest possible score and 10 is the highest.

The values in the score column are my estimates of how the code stacks up. I'll look at why these numbers were arrived at in the next few sections.

Table 1-1. Introducing a scale of resilience for PL/SQL

Requirement number	Resilience requirement	Score (0–10)
1	Capture all errors and exceptions	0
2	Recoverability	2
3	Observability	0
4	Modifiability	5
5	Modularity	2
6	Simplicity	5
7	Coding conventions	5
8	Reusability	2
9	Repeatable testing	2
10	Avoiding common antipatterns	0
11	Schema evolution	0
	Total score	23

In Table 1-1, you see a score of 23 out of a possible 110, which is really quite low. Let's try to see why I arrived at this disappointing result to the thought experiment.

Capture All Errors and Exceptions: Score = 0

We get a big 0 for this one, and deservedly so. The code in Example 1-4 doesn't handle any errors or exceptions. This is perhaps the single greatest problem with this code. It can fail, and when it does, we'll have little or no idea as to why it failed. This makes it more difficult to recover and greatly reduces the resilience of the code.

Recoverability: Score = 2

We get a low score of 2 for recoverability. Why? Well, what happens if we encounter an error when the code runs? It just bombs out with no option to handle the problem. It will be difficult in this scenario to determine if the code ran to completion or stopped halfway through. As discussed, this is poor practice and is at odds with the needs of resilience.

Observability: Score = 0

A low score for observability is also bad news. It means that we have no easy way to see if the code ran successfully. Nor can we see any data changes that occurred as a result of the code run. Indeed, given that we have a call to COMMIT, the data change may well have occurred and then been reverted because of an error. In that case, the error causes the transaction to be rolled back. With low observability, we don't get to see any of what happens behind the scenes. It's as if the code hadn't run at all.

Modifiability: Score = 5

The code in Example 1-4 isn't all bad; it is easy to understand. This makes it more modifiable than might be the case in functional programming–style code blocks in languages such as JavaScript and indeed Java. In these languages, the code can be extremely difficult to understand and maintain. By contrast, the PL/SQL in Example 1-4 can be changed with confidence; this will be very useful when I start to look at refactoring this code in later chapters.

Modularity: Score = 2

The code in Example 1-4 has a structure that is fairly easy to understand. Thus, it can be converted into a callable unit of code, such as a PL/SQL procedure. Modularizing code in this way helps in promoting reuse, such as creating packages of useful PL/SQL code. Such packages can then be shared with other developers. This has numerous benefits that will be seen later.

Simplicity: Score = 5

Example 1-4 is pretty easy to understand even though it uses a CURSOR abstraction. The CURSOR abstraction may be (unnecessarily) viewed as a complex programming construct. As we'll see, CURSORs are a fundamental unit of PL/SQL and they provide a lot of algorithmic power and safety. Simplicity is a key requirement of resilience, because it forces us to think about the avoidance of overly complex code.

Coding Conventions: Score = 5

The code in Example 1-4 certainly looks like it might be based on a defined coding convention. Typically, this governs elements such as:

- Spacing
- Variable names
- Style of comments
- Length of code blocks

Good coding conventions are very useful and can make it easier for different teams in an organization to manage each other's code, such as developers and/or DevOps groups.

Reusability: Score = 2

Because the Example 1-4 code isn't structured as a procedure or function, it's not easily reusable. One of the merits of writing reusable code is that you must aim for more generality in terms of structure, parameter names, and so on. So rather than just solving the problem at hand, your aim should always be to write the code so that other developers can use it for their work. An unexpected benefit is that your code then gets looked at by more developers, and this can result in fixes or improvements to your original work. You'll see this later on.

Repeatable Testing: Score = 2

Again, a low score has been assigned because we don't have any test infrastructure. Without this, we can't be absolutely sure that the code is rock-solid. This code can only really be tested by manual means, i.e., looking at the original data and comparing it with the output data.

Avoiding Common Antipatterns: Score = 0

The code in Example 1-4 contains at least one antipattern related to the way it handles data types. Also, the lack of error handling is an egregious antipattern. I'll come back to this later and show how to resolve these types of issues.

Schema Evolution: Score = 0

The next piece of Example 1-4 that we'll analyze is a source of disappointment. Why do I get 0? Well, what happens to the following lines if the underlying table data definitions change?

```
SELECT ename, empno, sal FROM emp
   ORDER BY sal DESC;   -- start with highest paid employee
my_ename VARCHAR2(10);
my_empno NUMBER(4);
my_sal   NUMBER(7,2);
```

What happens if a DBA changes the definition of my_ename VARCHAR2(10) to my_ename VARCHAR2(100)? This happens quite regularly in organizations as business requirements change. It is an example of schema evolution and it has a bad effect on the code in Example 1-4, which will no longer work correctly.

Summary

This chapter's aims were as follows:

- Broadly understand what "resilient software" means.
- Understand the requirements for resilience: *what* versus *how*.
- Understand why PL/SQL is a good idea.
- Appreciate why using SQL for business logic is generally a bad idea.
- Know some of the disadvantages of PL/SQL.
- Gain a basic understanding of PL/SQL.
- Read existing or legacy PL/SQL code.
- Understand the need for a PL/SQL learning and development environment.
- Understand a basic scale of resilience.

Learning PL/SQL is much easier than many people might believe. The language is relatively simple and allows you to be flexible about using uppercase or lowercase characters. Spacing is similarly flexible and you can choose an indentation style that suits your needs or your house style.

I think one of the merits of PL/SQL is that it is a readable language, though some readers might not agree with me on this. One element of the language that really merits study is that of CURSORs. CURSORs demonstrate one of the major differences between PL/SQL and SQL. While SQL does use CURSORs internally, these objects are not visible to users. The use of a PL/SQL CURSOR, on the other hand, allows you to collect data in a type-safe way, and you'll see more on this in the coming chapters.

Introducing a scale of resilience allows us to numerically analyze a block of PL/SQL. This is useful because we are not so much focused on what the code does but on other aspects of it, such as modularity, simplicity, antipatterns, and so on. The scale gives us metrics that can then inform further work on the underlying code, such as enhancing and refactoring it.

By addressing these aspects and refactoring the PL/SQL examples, you will gain many benefits, as will be seen in the coming chapters.

CHAPTER 2

Installation of a Containerized Oracle Database Instance and SQL Developer

In Chapter 1, we looked at some examples of PL/SQL. While this is a useful exercise, it lacks a practical dimension. This chapter aims to get you set up with a working installation of Oracle Database and SQL Developer. This will permit a much deeper look at actually running the PL/SQL examples and subsequently building on them.

A Virtualized Oracle Database Installation

Rather than just doing a native installation of Oracle Database onto your machine, I instead opt to use a virtualized approach. This has many merits, not the least of which is the educational benefit. It's a good thing to come to grips with containers and images because they represent what might be called a heavyweight, global technology.

Containers differ from virtual machines (VMs) in that they have a lighter footprint, so you can typically install many containers on the same platform. VMs have many merits but they do require a hypervisor layer and hardware emulation, and this tends to make them hog a lot of resources. Containers, on the other hand, communicate directly with the host platform and don't require the hypervisor layer. Also, containers can share common files and are quick to start and stop.

Let's install an Oracle Database instance and Oracle SQL Developer. There are a number of ways of going about this. You may already have existing installations ready for use, or access to an installation. If not, we'll set up a Docker-based Oracle Database installation, which has numerous advantages, including the following:

- Repeatability
- Ease of use

- Continued operation after system updates
- Isolation from operational databases

The benefit of repeatability is that you can simply delete a Docker container and image and then re-create them at any time. This makes for an easier user experience than if you directly install the software onto your system. With a Docker container, it's as if you have installed a new machine inside your existing hardware. The great thing is that you can then create new containers and delete old ones at will.

Docker containers are easy to use once you understand a few key features. There are also additional tools you can install that provide an improved Docker user interface. This can be a lot less intimidating than using the command line, but it is optional. If you want to use such tools, there is a wide variety of options, including Portainer and Docker Desktop. There's a quick tour of Portainer and Docker Desktop in "An Alternative to the Command-Line Use of Docker" on page 50.

Once you create a Docker container and get it working, it doesn't tend to subsequently stop working. This is a big benefit when learning a new technology and it means that you don't have the hassle of wrestling with system changes brought about by updates or modifications due to other software installations. Docker tends to insulate you from most or all of these difficulties.

 The need to isolate yourself from existing databases might not seem so important at the beginning of learning PL/SQL. However, it is possible that an experimental PL/SQL code change might have a negative impact on the database or on other users.

I experienced this myself a few years ago. I was running a PL/SQL batch job on a large shared development database. The job deadlocked for some reason and resolving this required the assistance of a database administrator. Sharing development databases always has its difficulties. If you can remove the problem of other users, then your learning experience becomes a lot less fraught. In other words, if your database runs inside a Docker container, then you have total control over it and can stop and start it with no impact on anyone but yourself.

After reading this chapter, you should be able to do the following:

- Install and run Oracle Database in a containerized environment.
- Access the database using SQL Developer.

I also hope that you will acquire some new virtualization skills that can be reused in other, similar work.

Getting Started with Docker

The very first step is to install Docker on your local machine. It's relatively straight-forward to download and install Docker (*https://www.docker.com*) if it isn't installed already. To install Docker Desktop on Windows (*https://oreil.ly/q2hdK*), click the Docker Desktop for Windows button. Once the download is complete, remember to do your usual checks:

- Verify the file signature.
- Scan the file for any malware.

"Verifying Downloaded Files: Defense in Depth" on page 38 provides more detail on step 1. If you're happy with the file download, run the installation program. If the Docker Desktop installation succeeds, you should see the result shown in Figure 2-1.

Figure 2-1. Successful Docker Desktop installation on Windows

Given that many computer users don't require virtualization technology, the relevant feature may be disabled by default on your machine.

To verify that the Docker daemon is running, run Docker Desktop from the Start menu and then try the following command:

```
docker container ls -a
```

Because you don't have any containers deployed, you should see a listing similar to Table 2-1 (except with no containers listed).

Table 2-1. Docker is running (with a single container)—excerpt from command output

CONTAINER ID	IMAGE	COMMAND	CREATED	STATUS
380195f59d0d	enterprise:19.3.0.0	"/bin/sh -c 'exec $O..."	3 months ago	Exited (137)

You might need to enable virtualization on your host platform. For PCs and laptops, virtualization can be switched on when the machine is starting up. In my case, I had to interrupt the normal machine boot sequence and poke around the BIOS configuration screens to find the relevant setting. Some research might be required for your own platform. It's likely some kind soul has documented the steps to enable virtualization on your platform.

If all is well with your host platform virtualization and Docker setup, open a browser and go to the Oracle container registry (*https://oreil.ly/Gbp4C*) (see Figure 2-2).

Figure 2-2. Oracle container registry

Click on Database in Figure 2-2 and on the next page, click Enterprise. This should then open the login page, as shown in Figure 2-3.

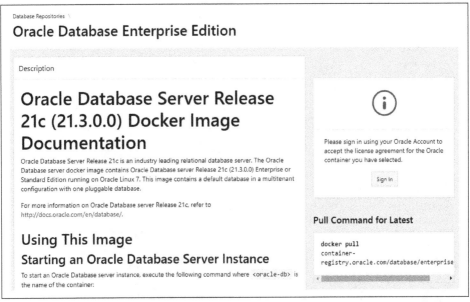

Figure 2-3. Oracle container registry login page

Notice in the upper-right corner of Figure 2-3, the login status is indicating you are logged out. Click the Sign In button shown in Figure 2-3 and create an account if you don't already have one. This should then return you as an authenticated user to the page indicating you are logged in, as shown in Figure 2-4.

Notice the tick mark in Figure 2-4. This indicates a successful login.

We'll come back to Figure 2-4 shortly. For the moment, note that I've selected (from the drop-down control) the language to use as English. Next, open a command prompt and type the following command:

```
docker login container-registry.oracle.com
```

Use the same credentials as for the container registry login page in Figure 2-3. If the login succeeds, then copy the docker pull command from the Pull Command for Latest section in the lower right of Figure 2-4. The command is shown here for version 19:

```
docker pull container-registry.oracle.com/database/enterprise:19.3.0.0
```

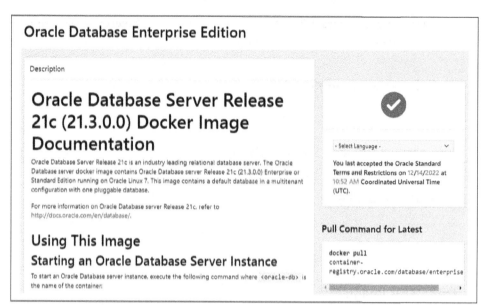

Oracle Database Enterprise Edition

Description

Oracle Database Server Release 21c (21.3.0.0) Docker Image Documentation

Oracle Database Server Release 21c is an industry leading relational database server. The Oracle Database server docker image contains Oracle Database server Release 21c (21.3.0.0) Enterprise or Standard Edition running on Oracle Linux 7. This image contains a default database in a multitenant configuration with one pluggable database.

For more information on Oracle Database server Release 21c, refer to http://docs.oracle.com/en/database/.

Using This Image

Starting an Oracle Database Server Instance

To start an Oracle Database server instance, execute the following command where <oracle-db> is the name of the container:

- Select Language -

You last accepted the Oracle Standard Terms and Restrictions on 12/14/2022 at 10:52 AM Coordinated Universal Time (UTC).

Pull Command for Latest

```
docker pull
container-
registry.oracle.com/database/enterprise
```

Figure 2-4. Oracle container registry page indicating you are logged in

I had to attempt this installation a few times and I found that one important part seems to be ensuring that there is in excess of 10 GB of free disk space.

The Oracle web page is subject to change. At the time of this writing, the docker pull command is located in the area shown in Figure 2-4. These installation instructions were verified for the following Oracle Database image: Oracle Database 19c Enterprise Edition Release 19.0.0.0.0—Production.

Paste the docker pull command into the command prompt and run it. This initiates the download of the image. At the time of this writing, this exceeds 3 GB, so it will take a while to complete depending on your internet access speed.

If the pull operation succeeds, then run the following command (on one line and without the slash characters), as shown in Example 2-1.

Example 2-1. Running the container

```
docker run -d --name oracle-std3 -p 1521:1521 -e ORACLE_SID=ORCLCDB \
-e ORACLE_PWD=mySyspwd1 \
container-registry.oracle.com/database/enterprise:19.3.0.0 \
-p 1521:1521 --name oracle-std --shm-size="8g" \
container-registry.oracle.com/database/standard
```

In Example 2-1, you can use any values you like for the name, ORACLE_SID, and ORACLE_PWD parameters. Make a note of them, as you'll need them later.

While the container creation is running, you can execute the following command to verify that the installation is progressing. Remember to substitute the name you used in Example 2-1:

```
docker logs oracle-std3
```

If all is well with your installation, you should see log output similar to Example 2-2.

Example 2-2. Checking the log for the container

```
The listener supports no services
The command completed successfully
Prepare for db operation
8% complete
Copying database files
```

If you see log details similar to Example 2-2, leave it to run for a few minutes and then rerun the docker logs oracle-std3 command. At this point, the log details should look something like Example 2-3.

Example 2-3. Checking the log for the container again

```
Prepare for db operation
8% complete
Copying database files
31% complete
Creating and starting Oracle instance
32% complete
36% complete
40% complete
43% complete
46% complete
Completing Database Creation
```

When the container creation is complete, you should see log content similar to Example 2-4.

Example 2-4. Checking the log for the container one last time

```
ALTER SYSTEM SET local_listener='' SCOPE=BOTH;
   ALTER PLUGGABLE DATABASE ORCLPDB1 SAVE STATE
Completed:   ALTER PLUGGABLE DATABASE ORCLPDB1 SAVE STATE
2022-12-30T19:28:54.854962+00:00

XDB initialized.
2022-12-30T19:37:53.816824+00:00
```

```
ORCLPDB1(3):Resize operation completed for file# 10, old size 337920K,
new size 348160K
```

If the log looks like the text in Example 2-4, then your Oracle Database is installed and ready to use.

 This is just a short technical note about the command in Example 2-1. The docker run command first creates a writable container layer over the Oracle Database image and then starts it using the specified run command. You can read more about layers here (*https://oreil.ly/HEVZZ*).

Once the run operation from Example 2-1 is complete, run this command to list all containers:

```
docker container ls -a
```

If the container is present, you should see something like Table 2-2 where there is just a single Oracle Docker container.

Table 2-2. Listing the Docker containers

CONTAINER ID	IMAGE	COMMAND	CREATED	STATUS
380195f59d0d	container-registry.oracle.com/database/ enterprise:19.3.0.0	"/bin/sh -c 'exec $0…"	2 months ago	Up 40 minutes (healthy)

Notice in Table 2-2 that the status includes the word *healthy*. You'll be happy to hear that this rather complicated run command in Example 2-1 only has to be run once. Subsequent runs can be completed using the following command to start the container:

```
docker start <container_id>
```

You will, however, need to supply the container ID from this command output, as shown in Table 2-2.

At the end of your session, you can use the following command to stop the container:

```
docker stop <container_id>
```

It's not mandatory, but it may avoid you getting some strange error messages when you shut down your machine.

As mentioned earlier, the value of <container_id> can be acquired from the leftmost column in Table 2-2. So, for illustration, the full command pair to start and stop the container on my system is as follows:

- To start the container: `docker start 380195f59d0d`

- To stop the container: `docker stop 380195f59d0d`

Handling these container ID numbers seems a bit difficult, doesn't it? The following section describes a way to make this a little easier.

 Manually typing the container ID strings soon becomes tedious. You can instead copy the ID value from Table 2-2 as follows:

1. Right-click the command prompt title bar.

2. In the pop-up menu, click Edit followed by Mark.

3. Use your mouse to select the ID string.

4. Press Enter to copy the ID.

5. Right-click to paste the value where it is required.

The last step might be to paste the ID into another command prompt.

After using it for a while, you'll notice that the Docker CLI isn't too chatty. It just provides the bare minimum of feedback to facilitate your required workflows. So, when you run the following command, it produces this rather pithy response, where the container ID is echoed to the screen:

```
C:\Users\Stephen>docker start 380195f59d0d
380195f59d0d
```

The paucity of information reflects the fact that we are using a CLI and not a more advanced user interface. Tools with a more sophisticated user interface tend to provide much more information, as you'll see in "An Alternative to the Command-Line Use of Docker" on page 50.

Configuring Your Oracle Database

In order to get the containerized Oracle Database instance to work with SQL Developer, you now need to make a few changes to the configuration. Run the following (rather complicated-looking) command to modify your database. As usual, please ensure that you supply the container ID that matches your own setup:

```
docker exec -it <container_id> bash \
    -c "source /home/oracle/.bashrc; sqlplus /nolog"
```

If the command runs successfully, you should see something similar to Example 2-5.

Example 2-5. A SQL prompt in the Oracle Database instance

```
C:\Users\Stephen>docker exec -it 9b6af7c0e426 bash -c "source /home/oracle/.bashrc;
sqlplus /nolog"

SQL*Plus: Release 12.1.0.2.0 Production on Wed Dec 14 15:23:09 2022

Copyright (c) 1982, 2014, Oracle. All rights reserved.

SQL>
```

As you can see in Example 2-5, this opens a SQL prompt into which you type the following:

```
connect sys as sysdba;
```

The addition of the AS SYSDBA clause means that access is authenticated, which is why you may be prompted for a password. The password is available from the command in Example 2-1 that you used when creating the container. Next, type the following script, one line at a time, and remember to supply your required username and password. Make a note of the password because you'll need these credentials for the next step when you set up SQL Developer.

The following script should *not* be used in a production database. Because I'm using a Docker-based Oracle Database, there are no other users of this installation. The intention here is to get you up and running as quickly as possible with a minimum of installation complexity.

For this reason, I use _ORACLE_SCRIPT (also not recommended (*https://oreil.ly/KKXrB*)) in order to insert the user into the container database (CDB). It would, of course, be better to use a pluggable database (PDB) instead of the CDB for users and their objects. So it would be a better practice to specify a container name before creating the user.

```
alter session set "_ORACLE_SCRIPT"=true;
create user <user_name> identified by <password>;
GRANT ALL PRIVILEGES TO <user_name>;
```

In this command, make sure to supply your username and your password. If no errors occurred in the command execution, then type quit to exit the SQL prompt.

Security measures (such as mandatory user credentials) invariably result in the imposition of problems over time. Having now set the username and password, it may be necessary at some future point in time to modify the credentials. This is briefly described in the following section.

Updating the User Password

There may come a point in the future where you will need to change your Oracle Database password. For example, if you don't use the Docker image for a long time, the user password may expire. If this happens, then it's simple enough to update the password using a very similar set of steps to those described in the previous section.

Notice in Example 2-6 the use of `update` instead of `create`. If the user already exists in the database and has the required privileges, then there is no need to include the GRANT statement.

Example 2-6. Updating a user

```
alter session set "_ORACLE_SCRIPT"=true;
update user <user_name> identified by <password>;
GRANT ALL PRIVILEGES TO <user_name>;
```

So, just supply a different password in the `update` command in Example 2-6 and make a note of the new password for future reference. Quit the session when you're done with the password update.

You're finally finished configuring the containerized Oracle Database instance and it's now time to move on to installing SQL Developer.

Getting Started with SQL Developer

For your required platform, download a copy of SQL Developer from Oracle:

```
https://www.oracle.com/tools/downloads/sqldev-downloads.html
```

 As SQL Developer is an Oracle product, you'll have to accept terms and conditions and also log in as a user. Once this is complete, you can then follow the steps to install SQL Developer on your platform.

We've trudged through a lot of steps to get to this point. So, let's take a short break to discuss an important topic, which relates to downloaded artifacts.

Verifying Downloaded Files: Defense in Depth

As an optional extra, it's always a good practice to verify the signature of any manually downloaded file. Where a key value is provided, you can verify it locally after downloading the required file. On the Windows platform, this can be done using the `certutil` command:

```
certutil -hashfile <Downloaded_File_Name> MD5
```

Substitute the full path and name of the file you downloaded and use the signing algorithm that matches the one on the distribution website from which you received the file. I use the MD5 algorithm. Another signing algorithm that can be used is SHA-1. In either case, make sure that the signature value generated by the `certutil` command matches the one on the originating website. This helps to verify that the file has not been tampered with during the download.

This is an example of what is known as *defense in depth* (*https://oreil.ly/G0jMs*), which means that, rather than relying on a single level of defense, we use multiple levels. How the principle applies in this case is that we don't assume that our antivirus software will detect and quarantine a compromised downloaded file. Instead, we check that the published signature on the website for the file matches the value returned by the `certutil` command. The signature check operates in addition to the antivirus software check.

Sadly, not all publishers include signatures on their downloadable binary files. This is a shame because it may inadvertently facilitate file modification attacks. Such signatures can be created automatically by the build process used to generate the artifacts.

Defense in depth is a little like having two external locked doors in your home. If one of the external doors is breached, then there's a second level of defense. So, rather than relying exclusively on one defense mechanism, we use a combination of schemes, layered one on top of the other. Signing algorithms are of course not foolproof. They are merely an addition to existing security measures.

The next step is to extract the zipped file and follow the installation steps on the website. Let's now finally configure SQL Developer to use our Docker-containerized Oracle Database.

Launch the newly installed SQL Developer application and click the plus sign at the top left of the main window shown in Figure 2-5.

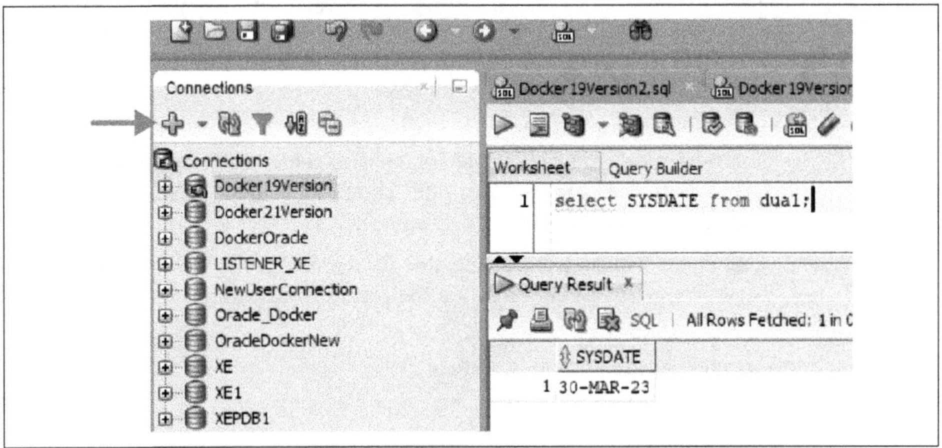

Figure 2-5. Create a connection to the Oracle Database container

This should prompt you to create a new connection to the database. To do this, you must supply your Oracle Database connection details and your user credentials, as shown in Figure 2-6.

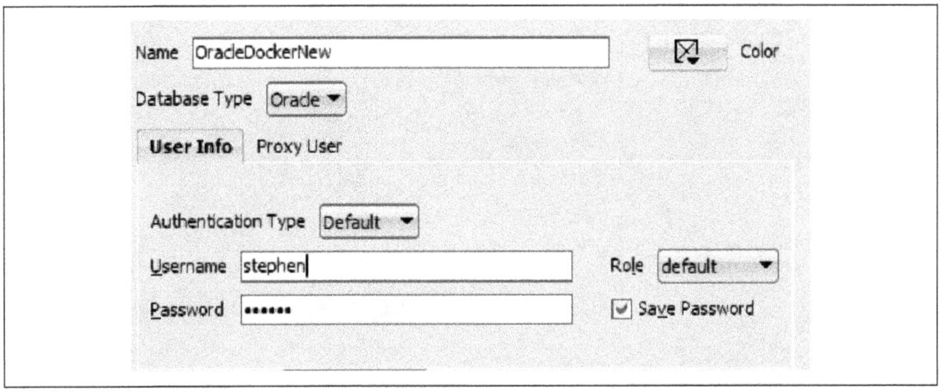

Figure 2-6. Challenging the user for credentials and Oracle Database connection details

In the database connection dialog shown in Figure 2-6, insert the indicated details. For the username and password, remember to use the same ones you configured in Example 2-5 for the Oracle Database. In Figure 2-6, I've inserted my own username for illustration. Just make sure to use the one you set up.

For the SID, use the value ORCLCDB from Example 2-1.

 If, at any time, you experience issues with the connection to the Oracle Database, then you can right-click on the appropriate connection in Figure 2-5 and select Properties.

This opens a dialog displaying the connection properties, which allows you to look more closely at the connection details.

The connection properties are shown in Figure 2-7.

| New / Select Database Connection | × |

Connection Name	Connection Details
Docker 19Version	stephen@//localh...
Docker21Version	stephen@//localh...
DockerOracle	SYS@//localhost:...
LISTENER_XE	LISTENER_XE@//...
NewUserConnect...	SYS@//localhost:...
Oracle_Docker	SYS@//localhost:...
OracleDockerNew	HR@//localhost:1...
XE	XE@//192.168.1....
XE1	XE1@//192.168....
XEPDB1	hr@//192.168.1....

Name: Docker 19Version   Color

Database Type: Oracle ▼

User Info Proxy User

Authentication Type: Default ▼

Username: stephen   Role: default ▼

Password: ••••••   ☑ Save Password

Connection Type: Basic ▼

Details Advanced

Hostname: localhost
Port: 1521
◉ SID: ORCLCDB
○ Service name:

Status : Success

Help   Save   Clear   Test   Connect   Cancel

Figure 2-7. Examining the details of the connection to the Oracle Database

A really nice feature of SQL Developer is the Test button, which you can see at the bottom of Figure 2-7. The Test button allows for easy verification of your installation. Click it to see if the new SQL Developer connection is able to communicate with your

Docker-containerized Oracle Database. If all is well, you should see something similar to Figure 2-7.

Notice the text Status: Success in the lower-left corner of Figure 2-7. This indicates that a successful connection has been made to the Dockerized Oracle Database instance.

If you've made it this far without incident, then well done. You're now up and running with a containerized Oracle Database that is accessible using SQL Developer. We've covered a good bit of ground in this chapter.

One quick test to verify that your database connection is good is to run the following SQL script:

```
SELECT * FROM V$VERSION;
```

The query result should indicate the version number of the Oracle Database, as shown in Figure 2-8.

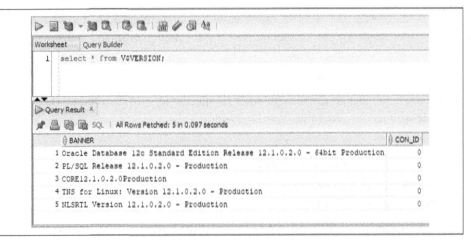

Figure 2-8. Successful SQL test query

As can be seen in the query result window in Figure 2-8, we have a fully configured Oracle Database installation.

Now that the installation is complete, let's briefly review the procedure for running the Oracle Database container and SQL Developer.

Recap of the Basic Docker Workflow

Let's assume you've just switched your machine on and you want to do some work with your containerized Oracle Database instance and SQL Developer. The following is the set of steps required along with the necessary commands.

Check the running Docker containers and look specifically for the Oracle container using this command:

```
docker container ls -a
```

Copy the resulting container ID and run the following command, substituting your own container ID:

```
docker start 380195f59d0d
```

After a minute or so, rerun the `container` command to check the container status:

```
docker container ls -a
```

Then, if all is well, the STATUS value should change to indicate the container is healthy. To shut down the container, just run the same command but use stop in place of start, so it looks like this:

```
docker stop 380195f59d0d
```

As always, remember to use the container ID specific to your own setup. The preceding code is, of course, the value from my system.

Oracle Database SID Versus Service Name

During the installation procedure, you might have wondered about the difference in Figure 2-7 between SID and Service name.

The SID is a unique name representing the installed Oracle Database instance, i.e., the Oracle process running on the machine. Documentation suggests that Oracle considers the database to be the underlying files.

The Service name is different from the SID in that the former represents an alias to *one or more* Oracle instances. The main purpose for having two mechanisms is that if you are running a cluster of Oracle Databases, then the client can request a connection to a given service name without having to specify the exact underlying instance.

The service option also facilitates flexibility in database administration procedures. For example, the number of instances in a given clustered service can be increased (or decreased) without requiring the client to change any local configuration settings. That can be very convenient if the client in question is built using a high-level language such as Java or C#. The database configuration of such clients might be embedded in the application source code. This means that database configuration

---

modifications might in turn necessitate an application rebuild and redeployment procedure.

A more flexible setup would involve the service name pointing to the cluster as a whole. This way, dependent client applications can retain their more general configuration while still allowing the database administration some degree of flexibility.

These types of issues typically only become relevant for somewhat larger installations with multiple Oracle Databases. The use of the *tnsnames.ora* file (*https://oreil.ly/ p3PTm*) and other options comes into play in these more complex environments.

In the next section, you'll see SQL Developer being used.

Running SQL Developer

At this point, you can use SQL Developer to interact with the database. If SQL Developer is open, right-click the Oracle connection you created earlier. In the case of Figure 2-9, the connection is called OracleDockerNew. This name is just text, so you can use whatever name you configured for your database.

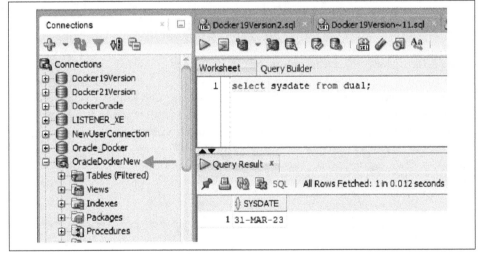

Figure 2-9. Using the Oracle Database connection

After right-clicking the OracleDockerNew connection, click Properties and you should see the dialog shown in Figure 2-10.

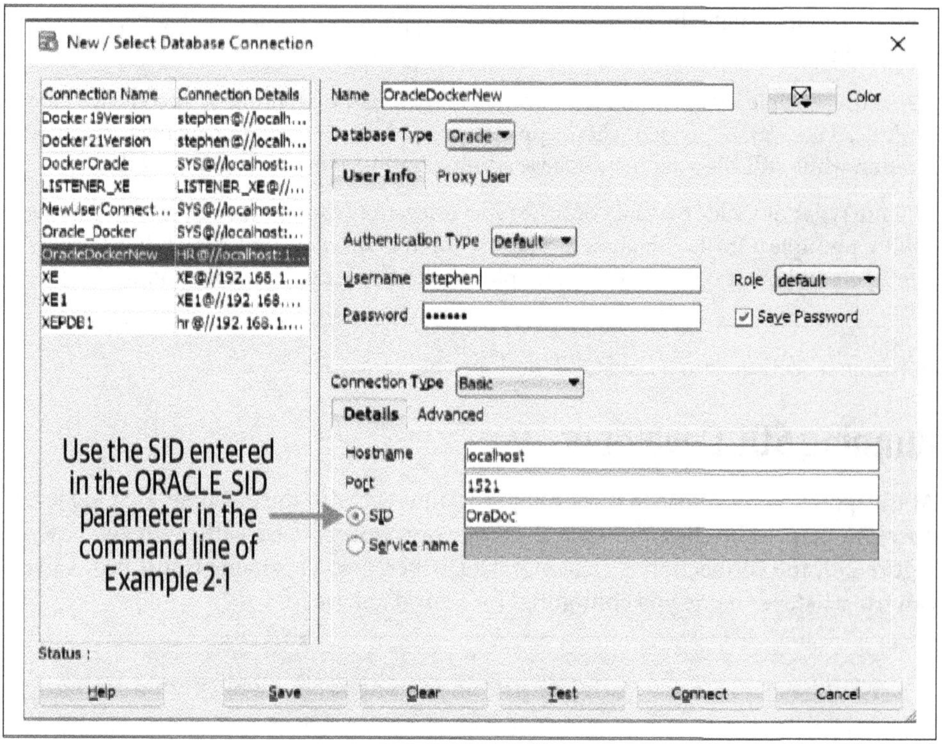

Figure 2-10. Opening the connection to the Oracle Database

Change the username to the value you selected earlier and supply your password, then click the Connect button. You should now have a connection to the database, as shown in Figure 2-11, where a sample SQL query has been executed.

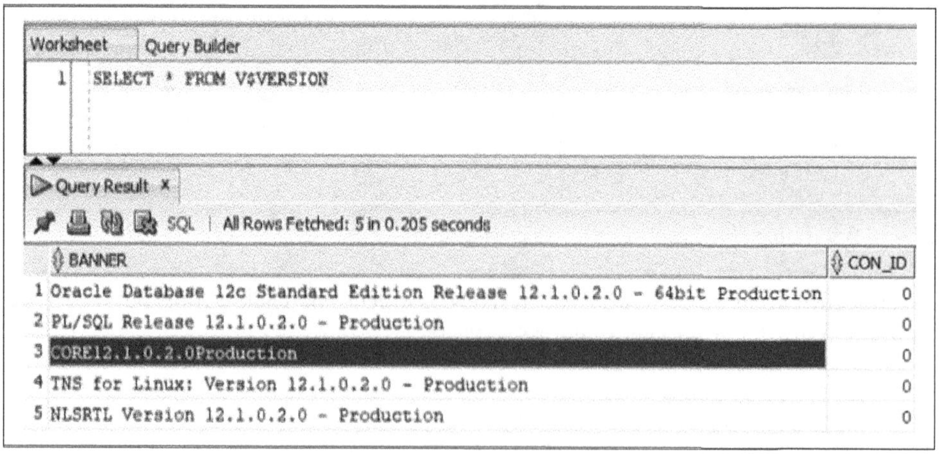

Figure 2-11. The database connection is ready to use

To close down your setup, just do the reverse by following these steps:

1. Right-click the connection OracleDockerNew.

2. Click Disconnect.

3. Exit SQL Developer.

4. Type the console command `docker stop 380195f59d0d`.

In the docker `stop` command, supply the container ID for your own setup. After a little practice, the startup and shutdown steps will become second nature.

The next thing we need is a simple database and this requires a schema. Let's now create an ultra-simple schema for use with the PL/SQL code examples.

A Simple Schema

A database schema (*https://oreil.ly/PCdrQ*) is the structure of the data in the database management system. We will revisit the basic schema later, but for the moment the schema is composed of two rather imaginatively named tables: `emp` and `temp`.

To create the schema, paste the SQL in Example 2-7 into the Query Builder prompt shown in Figure 2-11.

Example 2-7. Schema creation SQL

```
CREATE TABLE emp (
   ename VARCHAR2(10),
   empno NUMBER(4),
   sal   NUMBER(7,2)
   );

CREATE TABLE temp (
   ename VARCHAR2(10),
   empno NUMBER(4),
   sal   NUMBER(7,2)
   );

INSERT INTO emp (ename, empno, sal)
VALUES ('John', 1000, 40000.00);

INSERT INTO emp (ename, empno, sal)
VALUES ('Mary', 1001, 40000.00);

commit;
```

Notice at the end of Example 2-7, I insert two rows into the newly created `emp` table. To verify the contents of the `emp` table, run this SQL query:

```
select * from emp;
```

If your SQL Developer interface looks like Figure 2-12, then the tables are created and populated and you're all set.

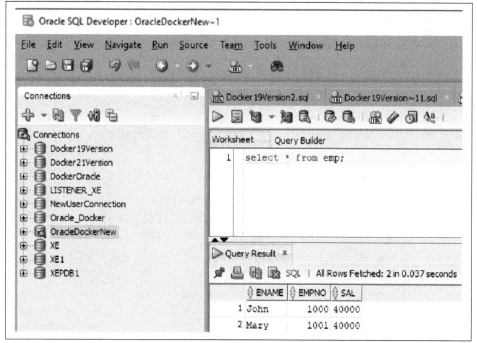

Figure 2-12. The data has been inserted

This also means that your installation of both Oracle Database and the sample schema is complete. It's now time to run some PL/SQL.

Running Some PL/SQL Code

Let's now review one of the earlier PL/SQL examples, as shown in Example 2-8.

Example 2-8. Cursor use in PL/SQL

```
DECLARE
    CURSOR c1 is
        SELECT ename, empno, sal FROM emp
            ORDER BY sal DESC;   -- start with highest paid employee
    my_ename VARCHAR2(10);
    my_empno NUMBER(4);
    my_sal   NUMBER(7,2);
BEGIN
    OPEN c1;
```

```
    FOR i IN 1..5 LOOP
       FETCH c1 INTO my_ename, my_empno, my_sal;
       EXIT WHEN c1%NOTFOUND;  /* in case the number requested */
                               /* is more than the total       */
                               /* number of employees          */
       INSERT INTO temp VALUES (my_sal, my_empno, my_ename);
       COMMIT;
    END LOOP;
    CLOSE c1;
END;
```

To run the code in Example 2-8, just select it (from the GitHub editor) and paste it into the SQL Developer Worksheet tab. Remove any non-PL/SQL characters and the screen should look like Figure 2-13.

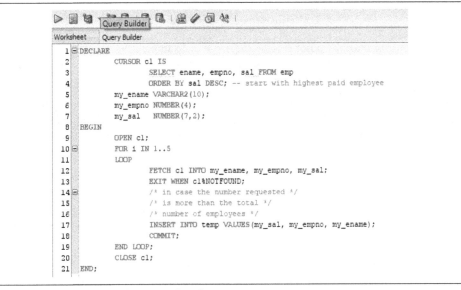

Figure 2-13. PL/SQL code inserted and run

To execute the PL/SQL in Figure 2-13, click the play icon at the upper-left corner of the window, just under the Welcome Page tab. The result of the run should be displayed in the Script Output window under the worksheet.

What is the output? Well, it's the rather disappointing error message shown in Example 2-9.

Example 2-9. An error is born!

```
Error report -
ORA-01722: invalid number
ORA-06512: at line 15
```

```
01722. 00000 -  "invalid number"
*Cause:   The specified number was invalid.
*Action:  Specify a valid number.
Listing 2-3 The code has an error, what's going on?
```

After all the hard work of getting Docker installed and creating our Oracle Database containerized instance, we've hit an error. What should we do?

The error in question is actually quite simple to fix. I'll leave it in for the moment because, in software development in general, the resolution of errors like this one is a crucial skill to acquire. Also, we often learn more from mistakes than from getting it right the first time. I'll fix this one in the next chapter. In the meantime, can you see what might be causing the error?

Ignoring Warnings

Is it possible or feasible to not resolve the error in Example 2-9? Is there some work-around we could try? What about ignoring it? It's definitely not an option to ignore this issue, but what about the more general case of ignoring warnings?

In the old days, with languages like C, the compilers aimed to help developers with their code. One way this occurred was when the compiler would complain about some use of the language. A simple example is when a numerical format gets trunca-ted, which might, in turn, result in some type of data loss.

To help the programmer avoid this and similar situations, the compiler could be con-figured to emit appropriate warnings (above and beyond the default warnings). Many bad habits were formed at an early stage in some C programmers' careers! An egre-gious bad habit and a deep antipattern was switching off or simply ignoring these types of warnings.

When your development tooling indicates to you that you're doing something wrong, then it's likely that you are in fact doing something wrong. In other words, treat warn-ings in the same way as you would treat an error message. Warnings can be seen as being like a senior developer looking over your shoulder as you work. I can't think of a good reason not to take the advice from this extra colleague. It's not uncommon for these warnings to be difficult to understand. Persistence in figuring them out will pay dividends in the form of spotting, fixing, and avoiding similar issues over the course of your career.

As you've now seen, PL/SQL also provides similar feedback when it deems code to be in some way risky or below par. When we fix the error described in Example 2-9, you'll see firsthand how to bring the various strands together in order to achieve a successful resolution.

Before rounding off the chapter, let's have a quick tour of some fairly typical issues that you may encounter when using Docker.

Three Docker Gotchas

As we're on the topic of errors, when you're using Docker commands, make sure not to enter the wrong parameter string.

1. Docker Case-Sensitivity

For example, here in Example 2-10, the user incorrectly supplies an uppercase letter in the Container parameter.

Example 2-10. Docker is case-sensitive

```
C:\Users\Stephen>docker Container ls -a
unknown shorthand flag: 'a' in -a
See 'docker --help'.
Usage:  docker [OPTIONS] COMMAND
A self-sufficient runtime for containers

Options:
      --config string      Location of client config files (default
                           "C:\\Users\\Stephen\\.docker")
  -c, --context string     Name of the context to use to connect to the
                           daemon (overrides DOCKER_HOST env var and
                           default context set with "docker context use")
```

This reflects the Linux heritage of Docker, where commands generally must be supplied in a case-sensitive manner. Windows traditionally tends to be a little more forgiving, though the result in Example 2-10 did occur in a Docker container on Windows.

2. Connecting to the Database Too Soon

When you're starting up your container, it's only natural to get a little impatient. If you try to connect (using SQL Developer) to an Oracle Database instance before the container is fully started, you might see an "Error encountered" dialog box warning you of a refused connection. It can take up to a few minutes for the Oracle Database container to reach *healthy* status.

The guideline is to not attempt to connect to the database until this point. Once the container is healthy, then it's safe to connect to the Oracle Database instance using SQL Developer. During the period where the Docker container is starting up, it's perfectly fine to run the familiar command multiple times:

```
docker container ls -a
```

One area of difficulty I've encountered with Docker on Windows is the impact of security updates, as discussed next.

3. A Docker Issue Caused by the Dreaded Windows Updates

It's quite common to see anomalous platform conditions arising after applying Windows updates. Sadly, Docker is not immune to this type of problem. I experienced this myself after accepting a bunch of Windows security updates. After rebooting, I subsequently attempted to run the usual docker command:

```
docker container ls -a
```

This was greeted with a rather cryptic response:

```
Error response from daemon: open \\.\pipe\docker_engine_linux:
The system cannot find the file specified.
```

A bit of searching online reveals that one solution is to run the following two commands. Remember to substitute the location of the Docker application specific to your own setup:

```
cd C:\Program Files\Docker\Docker
DockerCli.exe -SwitchLinuxEngine
```

After running this command pair, the original docker container ls -a command was successful. Needless to say, this applies only to the Windows platform. Other platforms might or might not suffer from a similar problem.

The next section covers a couple of alternatives to the exclusive use of the command line with Docker. This becomes increasingly relevant as the number of containers in use grows.

An Alternative to the Command-Line Use of Docker

The Docker-based setup we're using has a number of merits. One is that it's quite quick to get it working and it requires a minimal amount of installed software.

I mentioned that there are a range of options to choose from if using Docker from the command line feels a little unwieldy. Why might the command line become unwieldy? Well, as the number of containers in use grows, it can become difficult to keep track of them all using just commands.

Also, unlike machines, we tend to work better with pictures rather than pure text. So, rather than using the command line exclusively, one nice, easy alternative is Portainer, which can be installed in two docker commands as follows:

```
docker volume create portainer_data
docker run -d -p 9000:9000
--name=portainer --restart=unless-stopped -v
/var/run/docker.sock:/var/run/docker.sock
-v portainer_data:/data portainer/portainer-ce
```

If all is well after running these commands, then you can just browse to the following Portainer URL: *http://localhost:9000*. Then, create a password for the admin account and click Login, as shown in Figure 2-14.

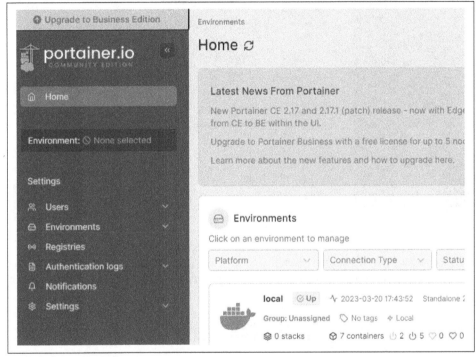

Figure 2-14. Portainer, an alternative to the command line

It's useful to spend a little time exploring the user interface shown in Figure 2-14. It is of course a much richer and more intuitive user experience than that of the basic command-line user interface. When you're ready, click through to the Containers listing, as shown in Figure 2-15. The Oracle Database container instance is the second item in the list in Figure 2-15.

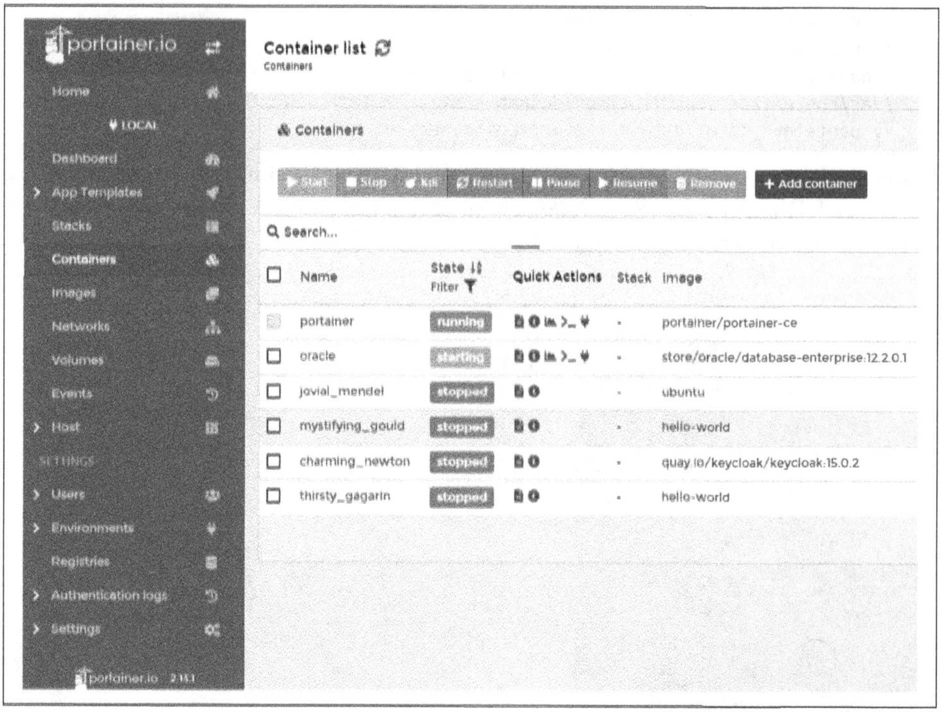

Figure 2-15. Portainer listing the containers

This page also has container-specific control buttons located near the top of the screen. You can also log out of Portainer when you're finished by clicking the button in the upper-right of the container list.

Another Alternative to the Command-Line Use of Docker

Docker Desktop also provides some pretty decent container management features. In Figure 2-16 you see the container listing, which comprises the Oracle Database container.

In Figure 2-16, you can also look at the container image by clicking the Images option, as shown in Figure 2-17.

As the number of containers and images grows, the utility of these higher-level tools becomes clear. The graphical user interfaces provide both more information and more clickable menu options. This allows you to look into the operational state of your containers and more easily interact with them. For example, deleting a container requires no more than a mouse click. Clearly, this enhanced power needs to be used with care.

In other words, use the graphical tools if you find that continuing to use the command line is becoming unwieldy.

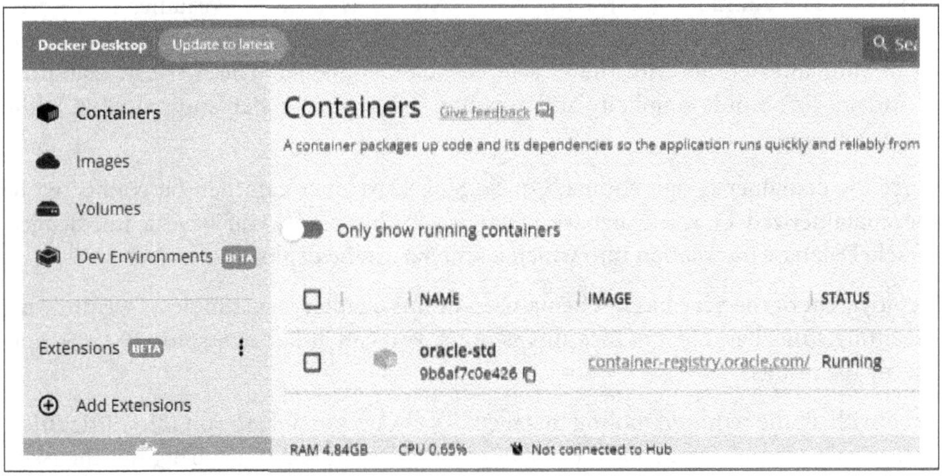

Figure 2-16. Docker Desktop listing the containers

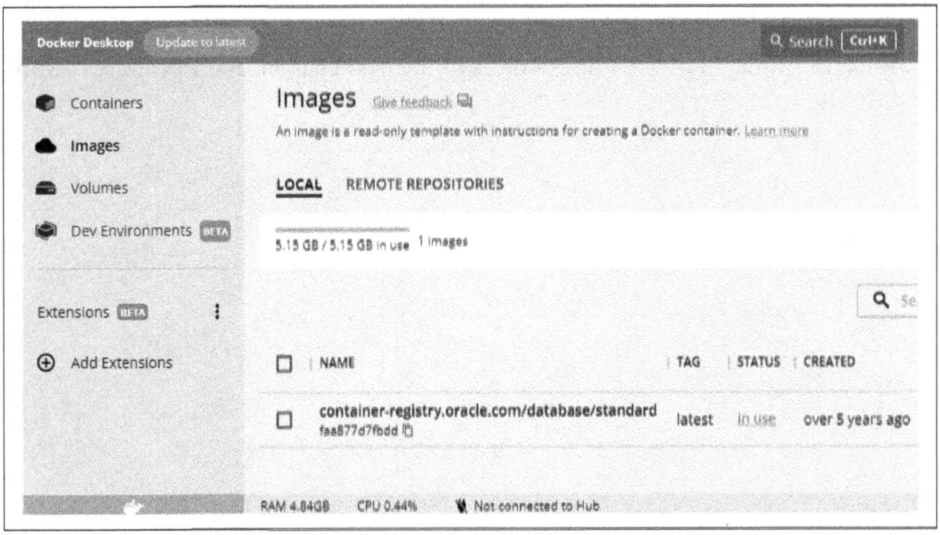

Figure 2-17. Docker Desktop listing the images

Summary

Installing an Oracle Database in a Docker container provides many advantages. It's relatively straightforward to get Oracle installed in this way. For Windows users, the Oracle installation is then, to some extent, immune to the vagaries of Windows updates.

Starting and stopping the containerized Oracle instance is easy. You can make it even easier than the command-line use case by installing one of the Docker user interface products. The addition of extra Docker-specific tools, such as Portainer or Docker Desktop, is of course entirely optional. It's possible to just use the command line for all of your interactions with the Oracle Database container. The merit of using the command-line tool is simplicity and avoiding the need to install and maintain additional software.

Once the container is operational, Oracle SQL Developer can then be connected to the containerized Oracle Database instance. At this point, you have a full-fledged Oracle Database installation into which a schema can be deployed.

Deployment of the very basic schema used in this chapter is as simple as writing and executing some basic SQL. Once this is done, you can at last run some PL/SQL and survey the results.

Even with all the required tooling installed, it's always possible to run into difficulties. You saw an example of a typical PL/SQL error in Example 2-9. Figuring out the issue causing such an error is an important part of learning any programming language. We'll explore this one in the next chapter where you'll see how easy it can be to resolve issues of this type.

So, we have a little bit of work ahead of us in the next chapter. But I promise it won't be difficult.

CHAPTER 3

Taking SQL Developer for a Drive

We've covered a lot of ground in the previous chapters. At this point, you've now got a working installation of a containerized Oracle Database instance. The venerable SQL Developer application is also configured for use in accessing the database. You can now get stuck into more detailed PL/SQL examples.

After reading this chapter, you should be able to take a deeper look at the development environment and use some new skills to fix a PL/SQL error.

Let's now revisit the error from the previous chapter. It has always been my experience that errors are good teachers. This is because it's not always obvious how to fix most errors, particularly the more difficult ones. The resolution of errors forces us to resort to a range of techniques, including:

- Examining logfiles
- Carefully reading error messages
- Looking up the meaning of the error messages
- Examining the data in tables
- Applying some trial fixes
- Repeating these steps

Let's do it.

Fixing the Pesky PL/SQL Error

In the previous chapter, we encountered the error shown in Example 3-1 during the PL/SQL run.

Example 3-1. An error is born!

```
Error report -
ORA-01722: invalid number
ORA-06512: at line 15
01722. 00000 -  "invalid number"
*Cause:   The specified number was invalid.
*Action:  Specify a valid number.
```

Let's look a little more closely at Example 3-1. Notice that there's an error on line 15. I need to locate that line in the PL/SQL code. I can of course just manually count down to line 15 in the PL/SQL code. But in more realistic situations, there might well be an error on line *xxx*, where *xxx* is a large number. So, manually counting the lines quickly loses its appeal and becomes impractical. It's better to switch on the display of line numbers in SQL Developer. To do this, click Tools > Preferences > Code Editor > Line Gutter, as shown in Figure 3-1.

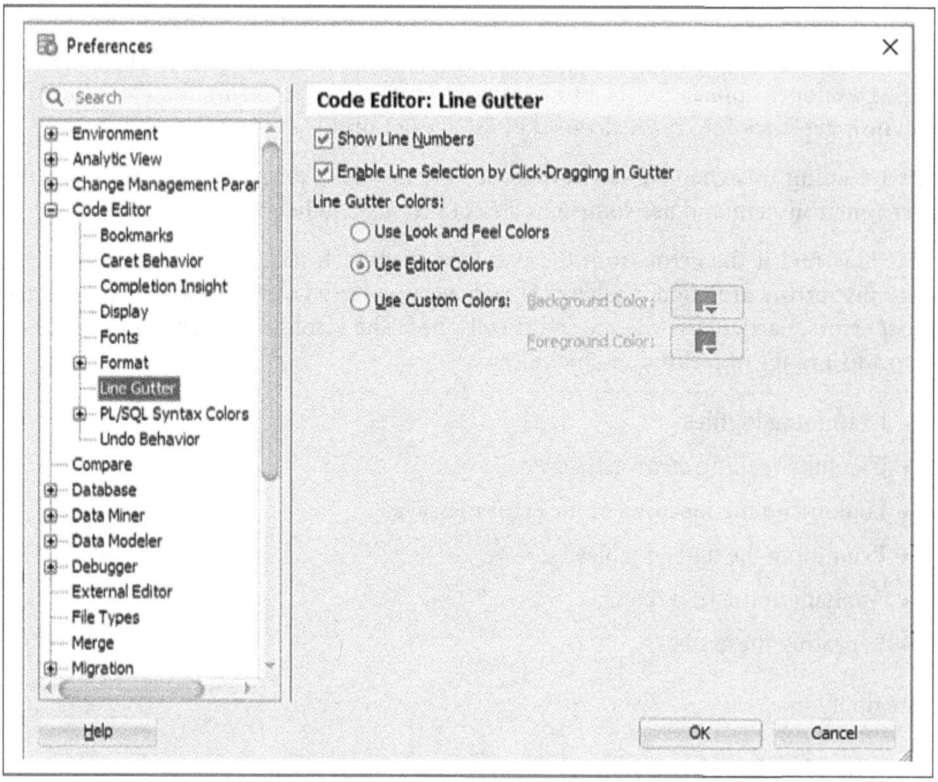

Figure 3-1. Switching on line numbers in SQL Developer

If the Show Line Numbers control in Figure 3-1 is unchecked, then click the control followed by OK, and then each line will start with its number, as shown in Figure 3-2.

It's much more intuitively appealing to see the line numbers. This allows for direct comparison of the error report and the source code line that is causing the issue.

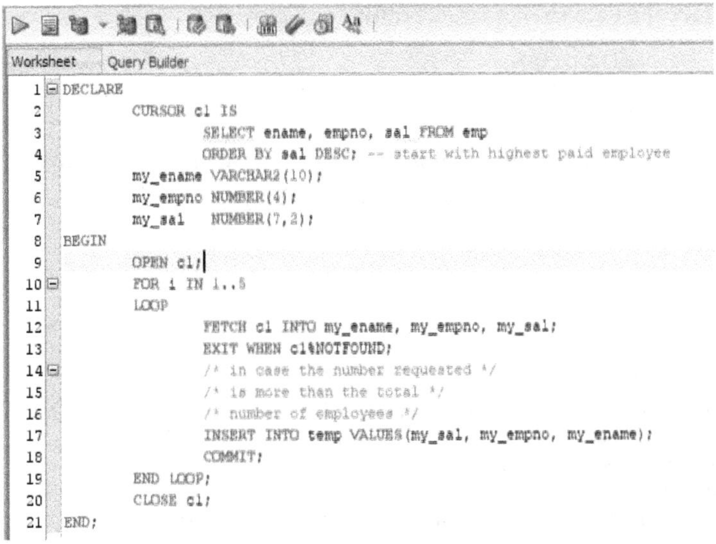

Figure 3-2. PL/SQL code with line numbers

In Figure 3-3, you see another really useful facility: displaying the data types of the columns of the TEMP target table.

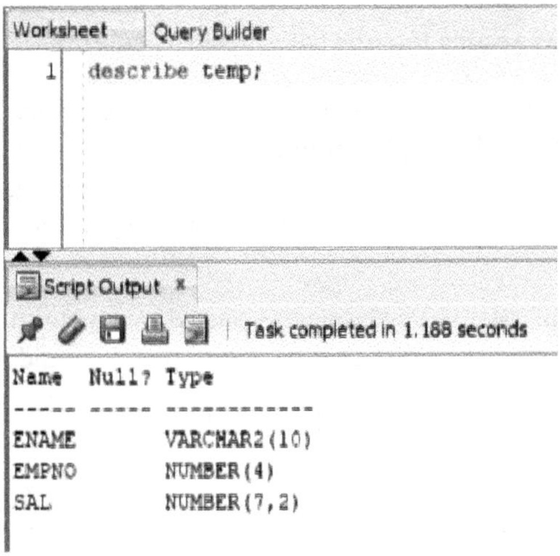

Figure 3-3. Describing the target table

The following ultra-simple SQL is required to produce the Figure 3-3 output:

```
describe TEMP;
```

It will produce the data shown at the bottom of Figure 3-3:

```
ENAME       VARCHAR2(10)
EMPNO       NUMBER(4)
SAL         NUMBER(7,2)
```

With these data types and their values noted, let's now look at the relevant PL/SQL (keeping the INSERT INTO line in mind in particular):

```
my_ename VARCHAR2(10);
my_empno NUMBER(4);
my_sal NUMBER(7,2);
BEGIN
 OPEN c1;
 FOR i IN 1..5 LOOP
  FETCH c1 INTO my_ename, my_empno, my_sal;
  EXIT WHEN c1%NOTFOUND; /* in case the number requested */
  /* is more than the total */
  /* number of employees */
  INSERT INTO temp VALUES (my_sal, my_empno, my_ename);
 COMMIT;
 END LOOP;
```

Putting the code listing and the data description together, you can now see with certainty that the PL/SQL code is attempting to do two erroneous actions:

- Insert the salary number into the ENAME (VARCHAR2) column.
- Insert the employee name into the SAL (NUMBER) column.

With this in mind, I've applied the required code fix (see Figure 3-4). To compile the code, you just need to click the play button, which sits below the Welcome Page tab. Notice also at the bottom of Figure 3-4, the successful compilation status message. Without this, your PL/SQL won't run; it's important to get into the habit of checking for this message.

So, what caused the problem? The issue was caused by trying to use a string value in place of a numerical one. Running the code in Figure 3-4 should now be successful.

In summary, fixing this type of issue requires us to iteratively do the following:

1. Change perspective.
2. Look at the schema SQL.
3. Look at the relevant data.
4. Look at the error report.
5. Put it all together.

6. Arrive at a solution.

Figure 3-4. Applying the code fix

To verify the fix, you can then run the following SQL:

```
select * from temp;
```

This should produce something like Figure 3-5.

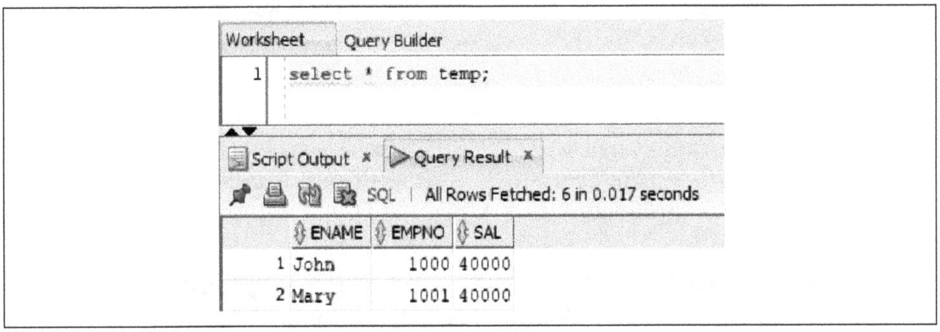

Figure 3-5. The code is now fixed and the data is verified

The PL/SQL code error is now fixed and verified. Until now, I've been using ad hoc PL/SQL. In the next section, you'll see how to install a stored procedure in the database.

Installing a PL/SQL Procedure in the Database

I've made a small change to the PL/SQL code in the form of adding a PROCEDURE name, as shown in Example 3-2.

Example 3-2. Completing the declaration of the PL/SQL procedure

```
CREATE OR REPLACE PROCEDURE update_employees
IS ❶
   CURSOR c1 is
      SELECT ename, empno, sal FROM emp
         ORDER BY sal DESC;   -- start with highest paid employee
   my_ename VARCHAR2(10);
   my_empno NUMBER(4);
   my_sal   NUMBER(7,2);
BEGIN
   OPEN c1;
   FOR i IN 1..5 LOOP
      FETCH c1 INTO my_ename, my_empno, my_sal;
      EXIT WHEN c1%NOTFOUND;  /* in case the number requested */
                             /* is more than the total      */
                             /* number of employees         */
      INSERT INTO temp VALUES (my_ename, my_empno, my_sal);
      COMMIT;
   END LOOP;
   CLOSE c1;
END;
```

❶   This is the changed line.

 The PL/SQL compiler can be configured to emit warnings. The following line of PL/SQL is one way to enable this:

```
ALTER SESSION SET PLSQL_WARNINGS='ENABLE:ALL';
```

You can read more about PLSQL_WARNINGS in the Oracle documentation (*https://oreil.ly/gALDX*). Jeff Smith's blog post "PLSQL Warning Messages in Oracle SQL Developer" (*https://oreil.ly/_0moy*) is another useful source for helping to resolve PL/SQL issues.

You can use CREATE OR REPLACE PROCEDURE to create a stored procedure or to update an existing procedure. In effect, this approach allows you to remove the old version and replace it with a new one. If there is no existing version of the procedure, then just the CREATE part is used. This is a very common concept in database development.

Let's use the updated version to install the procedure in the database using SQL Developer.

Installing the Stored Procedure in the Database

Copy and paste the PL/SQL code from Example 3-2 into the SQL Developer Worksheet, as shown in Figure 3-6.

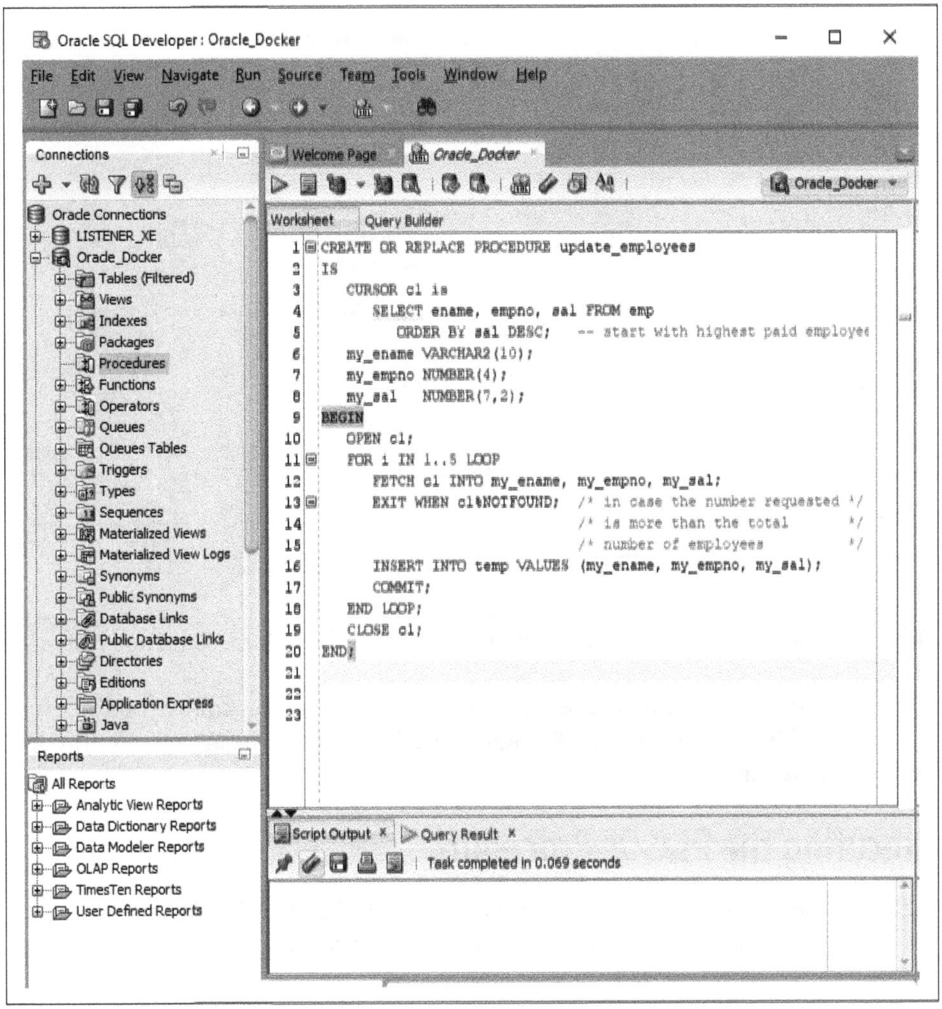

Figure 3-6. Installing PL/SQL in the containerized Oracle Database instance

Click the play button and watch out for the message in the Script Output window:

```
Procedure UPDATE_EMPLOYEES compiled
```

If all is well, you should see something like Figure 3-7. In order to see the procedure name, it might be necessary to click the Refresh button, as can be seen in Figure 3-7.

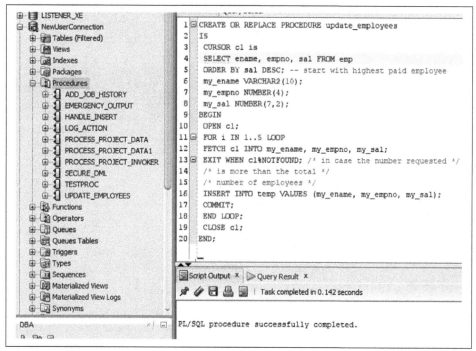

Figure 3-7. Successfully installed PL/SQL in the containerized Oracle Database instance

You can see the PL/SQL procedure shown under the Procedures control on the left of Figure 3-7. This indicates that the PL/SQL procedure has now been successfully compiled and stored in the database.

Executing the PL/SQL Procedure

Right-click the UPDATE_EMPLOYEES procedure name in Figure 3-7. This should display the procedure-specific context menu, as shown in Figure 3-8.

Notice the options available in relation to managing the PL/SQL procedure, such as:

- Edit
- Export
- Debug
- Compile

- Run
- Profile
- Grant

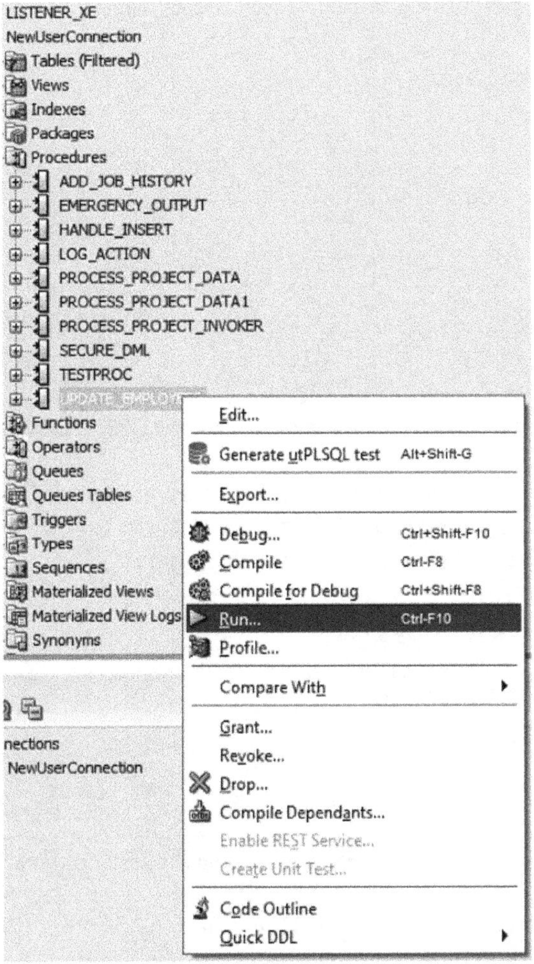

Figure 3-8. Executing PL/SQL in the containerized Oracle Database instance

Clearly, this menu provides a lot of power. For the moment, just click the Run option, at which point the Run PL/SQL dialog appears, as shown in Figure 3-9.

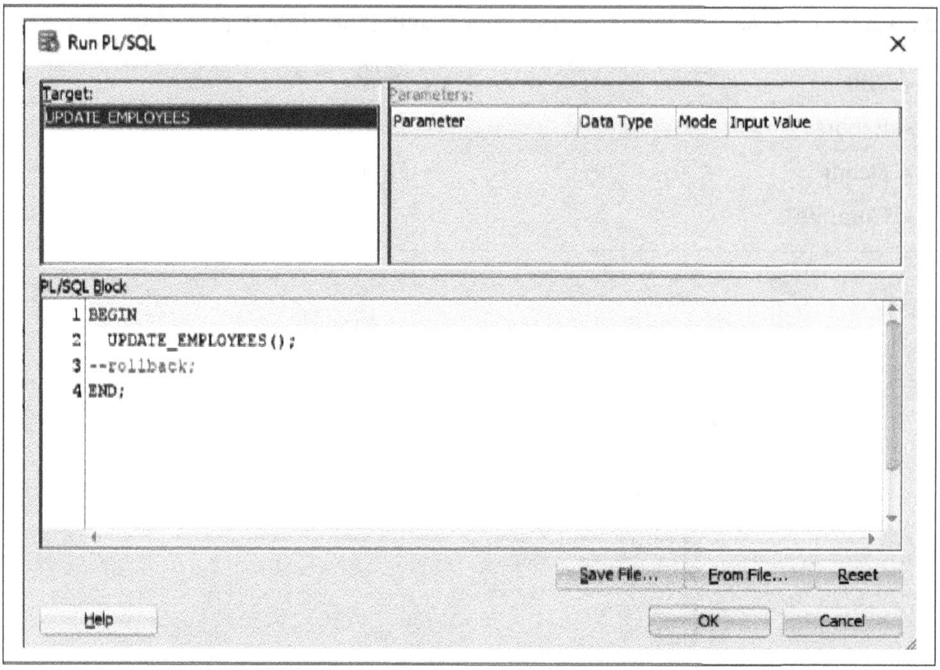

Figure 3-9. Launching the PL/SQL in the containerized Oracle Database instance

In Figure 3-9, there's no need to do anything other than click OK. If all is well, this should actually run the procedure, at which point you may be challenged for your credentials, as shown in Figure 3-10. We're nearly there.

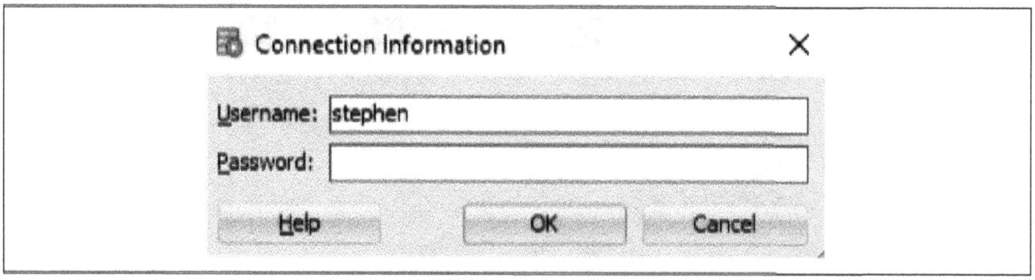

Figure 3-10. Supplying credentials before launching the PL/SQL procedure

Supply and submit your credentials in Figure 3-10 by clicking OK. At long last, the stored procedure should now run. Not too much feedback, though! This is because the PL/SQL procedure applies its output to the TEMP table. To see the result of the procedure, we need to use some SQL as follows. Use this **select** statement to view the data and **delete** it. Next, rerun the PL/SQL procedure. Then, run the select again to verify the data:

```
select * from TEMP;
delete from TEMP;
```

So, that completes the description of the PL/SQL fix.

The Takeaway: Errors Are Good Teachers

The key takeaway from this is that error reports (just like compiler warnings) are your friends and they invariably give good advice. Before we move on, let's make a note of that exotic error message (ORA-06512):

```
Error report -
ORA-01722: invalid number
ORA-06512: at line 15
01722. 00000 -  "invalid number"
*Cause:    The specified number was invalid.
*Action:   Specify a valid number.
```

This error is in fact caused by the stack, which has been unwound on account of an unhandled exception in the PL/SQL code. As we'll see later, this is actually providing us with some fantastically useful advice about the code. But we'll get to that in an upcoming chapter.

Shift-Left in Operation

Shift-left is a DevOps practice that aims to address code testing, defect removal, and performance evaluation as early as possible in the software development lifecycle. In effect, the purpose of shift-left is to move (or shift) these activities to the *left* side of the DevOps lifecycle, i.e., away from customers and end users but closer to developers.

The idea of shift-left has become increasingly popular as teams face pressure to deliver software more frequently and with higher quality. Shift-left potentially speeds up development efficiency and helps reduce costs by detecting and addressing software defects as early as possible in the development cycle, ideally long before such defects get to production.

"Fixing the Pesky PL/SQL Error" on page 55 could be considered a simple example of shift-left. Another nice thing about shift-left is reduced pain for developers. By front-loading development effort early in the process, we aim to accurately address requirements and produce solid solutions with a minimum of defects. Hopefully, there will be no defects at all.

Software development tools include facilities that can accelerate shift-left adoption. For example, IDEs such as Eclipse, IntelliJ IDEA, and SQL Developer include support for advanced plug-ins. The tool plug-ins can automatically identify code problems and security vulnerabilities. Moving such issues left can only be a good thing.

Summary

Fixing PL/SQL issues should be a straightforward exercise involving examination of log data and other database tables. Having a good development tool such as SQL Developer is indispensable. Once SQL Developer is configured to display line numbers, it becomes easier to correlate runtime error reports with the code that causes the errors.

PL/SQL provides type safety, so you can specify a procedure parameter type. This is always useful for those cases where the order of the supplied parameters is wrong.

Installing a stored procedure in the database is pretty straightforward using SQL Developer. You can verify the procedure has been stored by clicking the refresh button. Once installed, the procedure can be executed by right-clicking and selecting the Run option.

PL/SQL code errors are good teachers. The resolution of such errors forces us to adopt a rigorous approach. Indeed, the shift-left method described in "Shift-Left in Operation" on page 65 is an example of such an approach, where the main goal is to push errors in the direction of developers rather than users. It is the former who can do something about the errors whereas for the latter, errors can result in a loss of confidence about the solution.

In the next chapter, I'll apply the scale of resilience to score the PL/SQL code. This will illustrate how good or bad the code is in relation to its potential resilience. It also provides a basis for refactoring the PL/SQL code in order to improve its score.

CHAPTER 4

Applying the Scale of Resilience to the PL/SQL Code

The containerized Oracle Database instance that was set up in Chapter 2 can now be put to further use. Rather than just discussing PL/SQL code in isolation, I can now apply the scale of resilience and use the results to drive the remediation procedure.

In Chapter 1, you saw the unmodified version of Example 4-1.

Example 4-1. PL/SQL example from Chapter 1

```
DECLARE
    CURSOR c1 is
        SELECT ename, empno, sal FROM emp
            ORDER BY sal DESC;    -- start with highest paid employee
    my_ename VARCHAR2(10);
    my_empno NUMBER(4);
    my_sal   NUMBER(7,2);
BEGIN
    OPEN c1;
    FOR i IN 1..5 LOOP
        FETCH c1 INTO my_ename, my_empno, my_sal;
        EXIT WHEN c1%NOTFOUND;  /* in case the number requested */
                                /* is more than the total       */
                                /* number of employees          */
        INSERT INTO temp VALUES (my_sal, my_empno, my_ename);
        COMMIT;
    END LOOP;
    CLOSE c1;
END;
```

Applying the scale of resilience, the scores in Table 4-1 were recorded.

Table 4-1. Revisiting the scale of resilience for PL/SQL

Requirement number	Resilience requirement	Score (0–10)
1	Capture all errors and exceptions	0
2	Recoverability	2
3	Observability	0
4	Modifiability	5
5	Modularity	2
6	Simplicity	5
7	Coding conventions	5
8	Reusability	2
9	Repeatable testing	2
10	Avoiding common antipatterns	0
11	Schema evolution	0
	TOTAL SCORE	23

The following sections take each item in Table 4-1 in turn and explore them in more depth. As part of this, I'll make some targeted code changes with a view to improving the scores.

For ease of reference, the latest working version of the code is shown in Example 4-2.

Example 4-2. The latest working version of the PL/SQL procedure

```
CREATE OR REPLACE PROCEDURE update_employees
IS
   CURSOR c1 is
      SELECT ename, empno, sal FROM emp
         ORDER BY sal DESC;   -- start with highest paid employee
   my_ename VARCHAR2(10);
   my_empno NUMBER(4);
   my_sal   NUMBER(7,2);
BEGIN
   OPEN c1;
   FOR i IN 1..5 LOOP
      FETCH c1 INTO my_ename, my_empno, my_sal;
      EXIT WHEN c1%NOTFOUND;  /* in case the number requested */
                             /* is more than the total      */
                             /* number of employees         */
      INSERT INTO temp VALUES (my_ename, my_empno, my_sal);
      COMMIT;
   END LOOP;
   CLOSE c1;
END;
```

The code in Example 4-2 is now reviewed using the scale of resilience.

Scale of Resilience Requirement 1: Capture All Errors and Exceptions

Referring to Table 4-1, the score for this requirement is 0. The basic problem in relation to error and exception handling in Example 4-2 is that there isn't any! In other words, if an error or exception occurs, it will result in an immediate termination and exit. This is rarely a desirable outcome because it may prevent an orderly exit and could potentially lead to data inconsistencies.

Let's apply a few minor additions, as shown in Example 4-3.

Example 4-3. Adding exception handling to the earlier version of the PL/SQL procedure

```
CREATE OR REPLACE PROCEDURE update_employees
IS
   CURSOR c1 is
      SELECT ename, empno, sal FROM emp
         ORDER BY sal DESC;    -- start with highest paid employee
   my_ename VARCHAR2(10);
   my_empno NUMBER(4);
   my_sal   NUMBER(7,2);
BEGIN
   OPEN c1;
   FOR i IN 1..5 LOOP
      FETCH c1 INTO my_ename, my_empno, my_sal;
      EXIT WHEN c1%NOTFOUND;  /* in case the number requested */
                             /* is more than the total       */
                             /* number of employees          */
      DBMS_OUTPUT.PUT_LINE('Success - we got here 1!');
      INSERT INTO temp VALUES (my_sal, my_empno, my_ename);
      DBMS_OUTPUT.PUT_LINE('Successful insert!');
      COMMIT;
   END LOOP;
   CLOSE c1;
   DBMS_OUTPUT.PUT_LINE('Success - we got here!');

   EXCEPTION
   WHEN NO_DATA_FOUND THEN  -- catches all 'no data found' errors
     DBMS_OUTPUT.PUT_LINE('Ouch, we hit an exception');
     ROLLBACK;
   WHEN OTHERS THEN  -- handles all other errors
     DBMS_OUTPUT.PUT_LINE('We hit a general exception');
     ROLLBACK;
END;
```

Notice that, for the purpose of illustration, I've also reversed the original PL/SQL fix so that we are once again intentionally attempting to:

- Write the salary value into the ename column.
- Write the name into the salary column.

This bug just won't go away! Obviously, I'm just using it for the purposes of illustration and you'll soon see how to actually catch the exception raised by this bug.

I've also added a few extra lines to Example 4-3 using DBMS_OUTPUT to produce some developer output. Can you see the differences? I'll break down the Example 4-3 changes in the next section.

The Changes for Exception Handling

Notice in Example 4-3 the addition of some screen output in the form of the call:

```
DBMS_OUTPUT.PUT_LINE('Success - we got here 1!');
```

Normally only developers will see this screen output, but it can also become visible to other users. As you'll see, output from DBMS_OUTPUT.PUT_LINE is very useful for providing feedback during coding and testing.

The other main change in Example 4-3 is the addition of the following EXCEPTION block:

```
EXCEPTION
WHEN NO_DATA_FOUND THEN  -- catches all 'no data found' errors
  DBMS_OUTPUT.PUT_LINE('Ouch, we hit an exception');
  ROLLBACK;
WHEN OTHERS THEN  -- handles all other errors
  DBMS_OUTPUT.PUT_LINE('We hit a general exception');
  ROLLBACK;
```

Notice how the exception block is separate and distinct from the application code. This is a nice feature of the PL/SQL exception model in that the exceptions are handled after the application code section. Thus, there's no exception-handling code mixed in with (and cluttering up) the application code.

This exception block handles two exceptions, namely NO_DATA_FOUND and OTHERS. A NO_DATA_FOUND exception can occur when a SELECT INTO statement returns no rows. The second exception (OTHERS) catches all other exceptions. The NO_DATA_FOUND exception clause is an example of a *specific* exception, i.e., it checks for exactly one type of (specific) exception.

The OTHERS exception clause is an example of a *general* exception. It checks for a large number of potential exceptions. This type of exception case is very powerful. If it is not used correctly, then we may inadvertently run into an egregious antipattern: *swallowing all exceptions.*

Don't Swallow All Exceptions

It is rarely a good idea to attempt to swallow all exceptions. Why is this? Well, by swallowing all exceptions, the code is essentially saying this to the runtime system:

> I can handle all imaginable exceptions that can occur.

That's a very bold statement! The more likely outcome is that your code is actually saying this to the runtime system:

> I am a black hole for almost all possible exceptions and, in the event of an error, it will be very difficult for you to figure out why the overall PL/SQL solution has failed.

To illustrate why great care is needed in relation to the use of the OTHERS clause, what should the code in this clause do if the following exception occurs?

`STORAGE_ERROR    PL/SQL runs out of memory or memory has been corrupted.`

An error such as this is, of course, a critical runtime system or platform problem. It is highly unlikely that the PL/SQL code can do anything other than hand this type of exception off to the caller.

It is an old principle of software development to not attempt to over-deliver. In other words, just aim to solve the problem at hand without trying to solve all future potential problems. This is why swallowing all exceptions is an egregious antipattern and will almost certainly come back to haunt you at the most inconvenient moment, such as late on a Friday evening or just before you are due to go on vacation.

Having said all that, the code in Example 4-3 is *intentionally* swallowing all exceptions! But this is purely for the purposes of illustration. I will apply further code changes to better handle the exceptions. For the moment, we'll continue to use the *bad* approach just to get used to the mechanisms involved. So, let's run the code and see what happens.

Running the Updated PL/SQL

Before running the new version of the PL/SQL procedure, I need to replace the old one. To do this, I drop the existing version, as shown in Figure 4-1. Just right-click the procedure name and use the dialog you saw back in Figure 3-8. Technically, the CREATE OR REPLACE will of course obviate the need to manually drop the stored procedure. I'm just focusing here on a simple set of steps to get the procedure update done.

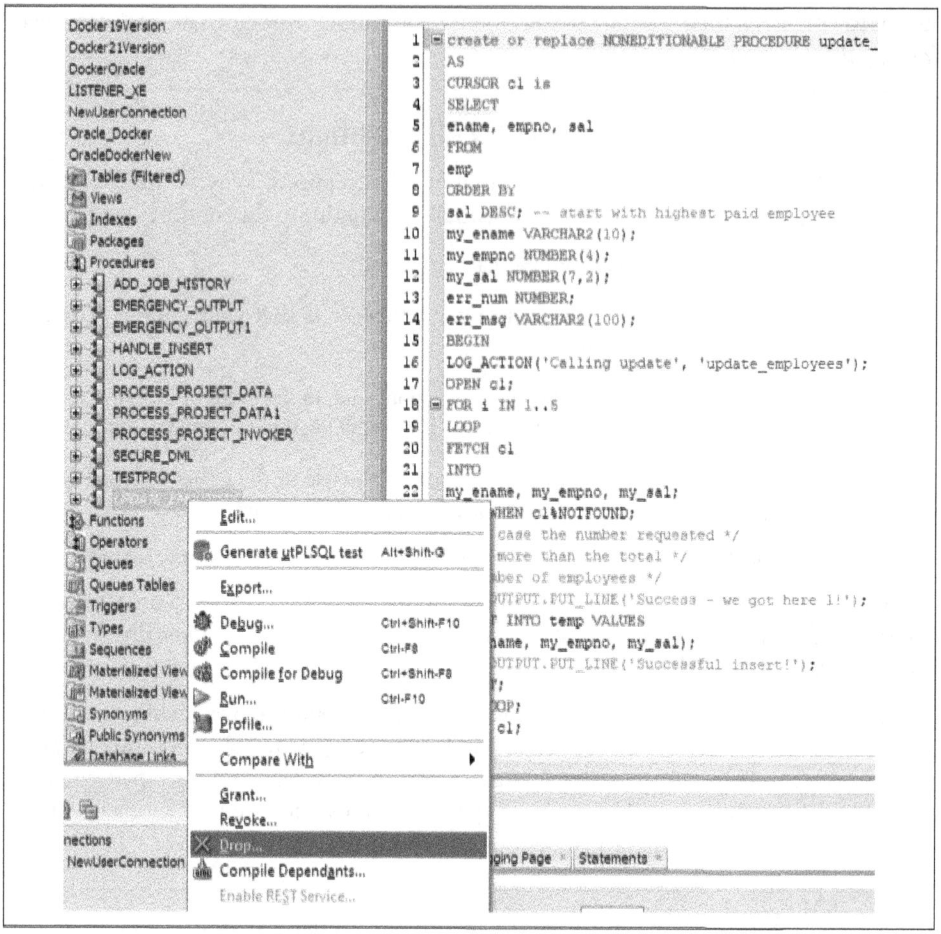

Figure 4-1. Drop the old version of the PL/SQL procedure

Notice in Figure 4-1 the appearance in line 1 of the word NONEDITIONABLE. This text is automatically inserted by the Oracle Database when the procedure is saved. It doesn't have any effect on this discussion and can be ignored during development. I've left the reference to NONEDITIONABLE in the example just in case you come across it in your own work.

Then, replace the code with the new version from Example 4-3, as shown in Figure 4-2. Click the play button and then click the refresh button in Figure 4-2 to verify that the updated procedure has been stored.

Version Control for Database Scripts, PL/SQL, and Other Artifacts

It is highly likely that your PL/SQL code is maintained in a version control system such as Git or Subversion. This is strongly recommended and applies as well to any other SQL scripts required to build your database, such as the SQL required to build your database schema.

You might encounter debate about the need for version control. This could happen in very small organizations, startups, or organizations that are new to using database technology. Aside from built components (derived from version-controlled code), it is in fact really important to maintain version-controlled artifacts for all of your code. This even applies to database views.

The approach I'm suggesting is to be able to re-create your entire database from scratch. Some organizations might take the position that some or all of these artifacts can be derived on demand from the database itself. After all, the database is, well, a database. This is true to some extent. However, when dealing with considerations of resilience (as well as defense in depth, as discussed in "Verifying Downloaded Files: Defense in Depth" on page 38), it is useful to consider how you might recover after a complete destruction of your databases. This is a question I like to ask organizations of any size! You'd be surprised by some of the answers.

Suppose your production database consists of a non-cloud-based, geographically separated active and backup pair. This is quite common for organizations that, for a variety of reasons, have not opted to move their data infrastructure to the cloud. So, all actions (updates, deletes, etc.) made against the active database instance are automatically reflected in the backup instance. If the active database is destroyed, for example, in a natural disaster, the backup database can be used during the recovery process. This is the happy path, so to speak. On the other hand, if both database instances are destroyed, it may not be possible to derive the necessary database-resident scripts in order to reinstate your database. Also, there may not be materialized scripts for your views and the schema scripts may be out of date. The latter can occur when modifications to tables have occurred without reflecting those changes in the underlying scripts.

Such an event might have very serious repercussions for an organization. Not maintaining version-controlled code and scripts is a recipe for a lot of unnecessary pain. Just because it's unlikely doesn't mean it won't happen. Make sure you always have a complete set of scripts available to rebuild your database in its entirety. Similar considerations also apply to the data inside the database.

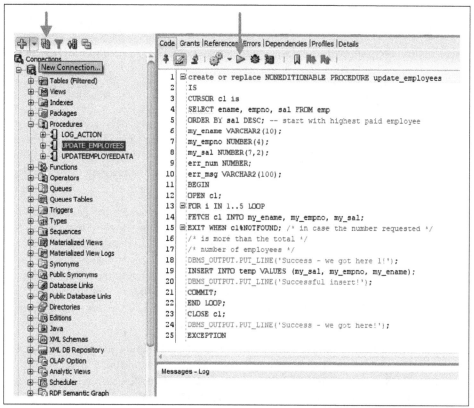

```
Code | Grants | References | Errors | Dependencies | Profiles | Details

 1 □ create or replace NONEDITIONABLE PROCEDURE update_employees
 2   IS
 3   CURSOR c1 is
 4   SELECT ename, empno, sal FROM emp
 5   ORDER BY sal DESC; -- start with highest paid employee
 6   my_ename VARCHAR2(10);
 7   my_empno NUMBER(4);
 8   my_sal NUMBER(7,2);
 9   err_num NUMBER;
10   err_msg VARCHAR2(100);
11   BEGIN
12   OPEN c1;
13 □ FOR i IN 1..5 LOOP
14   FETCH c1 INTO my_ename, my_empno, my_sal;
15 □ EXIT WHEN c1%NOTFOUND; /* in case the number requested */
16   /* is more than the total */
17   /* number of employees */
18   DBMS_OUTPUT.PUT_LINE('Success - we got here 1!');
19   INSERT INTO temp VALUES (my_sal, my_empno, my_ename);
20   DBMS_OUTPUT.PUT_LINE('Successful insert!');
21   COMMIT;
22   END LOOP;
23   CLOSE c1;
24   DBMS_OUTPUT.PUT_LINE('Success - we got here!');
25   EXCEPTION
```

Messages - Log

Figure 4-2. Updated PL/SQL with exception handling

At this point, I can run the new `update_employees` procedure and then review the output, as shown in Figure 4-3.

```
Running: IdeConnections%23OracleDockerNew.jpr - Log
Q
Connecting to the database OracleDockerNew.
Success - we got here 1!
We hit a general exception
Process exited.
Disconnecting from the database OracleDockerNew.
```

Figure 4-3. Updated PL/SQL output with exception handling

Notice the new screen output at the bottom of Figure 4-3, which consists of the following text:

```
Success - we got here 1!
We hit a general exception
```

Let's compare this to the PL/SQL code in Figure 4-2. The first message occurs just before the INSERT statement and the second message is produced by the OTHERS clause in the exception block.

This is all you need to know in order to infer the code path taken during execution, which consists of the following actions:

1. An attempt was made to INSERT some data.

2. An issue occurred during the INSERT statement.

3. An exception was raised by the runtime system.

4. The exception was caught and handled by the OTHERS clause.

It's extremely useful to be able to know in such detail what occurred during the stored procedure run. You can use this information to determine whether the code needs to be changed (it does!) and in what way you should modify it. Having ready access to this level of information goes a long way toward removing the guesswork from such PL/SQL development.

I'll make just one more code change in order to extract the exact exception that occurs. To do this, I'll make use of a special PL/SQL function called SQLCODE, which returns the error number associated with the most recently raised exception. I use SQLCODE in the OTHERS clause in Example 4-4.

Example 4-4. Adding enhanced exception handling to the PL/SQL procedure

```
create or replace PROCEDURE update_employees
IS
   CURSOR c1 is
      SELECT ename, empno, sal FROM emp
         ORDER BY sal DESC;   -- start with highest paid employee
   my_ename VARCHAR2(10);
   my_empno NUMBER(4);
   my_sal   NUMBER(7,2);
   err_num NUMBER;
   err_msg VARCHAR2(100);
BEGIN
   OPEN c1;
   FOR i IN 1..5 LOOP
      FETCH c1 INTO my_ename, my_empno, my_sal;
      EXIT WHEN c1%NOTFOUND; /* in case the number requested */
                             /* is more than the total      */
```

```
                         /* number of employees        */
     DBMS_OUTPUT.PUT_LINE('Success - we got here 1!');
     INSERT INTO temp VALUES (my_sal, my_empno, my_ename);
     DBMS_OUTPUT.PUT_LINE('Successful insert!');
     COMMIT;
   END LOOP;
   CLOSE c1;
   DBMS_OUTPUT.PUT_LINE('Success - we got here!');

   EXCEPTION
   WHEN NO_DATA_FOUND THEN  -- catches all 'no data found' errors
     DBMS_OUTPUT.PUT_LINE('Ouch, we hit an exception');
     ROLLBACK;
   WHEN OTHERS THEN  -- handles all other errors
     err_num := SQLCODE;
     err_msg := SUBSTR(SQLERRM, 1, 100);
     DBMS_OUTPUT.PUT_LINE('We hit a general exception error number ' ||
     err_num || ' Error message: ' || err_msg);
     ROLLBACK;
END;
```

Remember to drop the old version of the stored procedure and replace it with the one in Example 4-4. It is, of course, not necessary to manually drop the old version, given that the PL/SQL in Example 4-4 contains this line:

```
create or replace PROCEDURE update_employees
```

Just make sure that the old code has been replaced with the updated version. Figure 4-4 illustrates the improved code and the associated output. Notice that the exception-handling code has determined the error as being the following:

```
ORA-01722: invalid number
```

Remember we encountered this at the very beginning of our acquaintance with the PL/SQL bug, way back in Example 3-1? Here in Figure 4-4, you see the code extracting the error detail at the time it occurs. This is a very powerful addition to the PL/SQL toolbox.

Using this SQLCODE technique, you can know for certain exactly what type of exception occurs in similar situations. There's no need for inspired guesswork when the code provides the necessary data.

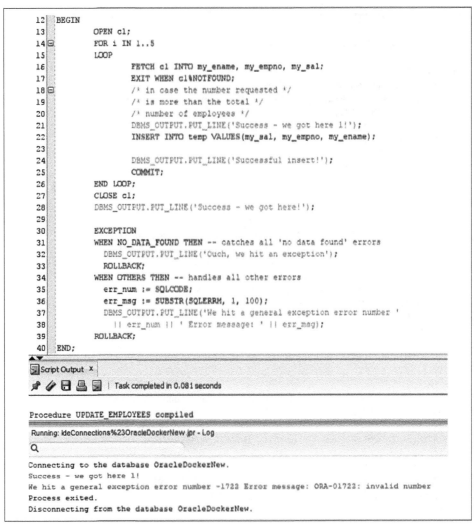

```
12   BEGIN
13        OPEN c1;
14        FOR i IN 1..5
15        LOOP
16             FETCH c1 INTO my_ename, my_empno, my_sal;
17             EXIT WHEN c1%NOTFOUND;
18             /* in case the number requested */
19             /* is more than the total */
20             /* number of employees */
21             DBMS_OUTPUT.PUT_LINE('Success - we got here 1!');
22             INSERT INTO temp VALUES(my_sal, my_empno, my_ename);
23
24             DBMS_OUTPUT.PUT_LINE('Successful insert!');
25             COMMIT;
26        END LOOP;
27        CLOSE c1;
28        DBMS_OUTPUT.PUT_LINE('Success - we got here!');
29
30        EXCEPTION
31        WHEN NO_DATA_FOUND THEN -- catches all 'no data found' errors
32          DBMS_OUTPUT.PUT_LINE('Ouch, we hit an exception');
33          ROLLBACK;
34        WHEN OTHERS THEN -- handles all other errors
35          err_num := SQLCODE;
36          err_msg := SUBSTR(SQLERRM, 1, 100);
37          DBMS_OUTPUT.PUT_LINE('We hit a general exception error number '
38             || err_num || ' Error message: ' || err_msg);
39        ROLLBACK;
40   END;
```

Script Output ×

Task completed in 0.081 seconds

```
Procedure UPDATE_EMPLOYEES compiled

Running: IdeConnections%23OracleDockerNew.jpr - Log
Q

Connecting to the database OracleDockerNew.
Success - we got here 1!
We hit a general exception error number -1722 Error message: ORA-01722: invalid number
Process exited.
Disconnecting from the database OracleDockerNew.
```

Figure 4-4. Updated PL/SQL with enhanced exception handling

Now that we know the exact exception, I can make a small design change to the PL/SQL code. Rather than using an OTHERS clause, I can opt to catch the specific error we know can occur. The updated code looks like Example 4-5.

Example 4-5. Removing the OTHERS clause from the enhanced exception handling

```
create or replace PROCEDURE update_employees
IS
   CURSOR c1 is
      SELECT ename, empno, sal FROM emp
         ORDER BY sal DESC;   -- start with highest paid employee
   my_ename VARCHAR2(10);
   my_empno NUMBER(4);
   my_sal   NUMBER(7,2);
   err_num NUMBER;
   err_msg VARCHAR2(100);
BEGIN
   OPEN c1;
   FOR i IN 1..5 LOOP
      FETCH c1 INTO my_ename, my_empno, my_sal;
      EXIT WHEN c1%NOTFOUND;  /* in case the number requested */
                             /* is more than the total      */
                             /* number of employees         */
      DBMS_OUTPUT.PUT_LINE('Success - we got here 1!');
      INSERT INTO temp VALUES (my_sal, my_empno, my_ename);
      DBMS_OUTPUT.PUT_LINE('Successful insert!');
      COMMIT;
   END LOOP;
   CLOSE c1;
   DBMS_OUTPUT.PUT_LINE('Success - we got here!');

   EXCEPTION
   WHEN NO_DATA_FOUND THEN  -- catches all 'no data found' errors
     DBMS_OUTPUT.PUT_LINE('Ouch, we hit an exception');
     ROLLBACK;
   WHEN INVALID_NUMBER THEN  -- handles INVALID_NUMBER
     err_num := SQLCODE;
     err_msg := SUBSTR(SQLERRM, 1, 100);
     DBMS_OUTPUT.PUT_LINE('We hit an INVALID_NUMBER exception error number '
     || err_num || ' Error message: ' || err_msg);
     ROLLBACK;
END;
```

 The inclusion in Example 4-5 of the two variables err_num and err_msg is not strictly required. Their values could be put straight into the call to PUT_LINE. They are added just to make the code a little easier to read.

So, in Example 4-5 we have no OTHERS clause. This means that the procedure handles just two exceptions: NO_DATA_FOUND and INVALID_NUMBER.

Any other exceptions pass up the chain to the procedure caller. This has the merit of simplifying the `update_employees` procedure. This simplification is a good pattern to adopt and I'll build on it in later sections.

Exception Code Design

You might have gathered that there are no hard-and-fast rules for how your PL/SQL code manages exceptions. This is true for other programming languages as well. The structure of the exception handlers is very much at the developer's discretion.

Well-designed exception handler code is an excellent investment to make. It protects your code without cluttering up your business logic, and judicious use of rollbacks can help in avoiding situations with data inconsistency.

I could add many more exception clauses to this code. As you'll see later, the key point to note is that I have now provided the means to accurately record the exceptions as and when they occur. This will tie in with the code that calls the procedure in Example 4-5.

Let's now move on and look at the next important scale of resilience requirement: *recoverability*.

Scale of Resilience Requirement 2: Recoverability

What do I mean by code that is recoverable? In a nutshell, recoverability means that the code can survive any errors or exceptions as well as letting you know the state at the point of exit. In other words, when attempting to implement recoverability, the aim is to know why the code exited and what (if any) data changes were applied during the run.

If I can achieve the twin aims of knowing the error details and data consistency, then I will have addressed some of the issues raised back in "A Cautionary Tale" on page 11. Imagine, in Example 4-5, what happens if either of the two designated exceptions occurs.

In both cases, we have a ROLLBACK call. This means that any database changes made in the current transaction are reversed. Let's try this out and see if the code is in fact recoverable.

To begin with, let's check the contents of the TEMP table, as shown in Figure 4-5.

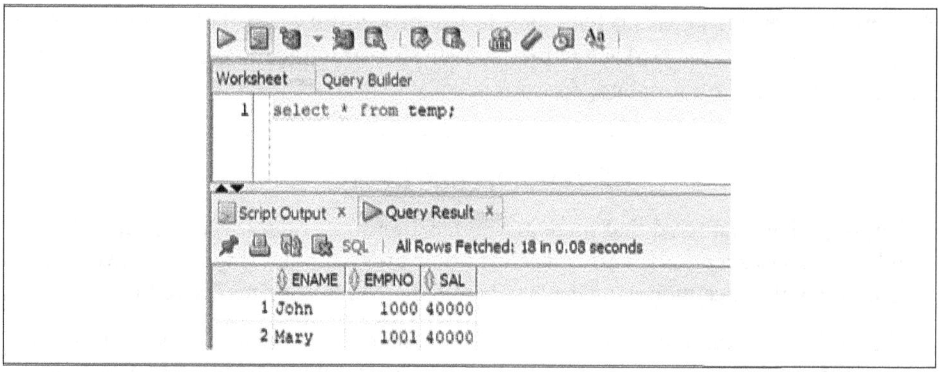

Figure 4-5. Checking the baseline data

Notice in Figure 4-5 that we've currently got two rows in the TEMP table. A successful run of the stored procedure would result in an additional two rows in the table. Let's now run the stored procedure and, after hitting the anticipated (i.e., deliberately inserted) exception, we then rerun the SQL script from Figure 4-5. The result is no change in the TEMP table data. In other words, the rollback worked. No surprises there.

This is a rather roundabout way of checking that the PL/SQL can handle exceptions by rolling back any data changes. The exception condition was of course artificially induced by way of a known bug in the PL/SQL. But the point of the discussion is that if we correct the bug and then subsequently encounter an exception, we can now be certain that no data changes will occur.

This means that it is safe to rerun the PL/SQL once the cause of the exception has been fixed. In other words, the PL/SQL code is recoverable. Running it multiple times in the face of an exception won't then result in unwarranted data changes.

One issue remains: we still have no idea (after the run) what error occurred. In other words, the code still lacks observability. To resolve this, let's now have a look at the issue of observability.

Scale of Resilience Requirement 3: Observability

Back in Chapter 1 and in Table 4-1, we got a score of 0 for observability. This is because, outside the safe confines of SQL Developer, we really don't know much about any given run of the stored procedure. Beyond the TEMP table data changes, it's very hard to know what has happened during a run.

I'm referring here to the case where the stored procedure is run and we have no access to the messages produced by the calls to DBMS_OUTPUT.PUT_LINE. Also, imagine if there was more going on with the procedure than is currently the case. For example, if the procedure contained a lot more code, it would be very difficult to say with any certainty what occurred during a given run. I need to fix this and therefore address the underlying requirement for improved *observability*. In other words, I want to provide persistent storage for the output messages.

One way to address this requirement is to introduce a new table purely for logging. With this in mind, let's extend our existing schema by creating a new table, as shown in Example 4-6.

Example 4-6. Extending the schema with a logging table

```
CREATE TABLE LOGGING (
    -- The next line works only on Oracle version 12c and up
    -- So, please make sure you are on 12c or higher
    Logging_ID NUMBER GENERATED ALWAYS AS IDENTITY,
    EVENT_DATE TIMESTAMP NOT NULL,
    ACTION_MESSAGE VARCHAR2(255),
    CODE_LOCATION VARCHAR2(255)
    );
```

In Example 4-7, we have a PL/SQL procedure to handle logging by populating the new LOGGING table.

Example 4-7. Implementing logging in PL/SQL

```
CREATE OR REPLACE PROCEDURE LOG_ACTION(action_message IN VARCHAR2,
                    code_location IN VARCHAR2) IS
                    PRAGMA AUTONOMOUS_TRANSACTION; ❶
  BEGIN
    INSERT INTO LOGGING(EVENT_DATE, action_message, code_location)
    VALUES (SYSDATE, action_message, code_location);
    COMMIT;
  END;
```

❶ This is an example of an autonomous transaction specification. It applies to the PL/SQL block that follows and provides for special operation in relation to transaction handling.

Autonomous Transactions

An *autonomous transaction* is a separate and distinct (independent) transaction that is initiated at the same time that another transaction is running.

When an autonomous transaction is initiated, the original transaction (i.e., the calling transaction) is temporarily suspended. The autonomous transaction must then commit or roll back before it returns control to the calling transaction. Once changes have been made by an autonomous transaction, those changes are then visible to other transactions.

Autonomous transactions can be nested. That is, an autonomous transaction can even operate as a calling transaction, initializing other autonomous transactions within itself. In theory, there is no limit to the possible number of nesting levels. Each of the transactions is tracked for auditing purposes.

As our use of transactions and exception handling becomes more complicated, an important question relates to handling exceptions in logging code. In other words, how should you handle an exception in the code that itself handles reporting on exceptions?

What to Do If Logging Hits an Exception?

Consideration should be given to the case where an exception occurs in the code in Example 4-7. Such an exception is an indication that the logging mechanism is itself failing. This might be due to some very serious runtime issue. Regardless, there should be some way of alerting the DevOps team if such an error occurs.

One simple mechanism might be to add some code that creates or updates an external file. The file could be located in a DevOps-monitored directory so that once an update occurs, it gets brought to the attention of someone who can then address the underlying problem.

A suggested way of handling this is described in Part III and shown in the PL/SQL code in Example 9-8. More information on this can be found in the UTL_FILE package (*https://oreil.ly/MAEPi*).

Back to our autonomous transaction; let's now run the SQL from Example 4-7 by compiling and installing the stored procedure.

Updated Schema

After running the SQL in Example 4-6 and also after installing the stored procedure, the setup should look like that shown in Figure 4-6.

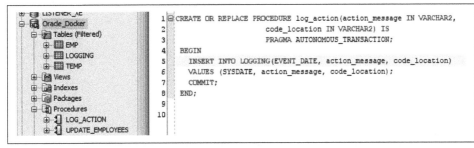

Figure 4-6. Modified schema and new procedure

Notice the successful addition of the new LOGGING table under Tables (Filtered) in Figure 4-6.

I also need to modify the original stored procedure to call the new logging procedure. The updated code for this is shown in Example 4-8.

Example 4-8. Adding a logging call in PL/SQL

```
create or replace PROCEDURE update_employees
AS
    CURSOR c1 is
        SELECT
                ename, empno, sal
        FROM
                emp
        ORDER BY
                sal DESC; -- start with highest paid employee
    my_ename VARCHAR2(10);
    my_empno NUMBER(4);
    my_sal   NUMBER(7,2);
    err_num  NUMBER;
    err_msg  VARCHAR2(100);
BEGIN
    LOG_ACTION('Calling update', 'update_employees'); ❶
    OPEN c1;
    FOR i IN 1..5
    LOOP
        FETCH c1
        INTO
                my_ename, my_empno, my_sal;

        EXIT WHEN c1%NOTFOUND;
        /* in case the number requested */
        /* is more than the total */
        /* number of employees */
        DBMS_OUTPUT.PUT_LINE('Success - we got here 1!');
        INSERT INTO temp VALUES
                (my_sal, my_empno, my_ename);
```

```
            DBMS_OUTPUT.PUT_LINE('Successful insert!');
            COMMIT;
        END LOOP;
        CLOSE c1;
        DBMS_OUTPUT.PUT_LINE('Success - we got here!');

EXCEPTION
WHEN NO_DATA_FOUND THEN -- catches all 'no data found' errors
        DBMS_OUTPUT.PUT_LINE('Ouch, we hit an exception');
        ROLLBACK;
WHEN INVALID_NUMBER THEN -- handles INVALID_NUMBER
        err_num := SQLCODE;
        err_msg := SUBSTR(SQLERRM, 1, 100);
        DBMS_OUTPUT.PUT_LINE('We hit an INVALID_NUMBER exception error number '
        || err_num || ' Error message: ' || err_msg);
        ROLLBACK;
END;
```

❶ This is the key line.

After the call to the logging procedure, we have a single row of content in the LOGGING table (see Figure 4-7).

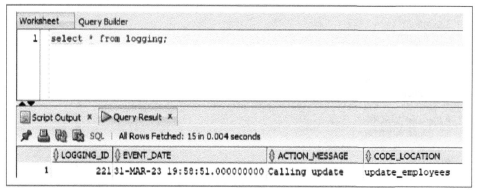

Figure 4-7. Logging data from the procedure call

Notice the logging data at the bottom of Figure 4-7. Note also the LOGGING_ID column in the table. This auto-increments with each new row insertion. Also included is an EVENT_DATE column, which provides the date and time of the row insertion.

The goal is the ability to verify the running of the PL/SQL code in an observable fashion. So, the Figure 4-7 content can be considered a baseline for the required data.

Here's the key PL/SQL that runs when I execute the logging procedure:

```
INSERT INTO LOGGING(EVENT_DATE, action_message, code_location)
VALUES (SYSDATE, action_message, code_location);
```

Because the LOGGING_ID column is marked as GENERATED ALWAYS AS IDENTITY, I don't have to update it in the PL/SQL code. This is handled by the Oracle Database. Note in passing that, if I attempt to insert (or update) a value into the LOGGING_ID column, the database will raise an error.

I use the SYSDATE function in order to supply an event date. So, there's a lot of power in these few lines of PL/SQL.

If I run a DESCRIBE call to look at the structure of the LOGGING table, like DESCRIBE LOGGING;, for instance, I get this output:

```
Name             Null?      Type
---------------  --------   -------------
LOGGING_ID       NOT NULL   NUMBER
EVENT_DATE       NOT NULL   TIMESTAMP(6)
ACTION_MESSAGE              VARCHAR2(255)
CODE_LOCATION              VARCHAR2(255)
```

Notice the NOT NULL constraints on the LOGGING_ID and EVENT_DATE columns. This is very useful for ensuring data consistency because the NOT NULL constraint forces a column to not accept NULL values. This is of course another way of saying that these columns must always contain a value. That is, we cannot insert a new row without adding a value to the EVENT_DATE column.

All of this new SQL and PL/SQL helps in achieving improved observability. I can now tell with certainty what happened during a code run. No more need for any inspired guesswork.

Let's move on to address the next scale of resilience requirement: *modifiability*.

Scale of Resilience Requirement 4: Modifiability

The latest version of the corrected PL/SQL code is shown in Example 4-9.

Example 4-9. The latest correct version of the PL/SQL code

```
create or replace PROCEDURE update_employees
AS
    CURSOR c1 is
        SELECT
                ename, empno, sal
        FROM
                emp
        ORDER BY
                sal DESC; -- start with highest paid employee
    my_ename VARCHAR2(10);
    my_empno NUMBER(4);
    my_sal   NUMBER(7,2);
    err_num NUMBER;
```

```
    err_msg  VARCHAR2(100);
BEGIN
    LOG_ACTION('Calling update', 'update_employees');
    OPEN c1;
    FOR i IN 1..5
    LOOP
        FETCH c1
        INTO
              my_ename, my_empno, my_sal;

        EXIT WHEN c1%NOTFOUND;
        /* in case the number requested */
        /* is more than the total */
        /* number of employees */
        DBMS_OUTPUT.PUT_LINE('Success - we got here 1!');
        INSERT INTO temp VALUES
              (my_ename, my_empno, my_sal); ❶
        DBMS_OUTPUT.PUT_LINE('Successful insert!');
        COMMIT;
    END LOOP;
    CLOSE c1;
    DBMS_OUTPUT.PUT_LINE('Success - we got here!');

EXCEPTION
WHEN NO_DATA_FOUND THEN -- catches all 'no data found' errors
    DBMS_OUTPUT.PUT_LINE('Ouch, we hit an exception');
    ROLLBACK;
WHEN INVALID_NUMBER THEN -- handles INVALID_NUMBER
    err_num := SQLCODE;
    err_msg := SUBSTR(SQLERRM, 1, 100);
    DBMS_OUTPUT.PUT_LINE('We hit an INVALID_NUMBER exception error number '
    || err_num || ' Error message: ' || err_msg);
    ROLLBACK;
END;
```

❶ Reverses the artificial bug in the INSERT statement.

How modifiable is this code in Example 4-9? The reason why I'm asking is because posing such questions to yourself is a good practice. In other words, it's best to ask yourself the question rather than rely on colleagues to apply their own thinking to make the code modifiable. Now that I've added exception handling to Example 4-9, do you get a feeling there's something missing from the code? Asking yourself this question is another good habit to develop in general.

The reason for this introspection is because, with the extra exception handler, I've now added a new pathway to the code in Example 4-9 and I've omitted a call to close the cursor. Now, this is minor enough in this case because the cursor is in fact closed automatically, but it's generally a good practice to close resources such as cursors when they're no longer in use. Just for the sake of completeness, I'll remedy that with the update shown in Example 4-10.

Example 4-10. Closing resources in the PL/SQL code

```
CREATE OR REPLACE PROCEDURE update_employees
AS
        CURSOR c1 IS
                SELECT
                        ename ,
                        empno ,
                        sal
                FROM
                        emp
                ORDER BY
                        sal DESC; -- start with highest paid employee
        my_ename VARCHAR2(10);
        my_empno NUMBER(4);
        my_sal   NUMBER(7,2);
        err_num  NUMBER;
        err_msg  VARCHAR2(100);
BEGIN
        LOG_ACTION('Calling update', 'update_employees');
        OPEN c1;
        FOR i IN 1..5
        LOOP
                FETCH
                        c1
                INTO
                        my_ename,
                        my_empno,
                        my_sal;

                EXIT WHEN c1%NOTFOUND;
                /* in case the number requested */
                /* is more than the total */
                /* number of employees */
                DBMS_OUTPUT.PUT_LINE('Success - we got here 1!');
                INSERT INTO
                        temp VALUES
                        (
                                my_sal  ,
                                my_empno,
                                my_ename
                        );

                DBMS_OUTPUT.PUT_LINE('Successful insert!');
                COMMIT;
        END LOOP;
        CLOSE c1;
        DBMS_OUTPUT.PUT_LINE('Success - we got here!');
EXCEPTION
WHEN NO_DATA_FOUND THEN -- catches all 'no data found' errors
        IF c1%ISOPEN THEN
                CLOSE c1;
```

```
          END IF;
          DBMS_OUTPUT.PUT_LINE('Ouch, we hit an exception - CURSOR open: '
          || sys.diutil.bool_to_int(c1%ISOPEN));
          ROLLBACK;
WHEN INVALID_NUMBER THEN -- handles INVALID_NUMBER
          IF c1%ISOPEN THEN
                  CLOSE c1;
          END IF;
          err_num := SQLCODE;
          err_msg := SUBSTR(SQLERRM, 1, 100);
          DBMS_OUTPUT.PUT_LINE(
          'We hit an invalid number exception error number - CURSOR open: '
          || sys.diutil.bool_to_int(c1%ISOPEN) || ' ' || err_num
          || ' Error message: ' || err_msg);
          ROLLBACK;
END;
```

When we run the code in Example 4-10, the program output is as follows:

```
Connecting to the database Oracle_Docker.
Success - we got here 1!
We hit an invalid number exception error number -
cursor open: 0 -1722 Error message: ORA-01722: invalid number
Process exited.
Disconnecting from the database Oracle_Docker.
```

Notice the new output: cursor open: 0. This indicates that the cursor is indeed being explicitly closed as part of the exception handler.

The small changes made in this section suggest that the code is quite modifiable. As you'll see in the next section on *modularity*, further improvement will be made possible in *modifiability*.

Scale of Resilience Requirement 5: Modularity

The code in Example 4-10 is getting a bit clunky at this point. It's really a bit of a mess! This is actually quite typical with coding in general. As new features are added and with development time pressure, it can get harder to understand the code. This is of course particularly the case for new people who haven't seen the code before. The original author may well understand the code but, in its current form, it is unnecessarily complicated.

Generally, the best way to resolve this excessive complexity is to resort to the old principle of *divide and conquer*. This is also referred to as *stepwise refinement* or, in modern parlance, *refactoring*.

In this approach, I will break the procedure into two separate procedures, as shown by the pseudocode requirements in Example 4-11.

Example 4-11. Requirements for producing a more modular example

```
Procedure 1 is tasked with:
* Data acquisition
* Flow control
* Exception handling

 Procedure 2 is tasked with:
* Data modification
* Business logic
```

To enhance the *modularity*, I therefore want to break up and simplify the code in some way. This is where it becomes useful to have knowledge of some additional PL/SQL language constructs. In Example 4-12, you can see an example of the cursor FOR LOOP.

Example 4-12. Using a language construct for simpler PL/SQL code

```
create or replace PROCEDURE update_employees
AS
  CURSOR c_employee
  IS
    SELECT
            ename, empno, sal
    FROM emp
    ORDER BY
        sal DESC;
BEGIN
  FOR r_employee IN c_employee
  LOOP
    dbms_output.put_line( r_employee.ename || ': $' ||  r_employee.sal );
    DBMS_OUTPUT.PUT_LINE('Success - we got here 1!');
    INSERT INTO temp VALUES
        (r_employee.empno,
         r_employee.ename,
         r_employee.sal);

    DBMS_OUTPUT.PUT_LINE('Successful insert!');
  END LOOP;
END;
```

One benefit of the FOR LOOP in Example 4-12 is implicit (or automatic) opening and closing of the cursor. So, in Example 4-12, we therefore no longer need to worry about cursor handling.

What about exceptions? Do I need to concern myself with exceptions now that I'm using the cursor FOR LOOP? To find out, let's run the code and put in our familiar (exception-producing) bug by changing this code:

```
INSERT INTO
        temp VALUES
        (
            r_employee.empno,
            r_employee.ename,
            r_employee.sal
        );
```

to this:

```
INSERT INTO
        temp VALUES
        (
            r_employee.sal,
            r_employee.empno,
            r_employee.ename
        );
```

In other words, I'm swapping the salary and name columns so as to produce a data type violation. Running the (now buggy) code, we see this output:

```
ORA-01722: invalid number
ORA-06512: at "STEPHEN.UPDATE_EMPLOYEES", line 15
ORA-06512: at line 2
Mary: $40000
Success - we got here 1!
Process exited.
```

So, I'm still getting the expected exceptions in the substantially reduced code. I'll address this by making a quick addition of some exception handling, which produces Example 4-13.

Example 4-13. Using a language construct for simpler PL/SQL code

```
create or replace PROCEDURE update_employees
AS
  err_num NUMBER;
  err_msg VARCHAR2(100);
  CURSOR c_employee
  IS
    SELECT
            ename, empno, sal
    FROM
        emp
    ORDER BY
      sal DESC;
BEGIN
  FOR r_employee IN c_employee
  LOOP
    dbms_output.put_line( r_employee.ename || ': $' || r_employee.sal );
          DBMS_OUTPUT.PUT_LINE('Success - we got here 1!');
    INSERT INTO temp VALUES
        (r_employee.sal,
          r_employee.empno,
          r_employee.ename);

    DBMS_OUTPUT.PUT_LINE('Successful insert!');
  END LOOP;

EXCEPTION
WHEN NO_DATA_FOUND THEN -- catches all 'no data found' errors
      DBMS_OUTPUT.PUT_LINE('Ouch, we hit an exception');
      ROLLBACK;
WHEN OTHERS THEN -- handles all other errors
      err_num := SQLCODE;
      err_msg := SUBSTR(SQLERRM, 1, 100);
      DBMS_OUTPUT.PUT_LINE('We hit a general exception error number - '
      || ' '
      || err_num
```

```
        || ' Error message: '
        || err_msg);
        ROLLBACK;
END;
```

Let's now run the code in Example 4-13. We should see the following output:

```
Connecting to the database Oracle_Docker.
Mary: $40000
Success - we got here 1!
We hit a general exception error number - 1722
Error message: ORA-01722: invalid number
```

I've caught the same exception as before, but look at how much smaller the code is in Example 4-13. That's a whole lot less code to maintain—no cursor management is required of us. Producing compact and easily understood code is always worth the effort. One important merit is that you are freer to focus on implementing important business capabilities.

But what about the modularity requirements? Example 4-11 specifies that we are to break the existing procedure into two procedures:

- Data acquisition, flow control, and exception handling
- Data modification and business logic

Example 4-14 shows how to divide the procedure in order to make it more modular. First, we have a data modification procedure and business logic.

Example 4-14. Data modification procedure and business logic

```
create or replace PROCEDURE updateEmployeeData(
ENAME IN VARCHAR2, EMPNO IN NUMBER, SAL IN NUMBER)
AS
BEGIN
    dbms_output.put_line('Employee: ' || ENAME || ' Number: ' ||
    EMPNO || ' Salary: ' || SAL);
    DBMS_OUTPUT.PUT_LINE('Success - we got here 1!');
    INSERT INTO temp VALUES
        (SAL, EMPNO, ENAME);
    dbms_output.put_line('Successful insert');
END;
```

The procedure in Example 4-14 is called during the loop by the now further-reduced procedure in Example 4-15.

Example 4-15. The main (driving) procedure

```
create or replace PROCEDURE update_employees
AS
 err_num NUMBER;
 err_msg VARCHAR2(100);
  CURSOR c_employee
  IS
    SELECT
            ename, empno, sal
    FROM
        emp
    ORDER BY
        sal DESC;
BEGIN
  FOR r_employee IN c_employee
  LOOP
    updateEmployeeData(r_employee.ename, r_employee.empno, r_employee.sal);
  END LOOP;

EXCEPTION
WHEN NO_DATA_FOUND THEN -- catches all 'no data found' errors
      DBMS_OUTPUT.PUT_LINE('Ouch, we hit an exception');
      ROLLBACK;
WHEN OTHERS THEN -- handles all other errors
      err_num := SQLCODE;
      err_msg := SUBSTR(SQLERRM, 1, 100);
      DBMS_OUTPUT.PUT_LINE('We hit a general exception error number - '
      || ' '
      || err_num
      || ' Error message: '
      || err_msg);
      ROLLBACK;
END;
```

 In Chapter 6, I'll introduce the idea of *helpers*, which are very short procedures and functions that provide specialized, clearly defined actions on behalf of the main code. When the main code requires some assistance (e.g., calculating the tax due on a sale) it calls an appropriate helper. In this context, updateEmployeeData is an example of a helper.

I have at last arrived at a more modular version of the PL/SQL code. In Example 4-15, you see a main procedure called update_employees that invokes a service (or helper) procedure with the name updateEmployeeData.

The main procedure (update_employees) handles any exceptions as well. So, if the service procedure (updateEmployeeData) happens to raise an exception (which it does), then it will be handled in the main procedure (update_employees). This approach gives us the benefits of good exception handling without adding burdens to the service code.

A slight change to this approach of handling exceptions in the calling procedure is commonly adopted by very experienced PL/SQL developers, where exceptions are handled as close to their origin as possible. When using this approach, every procedure/function has its own exception handler with a WHEN OTHERS clause ending in raise. The purpose of the raise is to push the exception back up the chain for any further processing.

This is also a good pattern in that it allows for localized processing of exceptions. Regardless of whether you opt for this approach or the helper-based technique, this discussion underlines the importance of having a defined strategy for *modularity* and exception management.

I think the structure in Example 4-15 is a nice division of labor, and it has the additional merit of being quite easy to understand for anyone who has to maintain it down the line.

Oracle PL/SQL also provides a packaging facility that allows for enhanced modularity. Let's have a look at this in relation to the logging code.

A Logging Package

The use of PL/SQL packages allows for code to be easily shared across the environment. As you'll soon see, packages can be compiled and stored in the Oracle Database. This facilitates sharing the package contents across many applications.

When you call a packaged subprogram for the first time, the whole package is loaded into memory. Subsequent calls to related subprograms in the package then require no additional disk I/O. It is for this reason that packages can be used to enhance developer productivity and improve performance. The use of packages also helps protect the runtime system.

One typical use case for PL/SQL packages is *utility* code, i.e., code that is of use to a range of callers. Logging fits nicely into this category. Getting up to speed with PL/SQL packages isn't difficult. I've created a packaged version of the logging procedure in Example 4-16. See if you can figure it out.

Example 4-16. The logging package

```
create or replace PACKAGE loggingPackage ❶
AS
  PROCEDURE LOG_ACTION(
                action_message IN VARCHAR2, code_location  IN VARCHAR2);
END loggingPackage;

create or replace PACKAGE BODY loggingPackage AS ❷
PROCEDURE LOG_ACTION(
                action_message IN VARCHAR2, code_location  IN VARCHAR2)
IS
    PRAGMA AUTONOMOUS_TRANSACTION;
BEGIN
    INSERT INTO LOGGING
            (EVENT_DATE
                , action_message
                , code_location
            )
            VALUES
            (SYSDATE
                , action_message
                , code_location
            )
    ;

    COMMIT;
END;
END loggingPackage;
```

❶　This is the API.

❷　This is the implementation of the API.

As with APIs in general, the package specification is the contract and the implementation remains hidden from the callers. Packages provide for enhanced modularity and they are strongly encouraged by Oracle.

Let's look now at the nuts and bolts of how to create a PL/SQL package and how to store it in the Oracle Database.

Creating a Logging Package

To create a new package, right-click Packages, as shown in Figure 4-8, and select New Package.

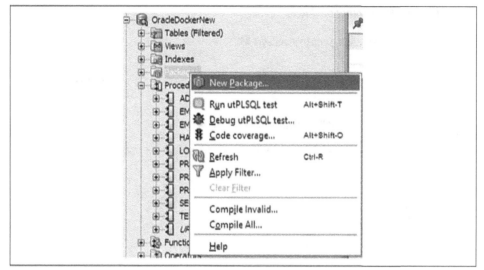

Figure 4-8. Create a new package

Type a new name for the package, such as LOGGINGPACKAGE. Then, paste or type the code from Example 4-17, overwriting the previous contents.

Example 4-17. The logging package API

```
create or replace PACKAGE loggingPackage
AS
 PROCEDURE LOG_ACTION(
 action_message IN VARCHAR2, code_location IN VARCHAR2); ❶
END loggingPackage;
```

❶ Supplies only the name and the required parameters of the procedure. This is crucial because the specification is the API that users of the package will see. In other words, package users won't know (or generally care) about the implementation of the package procedure(s).

Select the contents of Example 4-17, then right-click it and select Compile. This should then store the package specification in the database and you can verify this by clicking the refresh button on the upper-left menu.

Next up, we have to create the LOG_ACTION procedure implementation. Right-click the package name and select the Create Body option, as shown in Figure 4-9.

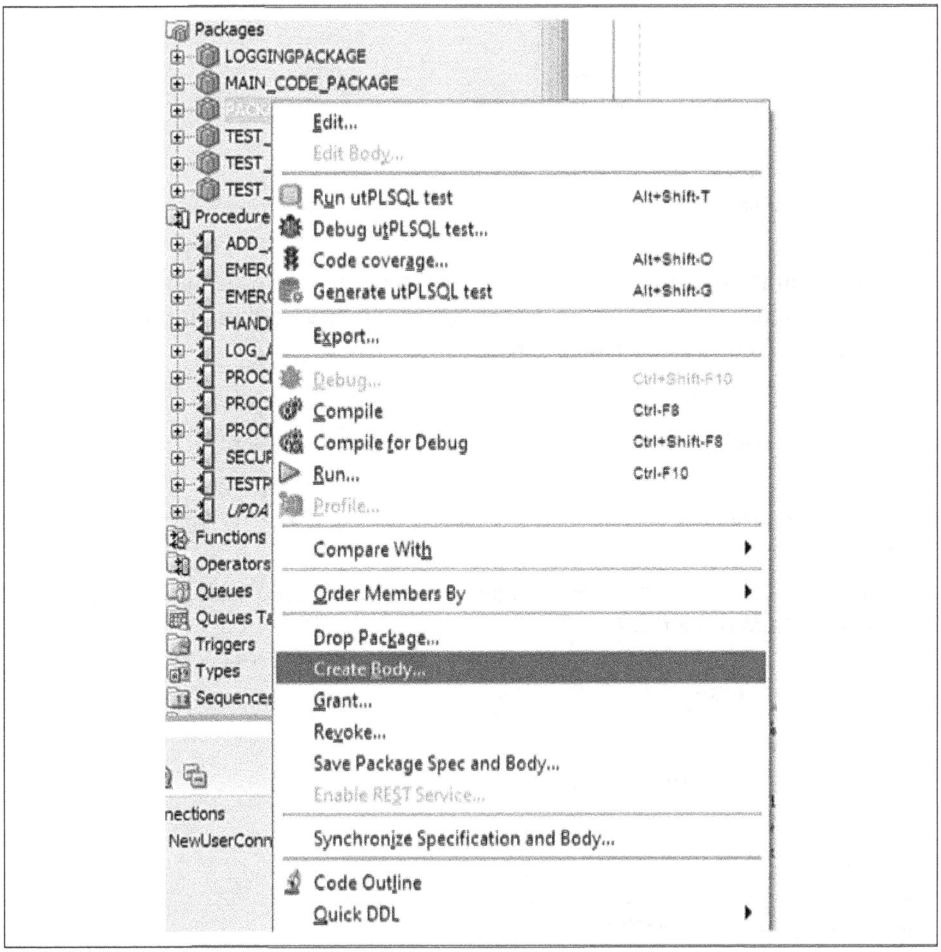

Figure 4-9. Create a new package body

Overwrite the `LOG_ACTION` procedure contents with the following (don't delete the package details surrounding the procedure code):

```
PROCEDURE LOG_ACTION(action_message IN VARCHAR2,
                     code_location   IN VARCHAR2)
IS
        PRAGMA AUTONOMOUS_TRANSACTION;
BEGIN
        INSERT INTO
                LOGGING
                (
                        EVENT_DATE    ,
                        action_message,
                        code_location
                )
```

```
                        VALUES
                        (
                                SYSDATE         ,
                                action_message,
                                code_location
                        );

            COMMIT;
    END;
```

Then select all (only required if there is other code in your worksheet), right-click, and select Compile. At this point, the package should be stored in the database, ready for use. To verify it, clear the LOGGING table:

```
delete from LOGGING;
```

Finally, call the package procedure with some PL/SQL:

```
BEGIN
    loggingPackage.LOG_ACTION('A log message', 'Trouble at mill');
END;
```

If all is well, there should now be a single row in the LOGGING table, as shown by the data at the bottom of Figure 4-10.

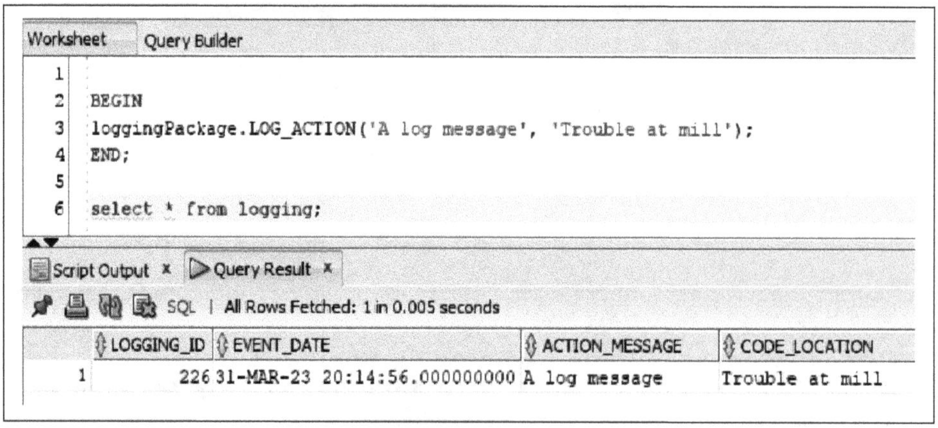

Figure 4-10. Successfully running the newly packaged procedure

The single row at the bottom of Figure 4-10 is, of course, the same data supplied by the call to loggingPackage.LOG_ACTION.

Integrating the Logging Facility

Now that we have a nice logging utility, let's get it integrated into the existing code. This is a simple task. In Example 4-18, you see the current revision of the main procedure, i.e., update_employees.

Example 4-18. The main (driving) procedure with no logging calls

```
create or replace PROCEDURE update_employees
AS
 err_num NUMBER;
 err_msg VARCHAR2(100);
  CURSOR c_employee
  IS
    SELECT
            ename, empno, sal
    FROM
        emp
    ORDER BY
        sal DESC;
BEGIN
  FOR r_employee IN c_employee
  LOOP
    updateEmployeeData(r_employee.ename, r_employee.empno, r_employee.sal);
  END LOOP;

EXCEPTION
WHEN NO_DATA_FOUND THEN -- catches all 'no data found' errors
        DBMS_OUTPUT.PUT_LINE('Ouch, we hit an exception');
        ROLLBACK;
WHEN OTHERS THEN -- handles all other errors
        err_num := SQLCODE;
        err_msg := SUBSTR(SQLERRM, 1, 100);
        DBMS_OUTPUT.PUT_LINE('We hit a general exception error number - '
        || ' '
        || err_num
        || ' Error message: '
        || err_msg);
        ROLLBACK;
END;
```

By adding logging to Example 4-18, I produce Example 4-19. Notice that the calls to the logging procedure required a small change to the logging message (i.e., I had to split the string into two parameters).

Example 4-19. The main (driving) procedure with integrated logging calls

```
create or replace PROCEDURE update_employees
AS
 err_num NUMBER;
 err_msg VARCHAR2(100);
  CURSOR c_employee
  IS
    SELECT
            ename, empno, sal
    FROM
        emp
```

```
    ORDER BY
        sal DESC;
BEGIN
  FOR r_employee IN c_employee
  LOOP
    updateEmployeeData(r_employee.ename, r_employee.empno, r_employee.sal);
  END LOOP;

EXCEPTION
WHEN NO_DATA_FOUND THEN -- catches all 'no data found' errors
        loggingPackage.LOG_ACTION('Ouch', 'we hit an exception');
        ROLLBACK;
WHEN OTHERS THEN -- handles all other errors
        err_num := SQLCODE;
        err_msg := SUBSTR(SQLERRM, 1, 100);
        loggingPackage.LOG_ACTION('We hit a general exception error number - '
        || ' '
        || err_num
        || ' Error message: '
        || err_msg, 'update_employees');
        ROLLBACK;
END;
```

Adding logging to the other (*helper*) procedure is very similar, as shown in
Example 4-20.

It is of course better to improve the INSERT statement by explicitly
specifying the target columns as follows:

```
INSERT INTO temp(column1, column2, column3)
VALUES(value1, value2, value3);
```

A less obvious point is that this more verbose approach can also
help avoid problems with virtual columns (*https://oreil.ly/6INeP*),
the values of which are derived rather than being stored on disk.

Example 4-20. Data modification procedure with logging integrated

```
create or replace PROCEDURE updateEmployeeData(
ENAME IN VARCHAR2, EMPNO IN NUMBER, SAL IN NUMBER)
AS
BEGIN
    loggingPackage.LOG_ACTION('Employee: ' || ENAME || ' Number: ' ||
    EMPNO || ' Salary: ' || SAL, 'updateEmployeeData');
    loggingPackage.LOG_ACTION('Success - we got here 1!',
    'updateEmployeeData');
    INSERT INTO temp VALUES
        (SAL, EMPNO, ENAME);
    loggingPackage.LOG_ACTION('Successful insert', 'updateEmployeeData');
END;
```

The code is now modularized with integrated logging packaged as per the scale of resilience requirement 5.

Let's now turn our attention to the requirement for *simplicity*.

Scale of Resilience Requirement 6: Simplicity

Prior to refactoring the code for modularity and the addition of a utility logging package, it was getting a little bit hard to understand. This was on account of cursor resource management and exception handling being mixed in with business logic.

The business logic is of course the database updates that are provided in relation to employee details. The latest code version in Example 4-21 is simple enough and yet it also provides a good deal of capability. How does it stack up in terms of simplicity? This is always a good question to ask when adopting the mindset and work practices of resilience and shift-left.

Example 4-21. The latest version of the main procedure with integrated logging calls

```
create or replace PROCEDURE update_employees
AS
 err_num NUMBER;
 err_msg VARCHAR2(100);
  CURSOR c_employee
  IS
    SELECT
            ename, empno, sal
    FROM
        emp
    ORDER BY
        sal DESC;
BEGIN
  FOR r_employee IN c_employee
  LOOP
    updateEmployeeData(r_employee.ename, r_employee.empno, r_employee.sal);
  END LOOP;

EXCEPTION
WHEN NO_DATA_FOUND THEN -- catches all 'no data found' errors
        loggingPackage.LOG_ACTION(('Ouch', 'we hit an exception'));
        ROLLBACK;
WHEN OTHERS THEN -- handles all other errors
        err_num := SQLCODE;
        err_msg := SUBSTR(SQLERRM, 1, 100);
        loggingPackage.LOG_ACTION('We hit a general exception error number - '
        || ' '
        || err_num
        || ' Error message: '
        || err_msg, 'update_employees');
```

```
    ROLLBACK;
END;
```

The exception-handling code and the later modularization effort have been beneficial in that it is probably difficult to make the code in Example 4-21 very much simpler than is currently the case.

 This is one of the merits of using an iterative design approach such as following a scale of resilience. You get what might be called pull-through benefits. That is, by applying careful design patterns and integration techniques, you get modularity, logging, simplicity, and a good foundation for exception and error handling.

Let's move on from simplicity and take a look at coding conventions.

Scale of Resilience Requirement 7: Coding Conventions

It's not uncommon to find multiple *coding conventions* even inside the same organization. This can arise when new entrants join and they have wide experience in similar or different organizations and industries.

Mixing and matching coding conventions can make for complexity across the software development lifecycle. Some developers may favor strong exception handling, while others prefer to put more effort into automation or testing.

Having a standard coding convention is an advantage when the goal is resilient software. Let's look a little at how to use a basic coding convention. As usual in this book, we can define a few fairly loose requirements as follows:

- Good comments
- Consistent variable names
- Clear formatting
- Exception handling
- Testing and automatic test cases
- Avoiding excessive complexity

The main thrust of these requirements is of course to make the code easier to understand. By following the scale of resilience, we get additional benefits including those that arise from using a coding convention.

The code examples so far have used a few coding styles. This has been done purely to illustrate the flexibility of PL/SQL. Also, it reflects the fact that you are at liberty to choose your own style.

In my own work, I tend to use a single style of coding and then stick to that. Then, later on, if I can't understand some code I've written, I only have myself to blame.

The examples from this point on will aim to adhere to a more rigorous style.

Scale of Resilience Requirement 8: Reusability

Is the code in Example 4-22 reusable? That is, would there be merit in placing this code, or part of it, in a shared package for use by other developers (as we did with the logging feature)?

> Experienced PL/SQL developers may insist on all code being placed in a package even if it is just one procedure or function.

Example 4-22. Is this code reusable?

```
create or replace PROCEDURE updateEmployeeData(
ENAME IN VARCHAR2, EMPNO IN NUMBER, SAL IN NUMBER)
AS
BEGIN
    loggingPackage.LOG_ACTION('Employee: ' || ENAME || ' Number: ' ||
    EMPNO || ' Salary: ' || SAL, 'updateEmployeeData');
    loggingPackage.LOG_ACTION('Success - we got here 1!',
    'updateEmployeeData');
    INSERT INTO temp VALUES
        (SAL, EMPNO, ENAME);
    loggingPackage.LOG_ACTION('Successful insert', 'updateEmployeeData');
END;

create or replace PROCEDURE update_employees
AS
 err_num NUMBER;
 err_msg VARCHAR2(100);
  CURSOR c_employee
  IS
    SELECT
            ename, empno, sal
    FROM
        emp
    ORDER BY
        sal DESC;
BEGIN
  FOR r_employee IN c_employee
  LOOP
    updateEmployeeData(r_employee.ename, r_employee.empno, r_employee.sal);
  END LOOP;
```

```
EXCEPTION
WHEN NO_DATA_FOUND THEN -- catches all 'no data found' errors
        loggingPackage.LOG_ACTION(('Ouch', 'we hit an exception'));
        ROLLBACK;
WHEN OTHERS THEN -- handles all other errors
        err_num := SQLCODE;
        err_msg := SUBSTR(SQLERRM, 1, 100);
        loggingPackage.LOG_ACTION('We hit a general exception error number - '
        || ' '
        || err_num
        || ' Error message: '
        || err_msg, 'update_employees');
        ROLLBACK;
END;
```

In truth, the code in Example 4-22 is not very reusable. Not because it's bad but more because it is such simple code and it's very specific to the task at hand. The overall pattern in use in Example 4-22 is certainly reusable. But the specific code itself, not so much.

In general, the case for reusable code tends to arise when dealing with less specific (i.e., more generic) coding tasks, system-level assets, and resources, such as the management of the following:

- Cursors
- Files
- Locking
- Logging

Having said all that, it is a best practice (and one strongly encouraged by Oracle) to deliver PL/SQL as packaged code. So (as noted at the beginning of this section), on balance I think the effort of producing a package for the type of code in Example 4-22 is outweighed by the benefits.

 In Example 4-22, it is also possible to use a SAVEPOINT. Once a SAVE POINT has been created, you can then either continue processing, commit your work, and roll back the entire transaction, or roll back just to the SAVEPOINT. In other words, SAVEPOINT provides more granular control over the rollback.

As you'll see in the next section, packaged PL/SQL is compatible with one of the de facto standard PL/SQL test frameworks, utPLSQL (*https://oreil.ly/NZJyS*).

Let's now have a look at whether there is scope for repeatable testing in Example 4-22.

Scale of Resilience Requirement 9: Repeatable Testing

In modern development, it is common to use the model of a continuous integration delivery pipeline. In this approach, code is designed, written, tested, and deployed much as in traditional methods.

However, the pipeline approach tends to make heavy use of automated tools to build, deploy, and test the code, as shown (in simple terms) in Figure 4-11.

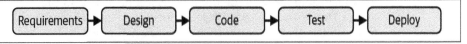

Figure 4-11. The software development pipeline

The global adoption of Agile methods has resulted in the activities in Figure 4-11 becoming very compressed in time. Very often, the activities overlap such that design and API creation may be considered coding. Likewise, a code check-in to a repository such as Git or Subversion is commonly used to signal the start of an automated build and deployment cycle. At this point, it is also quite common to receive an (often unwelcome) email attributing a build break to you.

Development is therefore no longer a strictly linear set of tasks. For this reason, we as developers need as much help as we can get in the form of:

- Compiler warnings
- Automatic test facilities
- Vulnerability checking
- Information concerning build issues

In Figure 4-11, much of the behind-the-scenes work, including testing, is automated. Nowadays, automated tests can be run as part of the build procedure and failing tests can result in the build terminating. In other words, tests must pass in order to proceed to the end of the pipeline.

Pretty much all the mainstream programming languages have tools and frameworks for this type of automated testing and PL/SQL is no exception. In any case, the database repository–based approach is a useful and instructive test method, which I've used myself. We will instead focus on a different technique for PL/SQL unit testing, one that uses the utPLSQL product. Let's have a look at how to get started with this interesting technology by getting it installed into the Docker-containerized Oracle Database setup.

There is a facility for unit testing built into the Oracle Database. To use the Oracle-centric testing, it is necessary to create a special-purpose unit test repository.

On shared databases (i.e., installations not using a Docker-based Oracle setup), it is often necessary to request this repository setup from a database administrator. This does add an extra step to getting set up with PL/SQL unit testing and it may act as a disincentive to team environments where there is a preference to keep such work internal to the team. It's worth remembering that, as we are using a Docker-based Oracle Database installation, there is a little more latitude than is normally the case when you are using a shared database.

Installing utPLSQL

The following commands require that your Docker container is running. So, make sure to run the usual startup command:

```
docker start <CONTAINER_ID>
```

As usual, you need to supply your own container ID, which you get by running the command:

```
docker container ls -a
```

Now open a command prompt in the Docker container

```
docker exec -itw /home/oracle/ <CONTAINER_ID> bash
```

This command opens a prompt in the directory */home/oracle*. Type **pwd** to verify the path is */home/oracle*. Next, download the most recently released utPLSQL ZIP file from GitHub. The utPLSQL version may well be different from v3.1.12 by the time you're reading this:

```
curl \
https://github.com/utPLSQL/utPLSQL/releases/download/v3.1.12/utPLSQL.zip \
-L -o utPLSQL.zip
```

Run the Linux commands in this section on one line only. If you need to separate a command so that it occupies two lines, then add "\" at the end of each line as shown.

For multiline Windows commands in a basic command prompt window, you can use the character "^" to continue a command across a line boundary, for example:

```
docker exec -itw /home/oracle/utPLSQL/source ^
380195f59d0d bash -c ^
"source /home/oracle/.bashrc; sqlplus /nolog"
```

Optionally, run `ls -l` to verify that the ZIP file is not a 0-byte file, i.e., indicating that the download failed for some reason (such as supplying an incorrect URL). Then, extract the downloaded ZIP file:

```
unzip -q utPLSQL.zip
```

Next, you need to create a schema in the Oracle Database, and this is done by connecting using `sqlplus` with the SYS account. For simplicity, you can exit the current command prompt—just type **exit** and press Enter.

Now, open a new command prompt in the Docker container (again supplying your own local container ID):

```
docker exec -itw /home/oracle/utPLSQL/source <CONTAINER_ID> \
bash -c "source /home/oracle/.bashrc; sqlplus /nolog"
```

This opens a command prompt in the directory */home/oracle/utPLSQL/source*. Next, type **connect sys as sysdba;**. At this point, you are prompted for a password. Use the password you provided in the setup back in Example 2-1. I used `mySyspwd1`.

Next, run the following command:

```
alter session set "_ORACLE_SCRIPT"=true;
```

Then, run this command to create the `ut3` user:

```
@create_utplsql_owner.sql ut3 ut3 users;
```

Use `!pwd` to see the current directory. This command did disconnect my session from the database. Just make sure you're in the correct directory. The installation seems to be a little fussy about running from this directory: */home/oracle/utPLSQL/source*.

Next, run this command (which takes a few minutes):

```
@install.sql ut3;
```

List schemas using this command:

```
select username as schema_name
from sys.dba_users
order by username;
```

In SQL Developer, under Other Users, you should now see the user UT3. Click Packages to see the required framework packages. Also, click Tables to verify the framework tables are installed.

Run the following command to allow access to `public` for user `ut3`. This gives access to all users. Normally, just one user is provided access, but for the Docker setup, the public option is fine:

```
@create_synonyms_and_grants_for_public.sql ut3;
```

The next two steps are optional. They grant access to a specific user by running this command (a username is required):

```
@create_user_grants.sql ut3 <Specific_user>;
@create_user_synonyms.sql ut3 <Specific_user>;
```

If the utPLSQL installation was successful, then you can exit both `sqlplus` and the bash session. You're now ready to create a utPLSQL unit test.

Creating a utPLSQL Unit Test in SQL Developer

An implicit assumption with utPLSQL is that the code you want to test must reside in a package. This is a reasonable and useful requirement, given that packaged PL/SQL provides the foundation for the following:

- Shareability
- Generality
- Simplicity
- Modularity

So, forcing us to write packaged PL/SQL helps in producing better-quality code. Let's now create a simple utPLSQL unit test suite:

```
CREATE OR REPLACE PACKAGE test_LOGGINGPACKAGE IS
  --%suite
  --%suitepath(alltests)

  --%test
  PROCEDURE LOG_ACTION;

END test_LOGGINGPACKAGE;
```

As you learned earlier in the chapter, a package specification needs a body where the `LOG_ACTION` procedure is implemented. This is done in Example 4-23.

As you've done in earlier chapters, it's a good idea to try to figure out what the code in Example 4-23 is trying to achieve.

Example 4-23. The test procedure

```
CREATE OR REPLACE PACKAGE BODY test_LOGGINGPACKAGE AS
  PROCEDURE LOG_ACTION IS
    l_actual    INTEGER := 0;
    l_expected INTEGER := 1; ❶
  BEGIN
    delete from LOGGING;
    loggingpackage.log_action('An action', 'A log message'); ❷
    select count(*) into l_actual from logging; ❸
    ut.expect(l_actual).to_equal(l_expected); -- to_equal is the matcher ❹
  END LOG_ACTION;
END test_LOGGINGPACKAGE;
```

❶ In general, in unit testing, the aim is to set up an expected result and then call the code under test and verify whether the actual result matches the expected result. Here, we're expecting a value of 1.

❷ Clears down the LOGGING table and calls the log_action procedure from the package loggingpackage. After clearing the LOGGING table and calling log_action, it's safe to assume I will have a single row in the table (at least in the context of this session), which explains our assumption in ❶.

❸ Verifies the expected condition. This line simply counts the number of rows in the LOGGING table and stores the result in the l_actual variable. By deduction, this value is 1.

❹ Compares the two values.

And that's the test. If the two values match, the test passes. If they don't match, the test fails.

Running a utPLSQL Unit Test

Let's have a look at how running the test happens in a normal unit test workflow. Before I get into test creation, look at Figure 4-12, which illustrates a failing test.

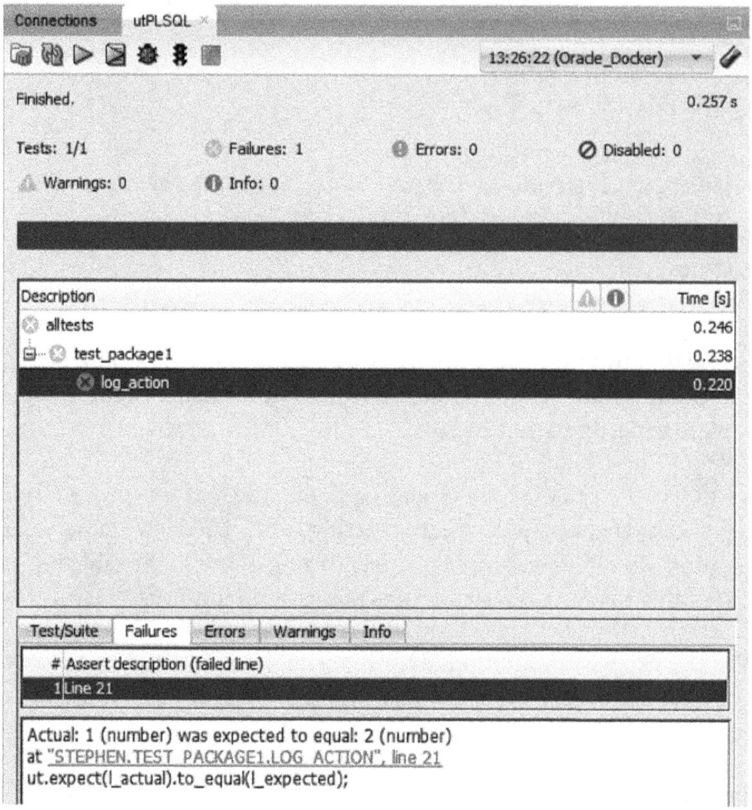

Figure 4-12. A test failure

I forced the test in Figure 4-12 to fail by making a small change to the expected result, as shown in Example 4-24.

Example 4-24. A failing test

```
procedure log_action is
   l_actual    integer := 0;
   l_expected integer := 2; ❶
begin
   -- arrange

   -- act
   -- package1.log_action;
   delete from LOGGING;
   PACKAGE1.log_action('An action', 'A log message');
   select count(*) into l_actual from logging;

   -- assert
   ut.expect(l_actual).to_equal(l_expected);
end log_action;
```

❶ We know the LOGGING table is cleared at the beginning of the test and then one row is added. So, if the test is to pass, the expected number of rows should be 1 and not 2, as shown here.

Having done all this, we now know what a failing test looks like in SQL Developer, as shown in Figure 4-12. Let's get back to creating a utPLSQL unit test from scratch.

In SQL Developer, you can employ a nice, easy method for creating the test. This does require installation of the utPLSQL plug-in as described in "Installing utPLSQL" on page 106. Starting with the package you want to test, right-click the package containing the logging code. This opens the context menu, as shown in Figure 4-13.

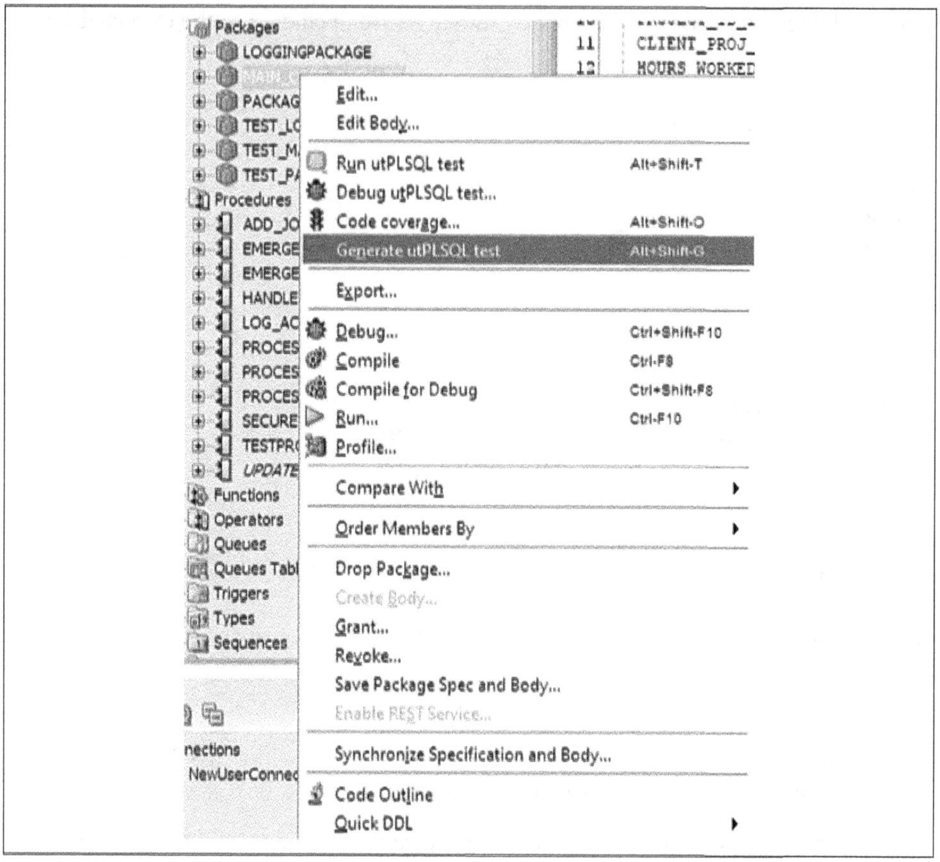

Figure 4-13. Generating a test suite

Select the highlighted option:

```
Generate utPLSQL Test
```

This produces the boilerplate code in Example 4-25.

Example 4-25. Boilerplate test code

```
create or replace package test_package1 is

    -- generated by utPLSQL for SQL Developer on 2022-06-02 13:47:44

    --%suite(test_package1)
    --%suitepath(alltests)

    --%test
    procedure log_action;
```

```
end test_package1;

create or replace package body test_package1 is

   -- generated by utPLSQL for SQL Developer on 2022-06-02 13:47:44

   --
   -- test log_action
   --
   procedure log_action is
      l_actual   integer := 0;
      l_expected integer := 1;
   begin
      -- arrange

      -- act
      -- package1.log_action;

      -- assert
      ut.expect(l_actual).to_equal(l_expected);
   end log_action;

end test_package1;
```

This is really useful! I now have a basic test ready for use. Let's just add a few lines into the procedure `log_action` in Example 4-25 as follows:

```
procedure log_action is
   l_actual   integer := 0;
   l_expected integer := 1;
begin
   -- arrange

   -- act
   -- package1.log_action;
   delete from LOGGING;
   PACKAGE1.log_action('An action', 'A log message');
   select count(*) into l_actual from logging;

   -- assert
   ut.expect(l_actual).to_equal(l_expected);
end log_action;
```

Now, select all, right-click, and then select the Run Statement menu option, as shown in Figure 4-14.

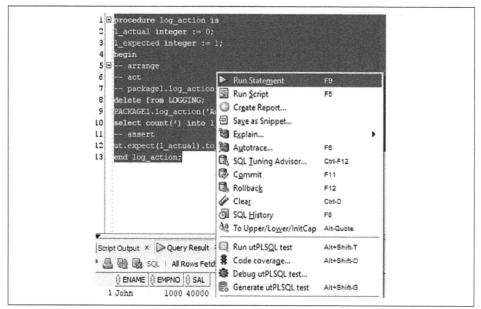

Figure 4-14. Compiling the test code

If all is well, you should see the following message in the result window:

```
Package Body TEST_PACKAGE1 compiled
```

At this point, the test package (called TEST_PACKAGE1) is stored in the database. Click the refresh button and then open the Packages control, and it should look somewhat like Figure 4-15.

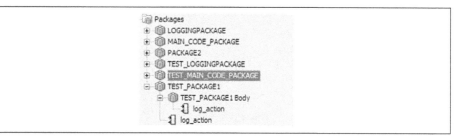

Figure 4-15. The new test package

All that remains is to run the test in Figure 4-15. Do this by right-clicking the package called TEST_PACKAGE1, as shown in Figure 4-16, and clicking the highlighted option "Run utPLSQL test."

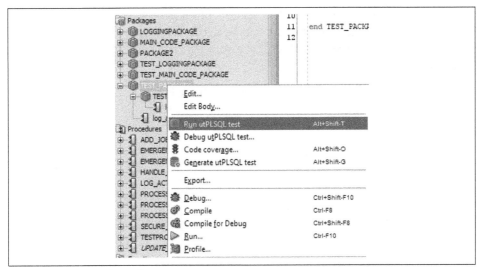

Figure 4-16. Launching the new test

After running the test, the result should look somewhat like Figure 4-17.

Description	⚠	ⓘ	Time [s]
✓ alltests			0.034
⊟ ✓ test_loggingpackage			0.025
⌐ ✓ log_action			0.012

Finished.　　0.047 s

Tests: 1/1　　Failures: 0　　Errors: 0
Disabled: 0　　Warnings: 0　　Info: 0

Test/Suite　Failures　Errors　Warnings　Info

\# Assert description (failed line)

Figure 4-17. The result of the new test

A green bar indicates that the test was successful. I'll now make a minor change (as was done earlier in this section) to the test code. This is to ensure that a failure occurs in the test. Remember I noted earlier that errors are good teachers? This also applies in the case of test code.

As before, I change the value of l_expected to 2 instead of 1:

```
PROCEDURE log_action
IS
        l_actual   INTEGER := 0;
        l_expected INTEGER := 2;
BEGIN
        -- arrange
        -- act
        -- package1.log_action;
        DELETE
        FROM
        LOGGING;

        PACKAGE1.log_action('An action', 'A log message');
        SELECT
                COUNT(*)
        INTO
                l_actual
        FROM
                logging;

        -- assert
        ut.expect(l_actual).to_equal(l_expected);
END log_action;
```

Then, select all, right-click, and select Compile. At this point the updated package should be stored in the database, ready for use. Right-click the test package and run the test. The result of this should appear somewhat similar to Figure 4-18. Test failures are clearly indicated with a red bar along with the following explanatory text describing the issue:

```
Actual: 1 (number) was expected to equal: 2 (number)
at "STEPHEN.TEST_PACKAGE1.LOG_ACTION",
line 20 ut.expect(l_actual).to_equal(l_expected);
```

The error report indicates that the number 1 was expected to equal the number 2. As this is not a valid comparison, the test is correctly marked as a failure.

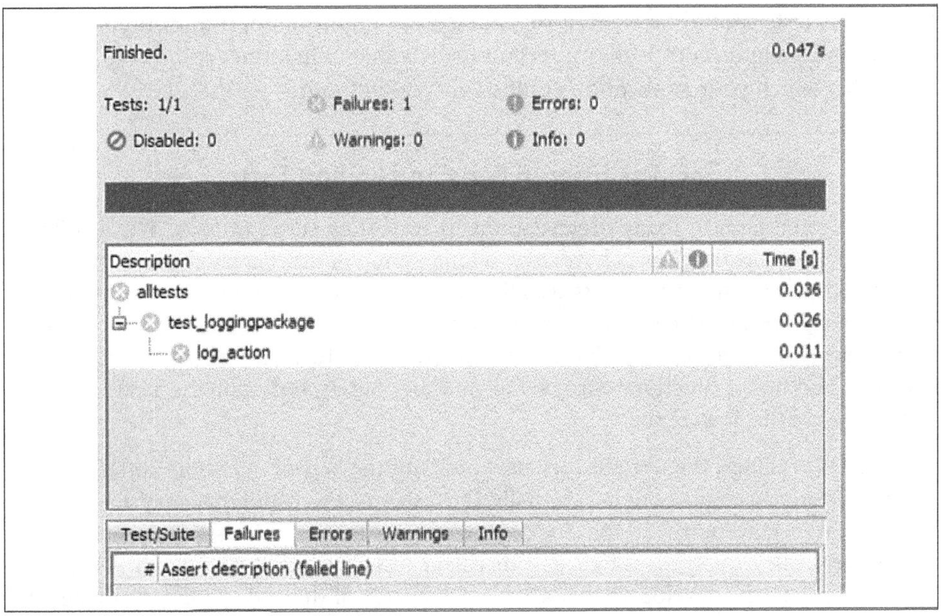

```
Finished.                                                    0.047 s

Tests: 1/1              ◎ Failures: 1        ◉ Errors: 0
⊘ Disabled: 0           ⚠ Warnings: 0        ① Info: 0
```

Description	⚠ ①	Time [s]
◎ alltests		0.036
⊟ ◎ test_loggingpackage		0.026
┊┄ ◎ log_action		0.011

```
Test/Suite  Failures  Errors  Warnings  Info
   #  Assert description (failed line)
```

Figure 4-18. The test is now failing

So, that's a rapid tour of the full workflow for utPLSQL unit tests, namely:

- Generating
- Running
- Modifying
- Rerunning

It's clear that unit testing tends to be something of an iterative process. The examples were chosen to be simple but illustrative of the procedures required for a test-centric development process.

I'll return to testing later in the book (in Part III). But for now the message to retain is that testing should afford the developer a high degree of confidence that the code is in good shape and that the system functions correctly.

There is of course no substitute for feedback from expert user-driven testing. But automatic tests should provide a close second. Good unit tests can flush out many minor issues, leaving the more complex test cases either to other automated tests or to your human testers.

So, we now have some utPLSQL tests that can help verify that the logging code is working correctly. Clearly, this could be extended to include the other code.

In general, tests should be written to exercise any important application code. What do I mean by important? Well, important code is that which underpins your application—that which your application couldn't survive without.

Test Facilities in Code and Failing Tests

It's pretty common in many organizations to see failing suites of tests. This is often the case when the developers have, over a long period of time, created a large body of automatic tests. The test suite is usually run as part of the build/deploy procedure. Sadly, a significant percentage of the tests may fail all the time. The issue of failing tests seems counterintuitive. Don't tests exist to verify that the software is correctly written and that it functions correctly at runtime? Surely, test failure is a rare exception? Would that it were so.

Like a lot of things, the test creators start out with the best of intentions, often creating impressively large test suites. Initially, the tests work well and they may even exercise a large percentage of the code; in testing parlance, this is of course called *coverage*. *Code coverage* is a figure of merit for tests because it provides a degree of reassurance to the developers that a large percentage of the code pathways are being executed with the associated results being verified automatically.

Over time, some of the tests may start to fail. This can be due to data changes in the database itself. A test might be relying on a certain set of data being present in a specific table. It's easy to assume that a given table will never change. Unfortunately, business requirements can change, and so too can the underlying data.

Another potential source of failed tests is regulation. Regulatory requirements may mandate the anonymization of data, in particular, personal identifiable information (PII). PII includes data such as Social Security numbers, driver's license numbers, medical histories, home addresses, and so on. For a variety of reasons, it is increasingly important that such data is protected. Nevertheless, it is quite common for organizations to extract real-world data from production databases and to then use that data for test purposes in other environments. Needless to say, it is essential that the data is filtered through anonymization procedures.

However, if a test was written before such regulations come into force, then the result of anonymization might be the disappearance of data crucial to the test. For this reason, it's important to maintain tests as time goes on. Failing tests can result in a loss of confidence in the codebase by other developers. Developers may even be forced to switch off the tests because the failures result in their software builds not completing.

Good tests should function a little like a really good human tester. In other words, if the tests succeed, then we can be confident that the system being tested is highly functional. Such tests give us a good indication of the health of the code. This can be particularly important when some large changes are made to the system. Examples of such changes can include:

- Database upgrades
- Security changes
- General software upgrades

I like to think of tests being like another member of the team, quietly working away in the background and verifying that we're on the right road, so to speak.

Let's now move on to look at how to avoid common antipatterns.

Scale of Resilience Requirement 10: Avoiding Common Antipatterns

Let's have a look at the code now that it has been passed through nine stages of the scale of resilience:

```
CREATE OR REPLACE PROCEDURE updateEmployeeData(
    ENAME IN VARCHAR2, EMPNO IN NUMBER, SAL IN NUMBER)
AS
BEGIN
    loggingPackage.LOG_ACTION('Employee: '
    || ENAME || ' Number: ' || EMPNO || ' Salary: ' || SAL,
    'updateEmployeeData');
    loggingPackage.LOG_ACTION('Success - we got here 1!',
    'updateEmployeeData');
    INSERT INTO temp VALUES(SAL, EMPNO, ENAME);

    loggingPackage.LOG_ACTION('Successful insert', 'updateEmployeeData');
END;

CREATE OR REPLACE PROCEDURE update_employees
AS
        err_num NUMBER;
        err_msg VARCHAR2(100);
        CURSOR c_employee IS
                SELECT ename, empno, sal
                FROM emp
                ORDER BY sal DESC;

BEGIN
    FOR r_employee IN c_employee
      LOOP
       updateEmployeeData(r_employee.ename, r_employee.empno, r_employee.sal);
      END LOOP;
EXCEPTION
WHEN NO_DATA_FOUND THEN -- catches all 'no data found' errors
        loggingPackage.LOG_ACTION(('Ouch', 'we hit an exception'));
        ROLLBACK;
```

```
       WHEN OTHERS THEN -- handles all other errors
              err_num := SQLCODE;
              err_msg := SUBSTR(SQLERRM, 1, 100);
              loggingPackage.LOG_ACTION('We hit a general exception error number - '
              || ' '
              || err_num
              || ' Error message: '
              || err_msg, 'update_employees');
              ROLLBACK;
       END;
```

We also have a logging procedure, which resides in a shared package:

```
PROCEDURE LOG_ACTION(action_message IN VARCHAR2,
                     code_location  IN VARCHAR2)
    IS
          PRAGMA AUTONOMOUS_TRANSACTION;
    BEGIN
          INSERT INTO
                LOGGING
                (
                        EVENT_DATE,
                        action_message,
                        code_location
                )
                VALUES
                (
                        SYSDATE,
                        action_message,
                        code_location
                );

          COMMIT;
    END;
```

What types of antipatterns should we look out for? We have already addressed some common antipatterns. Some of the more common antipatterns include:

- Code that is too long
- Overly complex code
- Lack of exception/error handling
- Exceptions that we decide to live with
- Lack of modularity
- Crashes with no known root cause

Let's take a look at each of these in turn.

Code That Is Too Long

There is often a temptation to just write big blocks of code. In fact, we saw this very issue back in Figure 1-1. Such large blocks of code are hard to understand. Perhaps a less obvious issue is that they are also hard to test.

It is best to break down large chunks of code into smaller units using additional procedures and functions. This is a passing reference to the old Linux principle of doing one thing well.

If each of your procedures and functions does just one thing well, then your code has the additional merit of being simpler. When the time then comes to create unit tests for the code, you can right-click on the procedure and generate a utPLSQL test template.

If your procedures are kept short and sweet, then the creation of the working unit test boils down to just pasting some key PL/SQL code into the test procedure. Remember, each unit test is a bit like having a dedicated inspector for the associated code. The inspector then keeps an eye on the code each time the test is run. Any issues, such as passing bad data into the procedure, should then result in a failed test result. This alerts you to a possible problem.

This is a further example of one of the pull-through benefits of adhering to the scale of resilience model.

Overly Complex Code

It's quite common nowadays to look at code and come away puzzled. Java lambda code is a good example. It's a similar story with JavaScript and Python. There seems to often be a desire to make code written in these languages hard to understand, which in turn can make it harder to test and verify. Worse still is the difficulty that arises when complex code has to be changed.

It's best to aim to keep PL/SQL code as simple as possible. Splitting code into smaller blocks is a good habit to develop. As you saw in the previous section, this stepwise refinement also pays dividends in the form of making the unit tests easier to write.

 If you really must use a complex mechanism, then try to document it in order to help a downstream maintainer.

Lack of Exception/Error Handling

We've looked in some detail at the issue of exception handling. Not catering rigorously to exceptions is an example of a risky shortcut. It saves you some time now, but later on it can be problematic when exceptions start to arise in your code.

Without handling or at the very least logging exceptions, you may be forced into trying to guess why certain problems arise. Guess-based diagnosis is invariably wrong, and you may then apply code changes based on an inaccurate understanding of the problem that occurred.

Exception management code is a good friend. Treat it well and it will return the compliment.

Exceptions That You Decide to Live With

When looking through log data from running code, it's quite common to see exceptions that occur all the time. Very often, the established developers will say that a given exception always occurs and has never been fixed. Living with exceptions is a really bad idea.

Exceptions are an indication that something may be seriously wrong with the code and its interaction with the runtime system. At the very least, all exceptions should be investigated and a determination made about their severity.

Even if an exception turns out to be a harmless logic error, the generated output will clutter up your logs. This can make it more difficult to diagnose a real problem. Which is easier in general: a 1 MB logfile, or one that is 500 MB, where the latter has loads of legacy exception data?

When an exception occurs, it's best to try to fix the underlying issue.

Lack of Modularity

Earlier in this chapter, you saw the benefits of modularity. Modular code is perhaps a little harder to write than is the case with larger blocks. But modular code gives us a number of advantages:

- Modular code is simpler and easier to understand.
- Modular code can be shared in packages.
- It is easier to test, even allowing for automatic test generation.

As with exception handling, not producing modular code might initially save you a little time, but in the longer term those savings are lost if the code proves to be brittle or insufficiently tested.

Crashes with No Known Root Cause

The unknown crash or runtime failure is a more common occurrence than might be supposed. Surprisingly, such crashes can occur when unexpected data is pushed through a system. A typical case of this is in date string handling, where the code expects a US date format such as 12/15/2022, i.e., MM/DD/YYYY. However, instead of US format, a European date format is used: 15/12/2022, i.e., DD/MM/YYYY.

In some cases, a simple oversight such as this can result in a fatal runtime error when an attempt is made to parse the unexpected date format—by trying to find the 12th day of the 15th month in the year. For this reason, it is prudent to check how a given library call handles such unexpected cases. It may be far more preferable to simply log this and return a default or placeholder value rather than allowing a runtime failure to occur.

A major difficulty with allowing runtime failures is that the normal exception pathway may be bypassed. In other words, the date format parsing code simply doesn't expect the wrong format to be presented and exits in an unexpected fashion. The lack of any log data can make this type of bug into one of the ones that never gets fixed.

Can't You Just Do a Restart?

When a DevOps team is faced with a partial or complete runtime failure of a business-critical system, it is a good practice to try to do some sort of root cause analysis. The purpose of this exercise is generally to try to establish the particular set of circumstances that gave rise to the failure. For example, the failure might be down to a code bug, or some dependent system failing, or some unexpected data, and so on. The reasons are many.

Root cause analysis is a highly skilled activity and usually involves trawling through reams of log data and looking for the key event that resulted in the failure. For systems where messages are transferred across multiple runtime boundaries, there is often a need to correlate those messages. So, if message A leaves process X and passes into process Y, then we can tie these multiprocess messages together using a correlation ID number. Extracting such details can require quite tricky database queries and then cross-referencing them against logfile content.

You can see that insufficient logging and weak exception handling can substantially work against effective root cause analysis. I've seen cases where the presumably well-intentioned analysis fails to turn up any actionable data. In other words, the runtime

---

failure is not resolved in any meaningful way. For cases like this, the only way around it is often just to restart the system and hope for the best.

In a similar vein, another organization I worked in had a legacy Java application that was running on a fairly substantial on-premises machine. The problem was that the system used to run out of memory approximately once per week. The solution was to simply do a restart each week and hope that not too many users were affected. No root cause analysis was done at all in this case. Such an approach doesn't inspire any confidence and the problems tend to recur with depressing regularity, usually at some deeply inconvenient moment. The actual problem is invariably due to some low-quality code buried deep in the system. Such problems may in fact never be resolved, particularly in those cases where the original programmer leaves the organization. This type of approach is clearly inimical to the needs of resilience.

I had a case of this myself years ago in a C++ application that I wrote for a client. The system was running out of memory. Interestingly, the client suggested just periodi-cally restarting the system! This antipattern seems to be a rather common "solution." While this would have been a stopgap solution, the eventual intention was for the application to run on a 24/7 basis. So the problem was not going away and was guar-anteed to come back and haunt us (or more precisely, me). After a little analysis, I noticed that the deallocation of a large block of memory was occasionally skipped during the normal workflow. Each time it was skipped, more memory was allocated. It took about a day to track it down, and a simple one-line fix resolved the issue. However, a simple test to measure and log the memory allocation during each run would have avoided the problem in the first place and obviated the need for any more involved efforts. Always try to write the best code you can; your future self and your colleagues will thank you for it.

Scale of Resilience Requirement 11: Schema Evolution

Let's now turn our attention to the important topic of schema evolution. In Example 4-26, you see the original schema that was introduced in "A Simple Schema" on page 45.

Example 4-26. Schema creation SQL

```
CREATE TABLE emp (
   ename VARCHAR2(10),
   empno NUMBER(4),
   sal   NUMBER(7,2)
   );

CREATE TABLE temp (
   ename VARCHAR2(10),
   empno NUMBER(4),
   sal   NUMBER(7,2)
```

```
     );

INSERT INTO emp (ename, empno, sal)
VALUES ('John', 1000, 40000.00);

INSERT INTO emp (ename, empno, sal)
VALUES ('Mary', 1001, 40000.00);

commit;
```

Schema evolution refers to the way in which a given schema changes over time. Such changes are generally in response to updated business requirements or simple fixes and refactoring. The types of changes that occur in schema evolution can include:

- Column addition
- Column removal
- Column renaming
- Table addition
- Table name changes

In fact, the schema shown in Example 4-26 is not of particularly high quality for the following reasons:

- Unclear table names
- No primary keys
- No data constraints

I'll discuss how to fix these issues shortly. In the meantime, let's have a look at the LOG_ACTION procedure in Example 4-27 in the context of schema evolution.

Example 4-27. LOG_ACTION without accommodating possible schema evolution

```
PROCEDURE LOG_ACTION(action_message IN VARCHAR2,
                     code_location  IN VARCHAR2)
IS
        PRAGMA AUTONOMOUS_TRANSACTION;
BEGIN
        INSERT INTO
                LOGGING
                (
                        EVENT_DATE      ,
                        action_message ,
                        code_location
                )
                VALUES
                (
```

```
                                    SYSDATE          ,
                                    action_message ,
                                    code_location
                    );

        COMMIT;
END;
```

Notice in Example 4-27 the parameters to `LOG_ACTION`:

```
PROCEDURE LOG_ACTION(action_message IN VARCHAR2,
                     code_location   IN VARCHAR2)
```

This parameter definition is not tied to the underlying database table columns. So, if we change the latter so that they no longer match the procedure parameters, then the procedure won't work correctly. This issue is resolved with the use of anchored declarations, as shown in Example 4-28. By using anchored declarations, the procedure will only become invalid if one (or more) of the anchors are modified.

Example 4-28. LOG_ACTION accommodating possible schema evolution

```
PROCEDURE LOG_ACTION(action_message IN logging.action_message%TYPE,
                     code_location   IN logging.code_location%TYPE)
IS
    PRAGMA AUTONOMOUS_TRANSACTION;
BEGIN
    INSERT INTO LOGGING
            (EVENT_DATE
                , action_message
                , code_location
            )
            VALUES
            (SYSDATE
                , action_message
                , code_location
            )
    ;

    COMMIT;
END;
```

If a subsequent change is made to the `LOGGING` table (such as extending the length of the `ACTION_MESSAGE` column), then we need only recompile the stored procedure and the code will once again be tied to the new columns. This eliminates a common source of error in the PL/SQL code, i.e., data type mismatch.

The changes in Example 4-29 illustrate an effort to improve the schema quality.

Example 4-29. Better-quality schema creation SQL

```
CREATE TABLE EMPLOYEE (
    ID NUMBER GENERATED ALWAYS AS IDENTITY,
    employee_name VARCHAR2(10) NOT NULL,
    employee_number NUMBER(4) NOT NULL,
    salary NUMBER(7, 2)
    );

CREATE TABLE PROCESSED_EMPLOYEE (
    ID NUMBER GENERATED ALWAYS AS IDENTITY,
    employee_name VARCHAR2(10) NOT NULL,
    employee_number NUMBER(4) NOT NULL,
    salary NUMBER(7, 2)
    );

INSERT INTO EMPLOYEE (employee_name, employee_number, salary)
VALUES ('John', 1000, 40000.00);

INSERT INTO EMPLOYEE (employee_name, employee_number, salary)
VALUES ('Mary', 1001, 40000.00);

commit;
```

In Example 4-29, the table names have been updated to improve readability. Also, autogenerated primary keys have been added. The other column names have also been updated to improve readability and data constraints have been added.

To implement these data changes, it would be necessary to use RENAME and ALTER. Obviously, the associated PL/SQL would also have to be modified to suit.

Scale of Resilience Change Summary

The original PL/SQL code has now been filtered through the scale of resilience. Having applied the changes, how does the new code score? In Table 4-2, I record the new scores with the old values in parentheses.

Table 4-2. Recalculating the scale of resilience for PL/SQL

Requirement number	Resilience requirement	Score (0–10)
1	Capture all errors and exceptions	10 (0)
2	Recoverability	10 (2)
3	Observability	10 (0)
4	Modifiability	8 (5)
5	Modularity	10 (2)
6	Simplicity	10 (5)
7	Coding conventions	8 (5)

Requirement number	Resilience requirement	Score (0–10)
8	Reusability	8 (2)
9	Repeatable testing	6 (2)
10	Avoiding common antipatterns	8 (0)
11	Schema evolution	8 (0)
	TOTAL SCORE	96 (23)

That's a significant improvement over the original score. Areas that could use more work are adherence to coding conventions and unit testing. While the code in question is very simple, the approach used is a good template for future PL/SQL work.

In Part III, I'll use the scale of resilience up front, i.e., for new code rather than for refactoring legacy code.

Scalable PL/SQL and Declarative Mechanisms

One of the central themes of this book is the importance of using PL/SQL abstractions and programming constructs. Indeed, this is true of using any programming language. The abstractions provide a kind of protective armor around your designs, data, and algorithms.

That all sounds a bit complicated, but in fact, embracing abstractions helps you to produce better and simpler solutions. In particular, certain PL/SQL abstractions (such as the cursor FOR LOOP) provide you with an on-ramp to scalable coding. Resilient code and scalable code are of course simply two sides of the same coin.

Scalable code addresses the need for data growth without exhausting the resources of the runtime system. In other words, as your incoming data size increases, it is essential that your code handles it in a graceful manner. You won't win many supporters in your user group by writing code that, over time, unnecessarily uses up all of the runtime resources and degrades the user experience.

A powerful PL/SQL scalability abstraction is the declarative cursor FOR loop, which you saw in Example 4-12. The concept of declarative code is very important when you want to achieve scalability. In one sentence, declarative code lets you indicate to the runtime system *what* it is that you want to achieve without specifying exactly *how* it will be achieved.

The declarative model is conceptually very similar to the requirements model that I've used in the book. Effective requirements define *what* a given piece of software will achieve. It is up to the designer/developer to translate the requirements into the *how*, i.e., working testable code. In other words, declarative code provides a means to request a specific outcome from the language runtime system without specifying how to achieve it. Effective resilience requirements embrace a similar conceptual model to that of declarative coding.

A physical analogy for declarative coding is when you switch on a light. When the switch is pressed, you indicate what it is that you require, i.e., light in the room. But you don't prescribe (or much care, in most cases) how that end result will be achieved. The declarative mechanism abstracts away the nitty-gritty details of how the end result is achieved. You'll see more on this topic in Parts II and III.

Remember, the three key commands used to manage the Docker container are:

```
docker container ls -a
docker start <CONTAINER_ID>
docker stop <CONTAINER_ID>
```

As always, remember to substitute your own value for <CONTAINER_ID>.

Summary

PL/SQL code errors are good teachers. The resolution of such errors forces you to adopt a rigorous approach. The shift-left method is an example of such an approach, where a key goal is to push errors in the direction of developers rather than users. It is the former who can do something about the errors whereas for the latter, errors can result in a loss of confidence about the solution.

The scale of resilience can be applied to PL/SQL code multiple times. It was revisited in this chapter following the refactoring modifications. The new code scored much better than was the case for the original version.

Exception handling requires particularly delicate handling, taking care to never swallow all exceptions, which is an egregious antipattern that may subsequently thwart future error resolution.

You also saw the way exception handling can be narrowed down in a given PL/SQL procedure. This allows for the propagation of exceptions not handled by that procedure to move up the chain to a more appropriate handler location. Exception handling is a key design issue that can greatly facilitate future remediation efforts.

Autonomous transactions allow for an originating transaction to be suspended until the autonomous transaction is committed or rolled back. This mechanism is crucial for supporting design patterns, such as effective PL/SQL logging. The simple logging mechanism described in this chapter is purely for illustration. An open source alternative logger is available here (*https://oreil.ly/bs_P_*).

The application of a scale of resilience can be viewed as a type of filter. The model can be thought of as: "You push your PL/SQL code through the filter and it comes out the other side in better shape."

PL/SQL packages are strongly encouraged by Oracle and they represent an important part of achieving modularity. Unit testing is also extremely important and for this you can use products, such as utPLSQL. Good tests should function somewhat like a really good human tester.

Root cause analysis can be facilitated by adhering to the scale of resilience approach.

In the next chapter, you'll see feature development in the context of PL/SQL, starting with how to invoke PL/SQL code from Java.

PART II

Feature-Driven Development

CHAPTER 5

Calling PL/SQL

Previous chapters have illustrated the ways in which PL/SQL can be:

- Created
- Refactored
- Debugged
- Saved to the database
- Executed using SQL Developer

In this chapter, I discuss two of the important PL/SQL integration (and execution) models.

Two PL/SQL Integration Models

It's not difficult to invoke packaged PL/SQL code in the form of functions and procedures. There are two approaches I'll look at:

- Running PL/SQL as a standalone database job
- Running PL/SQL using Java code

Both of these integration patterns are in common use. The standalone job approach has the merit of being independent of other integration languages, that is, it is pure PL/SQL. With the job-based model, you don't have any of the headaches associated with PL/SQL invocation from high-level languages. All of the work can be done using SQL Developer and the Oracle Database.

The Java code approach is more complex but has its own advantages. For example, it allows for PL/SQL business logic to be used directly in Java application code. One example of this could be calling a PL/SQL function from Java to return some sales data (such as an invoice). The data can then be used in the subsequent Java code. Calling PL/SQL in this way provides us with a means of protecting the investment in PL/SQL and also using the latter in our Java code. The Java code then does not need to make any access to the database, other than calling the PL/SQL packaged code.

Both the standalone job and Java integration methods obviate the need for complex object relational mapping (ORM) solutions. This is not to say that there is anything bad about ORM. It's just that the job and Java PL/SQL integration models are simple. One important advantage they may have over the ORM approach is that of performance.

Let's start by looking at the in-database option: calling PL/SQL using a job.

Calling PL/SQL Using a Job

Before you can run a database job, you have to create one. Such a job is itself conceptually quite similar to a stored procedure because the job resides in the database. As with stored procedures, jobs can dropped (or deleted from the database) if required.

To start a new job creation, select the Scheduler option in the SQL Developer Connections window. In Figure 5-1, the new job creation option is illustrated.

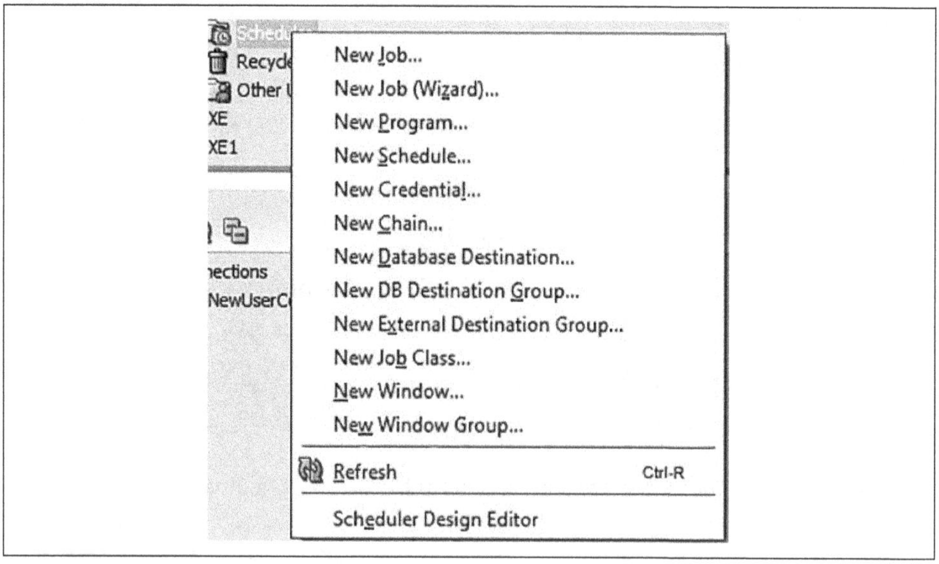

Figure 5-1. Creating a new Oracle Database job to call PL/SQL

The steps required to create a job are fairly self-explanatory. Click the New Job menu option in Figure 5-1 and fill out the job details, as shown in Figure 5-2.

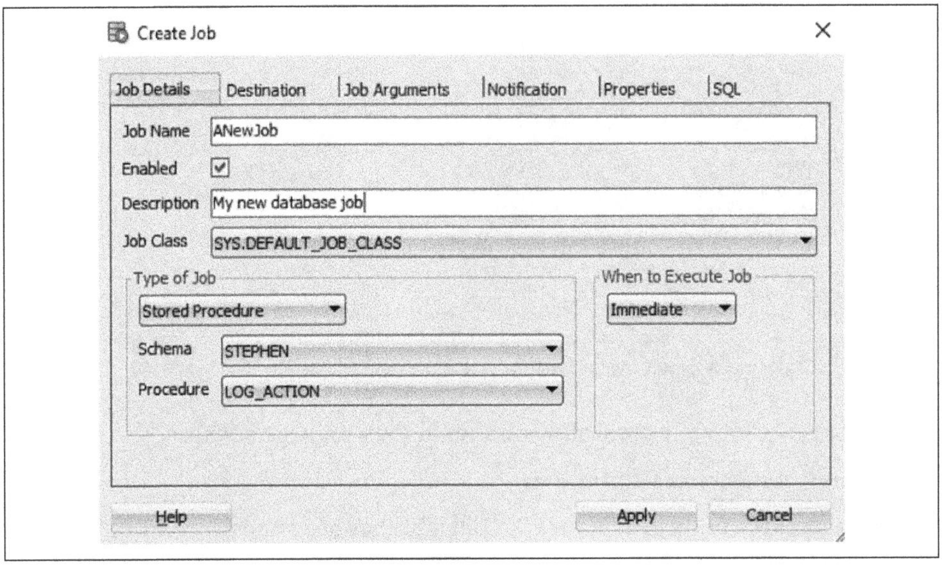

Figure 5-2. Filling out the database job details

In Figure 5-2, I've populated the following fields:

```
Job name - ANewJob
Description - My new database job
Type of Job: Stored Procedure
Procedure: LOG_ACTION
When to Execute Job: Immediate
```

Make sure the Enabled box is ticked in Figure 5-2—it does have a default value of Enabled, but make sure it is so. As I'm calling the LOG_ACTION procedure, I need to supply parameters to the procedure call, as shown in the procedure signature excerpt at the top of Example 5-1.

Example 5-1. The code we want to call from the job

```
create or replace PROCEDURE LOG_ACTION
        (action_message IN logging.action_message%TYPE,
         code_location  IN logging.code_location%TYPE)
```

To provide parameters for the procedure call, click the Job Arguments tab, as shown in Figure 5-3, and supply values for ACTION_MESSAGE and CODE_LOCATION. Any text string will be sufficient for the parameters, such as aaa and bbb. Click Apply in Figure 5-3 when you're happy with the settings.

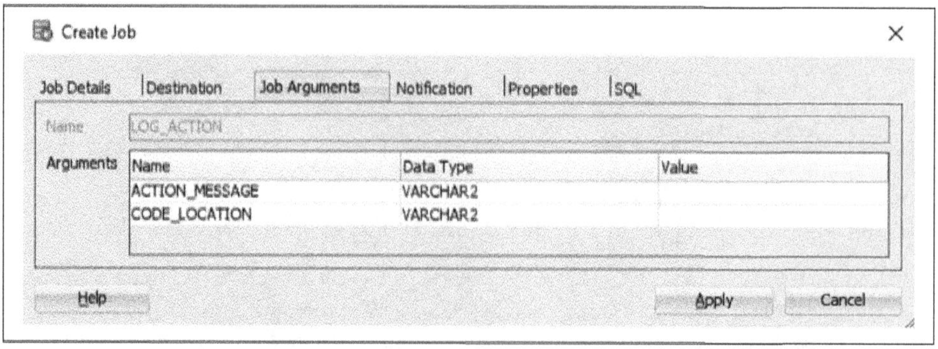

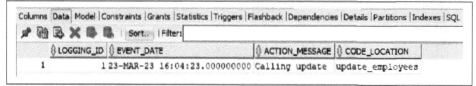

Figure 5-3. *Creating a new Oracle Database job to call PL/SQL*

If the job ran without any problems, you should see a message saying:

```
Successfully processed SQL command
```

You can also check to verify that the LOGGING table has been updated with a new row.

Until now, I've used a SQL query to view database table contents, but there is also a graphical method in SQL Developer, as shown in Figure 5-4.

| Columns | Data | Model | Constraints | Grants | Statistics | Triggers | Flashback | Dependencies | Details | Partitions | Indexes | SQL |

	LOGGING_ID	EVENT_DATE	ACTION_MESSAGE	CODE_LOCATION
1	1	23-MAR-23 16:04:23.000000000	Calling update	update_employees

Figure 5-4. *Checking the job results in the LOGGING table*

To see the data in Figure 5-4, click the LOGGING table in the Connections window and then click the Data tab in the upper-left of the screen. The values for the two LOGGING table columns should be aaa and bbb—or whatever values you supplied in Figure 5-3. The contents of Figure 5-4 illustrate the results of a successful job execution: we see a new row in the LOGGING table.

SQL Developer also provides a run log, as shown in Figure 5-5.

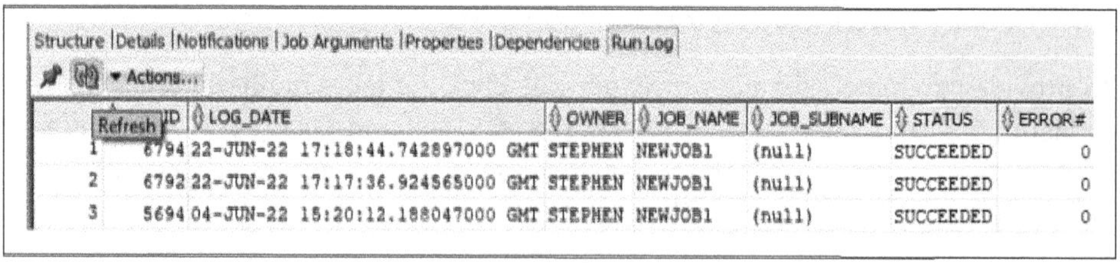

| Structure | Details | Notifications | Job Arguments | Properties | Dependencies | Run Log |

	ID	LOG_DATE	OWNER	JOB_NAME	JOB_SUBNAME	STATUS	ERROR#
1	6794	22-JUN-22 17:18:44.742897000 GMT	STEPHEN	NEWJOB1	(null)	SUCCEEDED	0
2	6792	22-JUN-22 17:17:36.924565000 GMT	STEPHEN	NEWJOB1	(null)	SUCCEEDED	0
3	5694	04-JUN-22 15:20:12.188047000 GMT	STEPHEN	NEWJOB1	(null)	SUCCEEDED	0

Figure 5-5. *Checking the job results in the run log*

In Figure 5-5, there is a good deal of data relating to the database job, namely:

- Log ID
- Date
- Owner of the job
- Status of the job

The run log has other information as well, such as the RUN_DURATION. This field is very useful for those rare cases of a job that runs into difficulties such as some sort of deadlock. Fortunately, in Figure 5-6, the job has run very quickly.

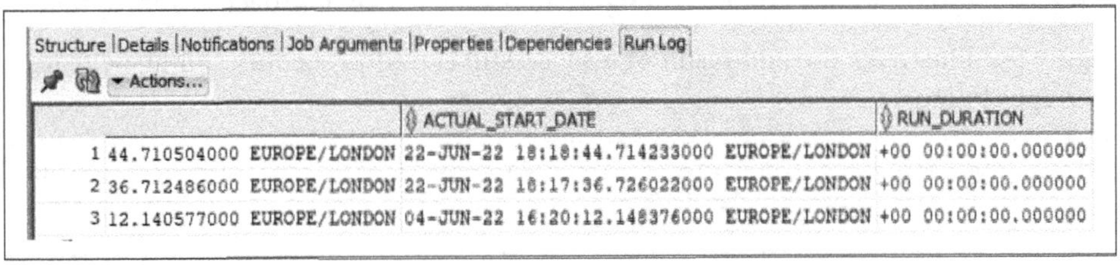

Figure 5-6. Checking the job duration in the run log

It's not always a smooth ride, so it's prudent to get into the habit of checking the value of RUN_DURATION, as shown in Figure 5-6. This is because it's not unknown for a job to get blocked indefinitely. I experienced this myself once on a shared development database and I used the RUN_DURATION column data as part of the problem diagnosis. The problem was resolved by a database administrator.

It is also possible to set up automatic or scheduled jobs. As for the immediate job run type, you can also check the job run log for scheduled cases when any suspected issues arise. Running jobs in this way is very useful, for example, for nondevelopers or during testing. This mode of using PL/SQL is a major use case for stored procedures. An example of use is the execution of a scheduled batch job, where there may be many calls to PL/SQL code, lookups of views, tables, and so on.

As discussed earlier in the chapter, another important mode of use for PL/SQL is invoking a stored procedure from within a Java application. I'll look at this next. Note in passing that Java is of course not the only high-level language you can use for this purpose; Java is selected here purely because it is a widely used and mature integration option.

Calling PL/SQL Using a Java Program

Many organizations use PL/SQL stored procedures as one of their principal means of expressing business logic. Because the stored procedures reside in the database, it may also be important to be able to invoke them from at least one high-level language. Many organizations have made significant investments in such languages. There is an understandable motivation to leverage this knowledge investment.

The Java integration model with PL/SQL is sufficiently flexible that you can call a single stored procedure or instead call a number of different stored procedures. In the latter case, the approach may be to use packaged stored procedures as database-resident subroutines. It's up to the designer to decide which approach is appropriate.

Figure 5-7 illustrates the end result of a successful stored procedure call made from a Java application.

	⬦ LOGGING_ID	⬦ EVENT_DATE	⬦ ACTION_MESSAGE	⬦ CODE_LOCATION
1	261	01-APR-23 14:07:32.000000000	Hello from Java	In Java

Figure 5-7. Checking the Java call results

Notice in Figure 5-7 that the table data matches the corresponding Java code, as described in the next section (specifically in Example 5-4).

Let's briefly explore at what a simple Java client application might look like.

Setting Up a Simple Java Application

In Example 5-2, you can see an example of calling a PL/SQL packaged procedure (specifically, it calls the loggingPackage.LOG_ACTION procedure). Remember that this procedure requires two parameters to be passed to it. The question marks in Example 5-2 are used as parameter placeholders, which are then substituted in the calls to statement.setString.

Example 5-2. Java code that calls the PL/SQL job

```
public class JDBCStoredProcedureWrite {

    public static void main(String[] args) {
        Connection connection = null;
        CallableStatement statement = null;

        String action_message = "Hello from Java";
        String code_location = "In Java";

        try { ❶
            connection = DBConnection.getConnection(); ❷
```

```
        statement = connection.prepareCall(
        "call loggingPackage.LOG_ACTION(?, ?)}");
        statement.setString("action_message", action_message);
        statement.setString("code_location", code_location);
        statement.executeUpdate();

        System.out.println("Successful call");
    } catch(Exception e) {
        e.printStackTrace();
    } finally {
        try {
            if (!statement.isClosed()) {
                statement.close();
            }
            if (!connection.isClosed()) {
                connection.close();
            }
        } catch (SQLException e) {
            e.printStackTrace();
        }
    }
    }
}

}
```

❶ The `try-catch-finally` structure is used. This is conceptually similar to the PL/SQL exception-handling code you've seen in the earlier examples.

❷ Notice this line in particular.

Invocation of the method `getConnection()` uses a helper class (`DBConnection`) that facilitates the connection to the Oracle Database, as shown in Example 5-3. If you're running the code examples, make sure to set the values for `DB_USERNAME` and `DB_PASS WORD` in Example 5-3 so that they match your installation.

Example 5-3. Database connection helper class

```
public class DBConnection {

    private static final String DB_DRIVER_CLASS = "oracle.jdbc.driver.OracleDriver";
    private static final String DB_USERNAME = "HR";
    private static final String DB_PASSWORD = "hrpass";

    public static Connection getConnection() {
        Connection connection = null;
        try {
            // Load the Driver Class
            Class.forName(DB_DRIVER_CLASS);

            // Create the connection
```

```
        connection = DriverManager.getConnection(
                "jdbc:oracle:thin:@localhost:localhost:1521:OraDoc",
                DB_USERNAME, DB_PASSWORD);
    } catch (ClassNotFoundException e) {
        e.printStackTrace();
    } catch (SQLException e) {
        e.printStackTrace();
    }
    return connection;
    }
}
```

The code in Example 5-3 handles the runtime setup required for the database connection. What does the Java code look like when we run it? Let's give it a try.

Running the Java Application

The following is an example of an unsuccessful call to the code in Example 5-2. This problem might occur if the Docker container isn't running or if the credentials supplied in Example 5-3 are incorrect:

```
java.sql.SQLRecoverableException: IO Error: The Network Adapter could
not establish the connection (CONNECTION_ID=o2zVzE/PToyy94mbj3dZGw==)
        at oracle.jdbc.driver.T4CConnection.handleLogonNetException(
        T4CConnection.java:893)
        at oracle.jdbc.driver.T4CConnection.logon(T4CConnection.java:698)
        at oracle.jdbc.driver.PhysicalConnection.connect(
        PhysicalConnection.java:1042)
        at oracle.jdbc.driver.T4CDriverExtension.getConnection(
        T4CDriverExtension.java:90)
        at oracle.jdbc.driver.OracleDriver.connect(OracleDriver.java:733)
        at oracle.jdbc.driver.OracleDriver.connect(OracleDriver.java:649)
        at java.sql.DriverManager.getConnection(DriverManager.java:664)
        at java.sql.DriverManager.getConnection(DriverManager.java:247)
        at DBConnection.getConnection(DBConnection.java:18)
        at JDBCStoredProcedureWrite.main(JDBCStoredProcedureWrite.java:15)
```

There are many reasons for problems when running the Java code. The following is an example of a successful call to the code in Example 5-2:

```
Successful call
Process finished with exit code 0
```

Nothing too dramatic there. The stored procedure has run without any errors. It is a good idea, at least the first few times this code is called, to make sure to verify that the row is created in the LOGGING table, as shown in Figure 5-4.

One other important potential source of error is in the parameters passed to the stored procedure. The Java code is shown in Example 5-4.

Example 5-4. Invoking the PL/SQL stored procedure

```java
public static void main(String[] args) {
    Connection connection = null;
    CallableStatement statement = null;

    String action_message = "Hello from Java";
    String code_location = "In Java";

    try {
        connection = DBConnection.getConnection();
        statement = connection.prepareCall("{call PACKAGE1.LOG_ACTION(?, ?)}");
        statement.setString("action_message", action_message); ❶
        statement.setString("code_location", code_location);
        statement.executeUpdate();

        System.out.println("Successful call");
    } catch(Exception e) {
        e.printStackTrace();
    } finally {
        try {
            if (!statement.isClosed()) {
                statement.close();
            }
            if (!connection.isClosed()) {
                connection.close();
            }
        } catch (SQLException e) {
            e.printStackTrace();
        }
    }
}
```

 The parameters are set (and the statement is executed) by these three lines (this and the next two). The two string parameters are populated using the `setString` method on the `CallableStatement` object instance.

Let's simulate an error by setting just one of the required parameters in Example 5-4 and see what happens. The updated Java code is shown in Example 5-5.

Example 5-5. Invoking the PL/SQL stored procedure with an intentional Java bug

```java
public static void main(String[] args) {
    Connection connection = null;
    CallableStatement statement = null;

    String action_message = "Hello from Java";
    String code_location = "In Java";

    try {
```

```
        connection = DBConnection.getConnection();
        statement = connection.prepareCall("{call PACKAGE1.LOG_ACTION(?, ?)}");
        statement.setString("action_message", action_message);
//      statement.setString("code_location", code_location); ❶
        statement.executeUpdate();

        System.out.println("Successful call");
    } catch(Exception e) {
        e.printStackTrace();
    } finally {
        try {
            if (!statement.isClosed()) {
                statement.close();
            }
            if (!connection.isClosed()) {
                connection.close();
            }
        } catch (SQLException e) {
            e.printStackTrace();
        }
    }
}
```

❶ Comments out the setString call for the code_location parameter.

Rerunning the updated (now buggy) Java code from Example 5-5 produces the result shown in Example 5-6.

Example 5-6. Java "filters" the error

```
java.sql.SQLException: The number of parameter names does not match
the number of registered praremeters ❶
        at oracle.jdbc.driver.OracleSql.setNamedParameters(OracleSql.java:213)
        at oracle.jdbc.driver.OracleCallableStatement.executeUpdate(
        OracleCallableStatement.java:4300)
        at oracle.jdbc.driver.OraclePreparedStatementWrapper.executeUpdate(
        OraclePreparedStatementWrapper.java:992)
        at JDBCStoredProcedureWrite.main(JDBCStoredProcedureWrite.java:19)

Process finished with exit code 0
```

❶ The problem encountered and reported is exactly as expected.

The exception details can then be used to track down the issue, which is of course to send the correct number of parameters.

The tip in the preceding sidebar leads us nicely into the area of responsibility for errors.

Who Owns the Java Error?

One important issue with the discussion of Java calling PL/SQL is responsibility. Is the error in Example 5-6 going to be communicated to the database in any way? In other words, will we see this error in the LOGGING table? The answer to both of these questions is no.

Because the design now involves a Java client, the buck stops there. The Java code has to be designed to handle the error and its remediation. By introducing the Java layer, we have also introduced a new layer that can produce exceptions.

This means that the Java code should also not be allowed to swallow exceptions. Indeed, we saw the same issue earlier when discussing PL/SQL exception management. At the very least, any exceptions in Java and/or PL/SQL should be logged.

When Java is used in this way, the database becomes what is sometimes called a *system of record*. In other words, the Java code uses the database as a separate system for data access and for storing results. The database is therefore separate and distinct from the Java code, unlike the PL/SQL use case where that code resides inside the database. Because of this separateness from the database, Java code can also be used to extract useful metadata.

Reading Database Metadata

The Java option for calling PL/SQL has additional merit; it provides quite a lot of useful information about the target database. This type of information is usually referred to as *metadata* and the code in Example 5-7 illustrates a sample of the type of Java code that retrieves it.

Example 5-7. Database metadata retrieval

```
{
    OracleDataSource oracleDataSource = new OracleDataSource();
    oracleDataSource.setURL(
    "jdbc:oracle:thin:Oracle_Docker/stephen@//localhost:1521/ORCLCDB.localdomain");
    oracleDataSource.setUser("<MY_USER_NAME>");
    oracleDataSource.setPassword("<MY_PASSWORD>");
    Connection connection = oracleDataSource.getConnection();

    // Create Oracle DatabaseMetaData object
    DatabaseMetaData metaData = connection.getMetaData();

    // gets driver info:
    System.out.println("JDBC driver version: " + metaData.getDriverVersion());
    System.out.println("Driver name: " + metaData.getDriverName());
    System.out.println("Database Product Name: " +
    metaData.getDatabaseProductName());
    System.out.println("Database Major Version: " +
    metaData.getDatabaseMajorVersion());
    System.out.println("Database Minor Version: " +
    metaData.getDatabaseMinorVersion());
    System.out.println("allProceduresAreCallable: " +
    metaData.allProceduresAreCallable());
}
```

Supply your own username and password to run the Java code in Example 5-7. The data that results from a call to the code in Example 5-7 is shown in Example 5-8.

Example 5-8. Database metadata received

```
JDBC driver version: 21.5.0.0.0
Driver name: Oracle JDBC driver
Database Product Name: Oracle
Database Major Version: 12
Database Minor Version: 2
allProceduresAreCallable: false

Process finished with exit code 0
```

In Example 5-8, the Java Database Connectivity (JDBC) driver version and name are shown along with the database product name, major and minor versions, and a boolean indicating that not all the stored procedures are callable.

This type of information can be quite useful in operational scenarios, such as when the version of Oracle Database or some other component is being upgraded. Another case where the version information might be useful is when security updates are being applied.

In cases where multiple databases are deployed, it can be very useful to know which database your code is talking to. The code in Example 5-7 is helpful in dispelling any such doubts.

Given that the use of Java to call remote stored procedures and other database code is beneficial, there are some issues to be aware of. I look at these in the next section.

Some Java PL/SQL Gotchas

Make sure that you download and install a correct JDBC driver and that it is added to the IDE—such as IntelliJ IDEA, Eclipse, etc.—in use. Another gotcha is the old, reliable "supplying the wrong username and password when attempting to connect to the database" error. Ensure that you have an up-to-date Java Development Kit (JDK). I used version 1.8 for the examples in this chapter.

Oracle Database Password Gotcha

Passwords expire and it's important to know how to update them in those cases where an automatic prompt doesn't appear. It's possible that you may see the Oracle message prompt "Login Messages" warning you that your password will expire.

To fix this issue, click OK to dismiss the dialog. Then, right-click the connection menu option (called Oracle_Docker in my case). Click Reset Password, as shown in Figure 5-8, and fill in the details in the resulting dialog. Finally, click OK to save the new credentials.

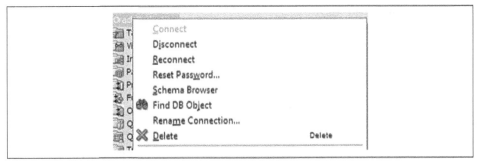

Figure 5-8. Reset an expired password

Summary

Integration options for PL/SQL are fairly flexible. You can opt to use a database-centric approach where a job calls the required PL/SQL stored procedure. The job can be run on an ad hoc or scheduled basis. The progress of the job can be viewed in the job run log. For cases where any errors occur, the job run log content is invaluable. This is especially so when writing the code for the first time and also on subsequent runs (if errors arise).

The database-centric integration has a number of benefits, for example:

- Security
- Performance
- Native execution

Perhaps one disadvantage with the database-centric approach is that it does require a fair degree of fluency with Oracle Database, SQL Developer, and PL/SQL.

If you don't like the sound of a database-centric approach, then there is an alternative integration model that uses the Java programming language. Invoking PL/SQL code with Java is achieved using JDBC integration. Given that the Java runtime environment is separate and distinct from the database, it is essential that you catch and log any Java exceptions that might occur.

The Java approach also facilitates the retrieval of database metadata including the database name and version details. Such data can be very useful when your environment comprises more than one database instance.

One of the advantages of the Java approach is that the database becomes, in a sense, just another system. In other words, the Java integration itself provides an abstraction of the database and its constituent PL/SQL code. The potential downside of this abstraction is that the performance of the Java code may be disappointing when compared to the *purer* database-centric model.

Who said technology is easy?

CHAPTER 6

Introducing Feature-Driven PL/SQL Development

In Part I, the discussion focused on the creation of a PL/SQL skills toolbox in the context of the scale of resilience. The scale of resilience was used to guide a variety of legacy PL/SQL code refactoring exercises. The toolbox skills were acquired with reference to existing PL/SQL code and the application of remediation measures. Part of the toolbox includes the crucial ability to test PL/SQL code using, for example, the utPLSQL product. In addition to testing PL/SQL, an important consideration is the integration model employed for using your packaged PL/SQL code. Two integration models in common use are those based on database-resident jobs and Java-based invocation.

I now move on to describing a further level of abstraction, where database application development artifacts are contained in features. This can be considered a shift-left approach where features are used as a type of requirement placeholder. This also reflects the fact that the discussion in Part II is somewhat more abstract than in Part I. With increased abstraction comes greater power than mere coding provides.

Before accessing the power of the feature abstraction, it's important to carefully define what I mean by a feature.

What Is a Feature?

A *feature* is a software component that models an interaction that produces some useful end result. The interaction may be initiated by either a user or a machine.

For the purposes of this discussion, a feature has another key attribute: *testability*. In other words, we can test or exercise a feature in isolation. Remember the unit tests using utPLSQL in Chapter 3? Well, a feature is always a good candidate for a suite of unit tests. This is because a feature typically has a number of actions and associated results. It is also possible for a feature to go wrong, and tests can be written to simulate this outcome. Unit tests can be written to execute each action and then handle the expected result. If the result differs from what is expected, then as we saw earlier, the test fails. The failure alerts us to a potential problem.

Aside from testability, the feature abstraction is powerful because it provides a very clear model for developers, users, and other stakeholders to understand requirements and expectations. In this context, a feature can be described as a placeholder for discourse among the stakeholders. Features can also help provide a means of describing the software in nontechnical terms. This is because features are used as a means to interact with the system.

A feature may have a visual control, such as a frontend button or some other graphical element. In this case, the feature is executed or initiated by user-driven action. When we run a database job in SQL Developer, we are also using the feature model— the job is the feature. Once the job starts and executes to completion, the feature has completed its useful work.

Another type of feature is the service variety, where the caller is a software element rather than a user. This type of feature interaction is autonomous in nature; that is, it runs without being driven by some external action. When we set up and run a scheduled database job in SQL Developer, we are also using the feature model; the scheduled job is the feature. Once this type of feature runs, it is typically indistinguishable from its user-driven counterpart.

A SQL Developer Feature

Just to solidify the feature concept, here's another example from Chapter 2. Remember the rather long-winded installation of Docker and Oracle Database? You might recall that SQL Developer has a nice feature that allows for testing the database connection.

In the case in Chapter 2, the database connection feature in question comes into play after configuring the containerized Oracle Database. When the user clicks Test to verify connectivity, as shown in Figure 6-1, SQL Developer checks the integrity of the connection with the Oracle Database. If the connection is good, then a text message (Status: Success) appears just above the Help button at the lower left of the window, as shown in Figure 6-1.

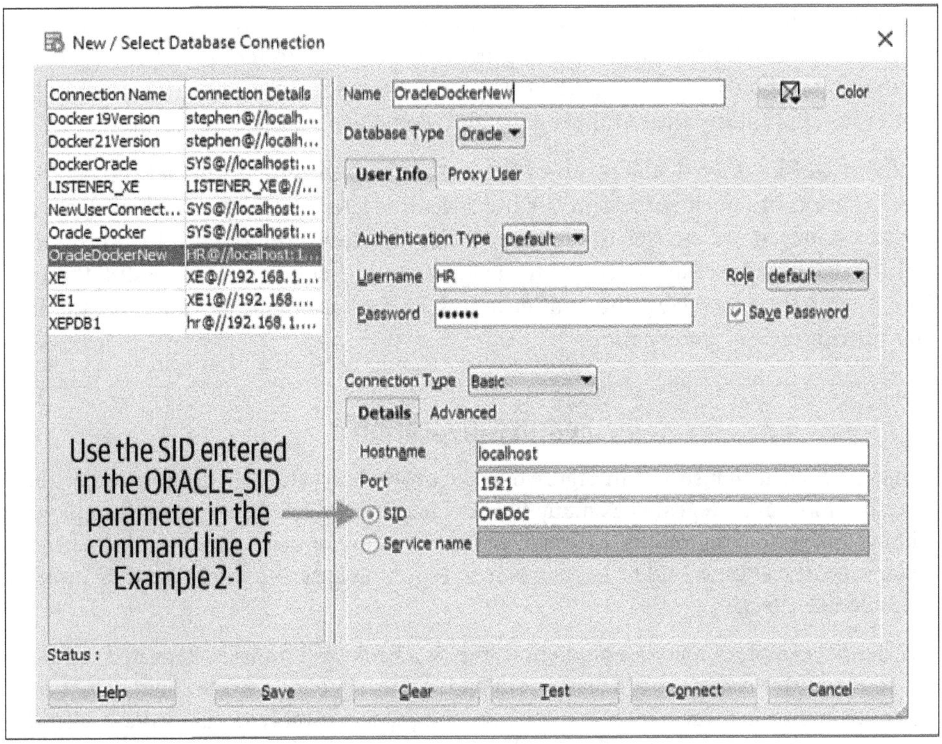

Figure 6-1. A feature that tests a connection to the Oracle Database

From Figure 6-1, it can be seen that a feature consists of a triggering action that results in one or more execution steps occurring. The end result of a feature execution is that some useful work has been done by the software.

Vertical Slices and Features

Remember: a feature is a vertical slice of a system. This slice is a testable element of capability that allows for doing some useful work. Features can be specified in isolation and typically do their useful work by employing ancillary helpers.

A further benefit of features is that they also provide nontechnical team members with a facility for discussing system components. Nontechnical members can then have useful discussions with developers using a common vernacular.

A hypothetical feature change might logically be arrived at as follows: "Feature *X* does this using Helpers *1* and *2*. We need to extend Feature *X* to do such and such. OK, we can extend Helper *2* and introduce a new Helper *3*."

The feature in Figure 6-1 is, of course, not a PL/SQL feature. Rather, Figure 6-1 depicts a general connectivity-checking feature. This is another way of saying that a feature orientation is quite a general way to look at software and that it applies to numerous application areas and programming languages (including PL/SQL).

In the case of Figure 6-1, the result of the feature invocation tells us that the database configuration has been successful (or not, which is also useful). Once this successful result is achieved, we are free to move on to the next task, confident in the knowledge that the database is set up correctly. If the feature end result is not successful, then we have to go back and review the configuration. In the case of either outcome, the feature provides useful information.

Feature Invocation

In cases such as that shown in Figure 6-1, the process of feature invocation and result verification can be repeated as many times as necessary. That is, we repeat it until we know that the configuration is correct. In software development parlance, this particular type of feature is said to be *idempotent*; repeating it has no unexpected or undesirable side effects.

A classic example of a nonidempotent feature is a bank cash transfer. Repeated calls to a cash transfer feature might have unintended consequences. An account might be debited more than once. For example, this might conceivably occur if the backend response is a little slow. An all-or-nothing transaction model is usually employed to handle this type of situation; that is, the transfer occurs successfully once and once only or else it is reverted or rolled back.

I once saw a case where a request message was being sent from a newly written frontend client application to a slow legacy backend system. The request was intended to update some backend data. Because the backend response was slow, the request was being re-sent after some short timeout, such as 5 seconds. The result was that the backend did eventually respond, but the long backlog of repeat requests were still queued up waiting to be processed.

Unfortunately, it didn't stop there. The end result was that the new client application continued to send large numbers of requests and this eventually caused the backend system to crash. Then, when the backend was brought up again, it started to work its way through the now irrelevant queued requests. Of course, the clients started sending new requests and the cycle started again.

Even though the requests were idempotent in nature, the client developers found out that they had inadvertently acquired the power to crash the backend. Needless to say, the owners of the backend system were none too pleased with this *new digital transformation technology* and they later laid down strict message timing requirements on the client application. The client developers were expressly forbidden from sending more than a designated number of requests per hour.

An end-to-end perspective is always a useful tool, particularly when integrating new applications into legacy backend systems. In such situations, it's a good idea not to assume you are the only user of the backend system.

Features are powerful parts of any system of software. Distinguishing features in this way provides us with a useful development model.

An Informal Feature Definition

A *feature* is a standalone item of system capability. A feature is a coarse-grained software element that executes some important business function. Running the feature provides some useful result (such as verifying the database is connected) or it can provide some useful data (such as verifying the successful invocation from Java of a PL/SQL procedure).

Features can be driven by users, software, or even a timed schedule.

In this context, the PL/SQL logging procedure can also be seen as a feature. The same is true for the update_employees PL/SQL procedure in Example 4-15. Remember when I used Java code in Chapter 5 to call the logging procedure? Where Java code is used to run PL/SQL code, that is another example of an autonomous or service feature.

I look at some more examples of features next.

Examples of Features

It is possible for a single block of PL/SQL to represent a feature. In other words, the PL/SQL block is employed to model a business function or is part of some wider process. Some common features include:

Data extraction
> A *data extraction* feature is commonly used to gather data from one or more sources, such as tables, views, data warehouses, and other systems of record. The extracted data is then available for further use in a downstream process.

Data cleaning
> *Data cleaning* is a procedure where unnecessary or erroneous items are removed from data. Duplicate data is often cleaned so that just one copy remains.

Data consolidation
> *Data consolidation* is employed to aggregate incoming data, such as sales or orders. The output from a data consolidation might subsequently be directed to an accounting system for further processing.

Data reconciliation

An example of a *data reconciliation* feature is the case where a payment for an order or service is matched against a corresponding bank account statement entry. The purpose of the reconciliation is to prove that the order or service has been fulfilled.

Invoice creation

Invoice creation is an important business process where one or more billable items are presented at the end of an order or work process. The data in the invoice typically may then be fed into the accounting system and the billing system.

Reporting

Reporting features are many and varied and are generally used to verify data integrity and to view the business-specific use of the data.

Each of those features typically results in the finished data being stored in a result table.

PL/SQL is a procedural language and this facilitates a nice feature-oriented model. It is easy to use PL/SQL and stepwise refinement to arrive at a modular end result. In fact, you can see an example of this in Example 6-1, where the code is carefully split into business logic and exception handling.

Example 6-1. The latest version of update_employees—an example of a feature

```
create or replace PROCEDURE update_employees
AS
 err_num NUMBER;
 err_msg VARCHAR2(100);
  CURSOR c_employee
  IS
    SELECT
            ename, empno, sal
    FROM
        emp
    ORDER BY
        sal DESC;
BEGIN
  FOR r_employee IN c_employee
  LOOP
    updateEmployeeData(r_employee.ename, r_employee.empno, r_employee.sal);
  END LOOP;

EXCEPTION
WHEN NO_DATA_FOUND THEN -- catches all 'no data found' errors
        loggingPackage.LOG_ACTION(('Ouch', 'we hit an exception'));
        ROLLBACK;
WHEN OTHERS THEN -- handles all other errors
```

```
    err_num := SQLCODE;
    err_msg := SUBSTR(SQLERRM, 1, 100);
    loggingPackage.LOG_ACTION('We hit a general exception error number - '
    || ' '
    || err_num
    || ' Error message: '
    || err_msg, 'update_employees');
    ROLLBACK;
END;
```

In terms of design in Example 6-1, it would probably be better to handle the SUBSTR call inside the LOG_ACTION procedure. This would have the benefit of simplifying the use of LOG_ACTION in Example 6-1.

By dividing the Example 6-1 PL/SQL code in this way, it is much easier for maintenance developers to understand. The update_employees procedure is a single item of business logic that serves to execute a single well-defined task. In order to complete its duty, the update_employees procedure makes a call to the updateEmployeeData procedure. This means that the update_employees procedure is a good candidate for being a feature. On the other hand, its call to updateEmployeeData is an example of using a *feature helper*.

There are no hard-and-fast rules for saying this or that code is a feature. It's really up to the developer, but a number of guidelines are useful in determining whether we're dealing with a feature:

- A feature is testable.
- A feature is a bit like a vertical *slice* of the system.
- A feature is a standalone item of use to the business.
- A feature does useful work.

An additional benefit of the feature model is that it can be easily understood by other stakeholders, such as the authors of requirements, architects, end users, managers, and so on.

It is important to understand that not everything is a feature or part of a feature. An example of a nonfeature is a SQL script. The script may of course be used as part of the construction of a feature. But strictly speaking, the SQL script itself is not a feature.

Anatomy of a Feature

A feature is composed of a number of artifacts, and Figure 6-2 illustrates the main components.

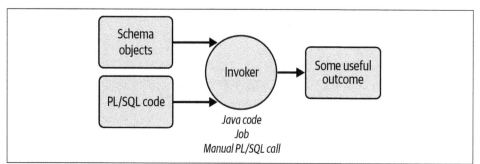

Figure 6-2. The elements of a feature

On the left side of Figure 6-2, you see schema objects, such as tables and PL/SQL functions and procedures. There are, of course, other objects, such as triggers, object-oriented PL/SQL types, and so on. In this discussion, the focus is mostly on PL/SQL functions and procedures. Feature orchestration is handled by the invoker element in the center of Figure 6-2.

As you've seen, in the PL/SQL domain, the feature can typically be invoked by one of the following:

- Java code
- A database job
- PL/SQL code
- A user interface element

On the right side of Figure 6-2, the outcome of the feature is shown, which can be:

- One or more table updates
- Execution of a procedure or function
- Extraction of some data

It's important to appreciate that Figure 6-2 is nothing more than a means of collecting the feature elements together and placing them under a common name.

Placing the feature elements under a single umbrella provides other benefits, such as:

- Articulating the common purpose of the feature
- Allowing the definition of the useful work the feature can do
- Defining the feature helpers
- Defining the invocation mechanism for the feature
- Defining tests to exercise the feature and its components
- Identifying the requirements for the feature and its components

Each of these is described in the following sections.

Articulating the Common Purpose of the Feature

The common purpose of the feature is closely related to the requirements definition. It answers the following questions:

- What is the feature required for?
- What problem does the feature solve?

As you've seen in earlier discussions, I initially don't look at the *how* of the feature, just the *what*. In other words, at the beginning of the project when the basic requirements are being drawn up, I don't care so much about what code will be written to produce the feature artifact. That comes a little later on. By looking closely at the *what*, I get a chance to articulate the purpose of the code rather the final realization of that purpose (i.e., the *how*).

The feature therefore acts initially as a placeholder for a solution to an important business problem. As the feature is developed, it changes from being a nearly empty placeholder into a fully populated resilient solution.

As the feature is designed, it may well be that the topmost element of the feature turns out to be a single line of Java code that calls a packaged PL/SQL procedure. Or the feature might be a pure PL/SQL solution, that is, a database-centric job—scheduled or ad hoc.

The feature invocation is a small, coarse-grained piece of source code. The main functional feature elements are shown in Figure 6-3. On the left is the general form of a feature. It contains the feature name, invoker or orchestrator, and feature helpers. The bulk of the work done is handled by the helpers in Figure 6-3. These are simply thin layers of PL/SQL code, such as procedures or functions. On the right is a specific feature, that is, a feature with a fixed set of helpers. In this case there are two helpers.

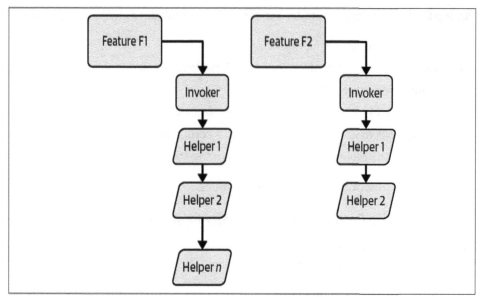

Figure 6-3. The functional elements of a feature

Allowing the Definition of the Useful Work the Feature Can Do

The work done by a feature is any work useful to the business. There's no real limit to the possibilities, but some examples of feature work are:

- Summarizing billable hours
- Summarizing overall cost for a given project code
- Generating a payroll run for a group of employees
- Extracting a list from a database of software applications in use
- Determining license compliance of software applications
- And so on

Defining the work of the feature allows for dividing up the tasks required to implement what the overall feature aims to achieve. The operation of the feature is handled by orchestration of the helpers.

Defining the Feature Helpers and Invocation Mechanism

As shown in Figures 6-2 and 6-3, a feature is generally composed of a number of helper elements. In the context of this discussion, the elements are PL/SQL code (i.e., procedures and functions).

The main feature does its work by enlisting the support of its helpers (i.e., other PL/SQL code). The helpers then do their designated parts of the overall task under the control of the main feature code. The invocation of a feature is some coarse-grained element. This can be a user interface button, a piece of Java code, a scheduled task, an ad hoc task, and so on.

The *invocation mechanism* of the feature is the solution entry point for the feature user. Once the feature is initiated, the useful work is carried out by the orchestrated action of the helpers.

Defining Tests to Exercise the Feature and Its Components

Because a feature consists of a group of components, it is important to test the components and the overall feature itself. To do this, each component is taken in turn and its inputs and expected outputs are defined. The tests then provide a way of verifying these inputs and outputs.

If the tests pass, then you can be confident that the code under test (the feature and its components) is correct. It is prudent where possible to also do some end-to-end tests. You'll see both test types in Part III.

Any future changes to the feature and its components may cause the tests to fail. This is a desirable situation because test failures may indicate some incorrect code or a need to update the test.

Identifying the Requirements for the Feature and Its Components

The set of requirements for a feature is crucial for the business owner. Indeed, skillful definition of feature requirements is one of the most difficult tasks in the software development lifecycle, and this is also true of features.

One of the motivations of this chapter is that features themselves provide a useful abstraction in which to define system capabilities. By breaking a solution into a set of features and helpers, we are then in a better position to articulate the requirements.

In general, the creation of features will start with the statement of a business problem of some sort. The feature is required to solve the business problem. Features are powerful. Let's now look at a concrete example of refactoring some PL/SQL code so that it becomes a feature.

Reimagining the Log Procedure as a Feature

The purpose of this section is to look at how to consider the code in Example 6-2 as a feature. This procedure resides in the LOGGINGPACKAGE package.

 In Example 6-2, I could add error handling, just in case there are possible errors with logging. The merit of this is that errors in logging would not then affect the main code. For example, you can log such errors to the *alert.log* using *dbms_system.ksdwrt* (*https://oreil.ly/0oFUM*).

Example 6-2. The code we want to call to record log events

```
create or replace PROCEDURE LOG_ACTION
        (action_message IN logging.action_message%TYPE,
         code_location  IN logging.code_location%TYPE
                            )
IS
    PRAGMA AUTONOMOUS_TRANSACTION;
BEGIN
    INSERT INTO LOGGING
           (EVENT_DATE
                , action_message
                , code_location
           )
           VALUES
           (SYSDATE
                , action_message
                , code_location
           )
    ;
    COMMIT;
END;
```

Take a step back to understand that the code in Example 6-2 conforms to the structure shown in Figure 6-3. The PL/SQL in Example 6-2 is, of course, very simple—nothing wrong with that. It inserts a log message in the LOGGING table. This is done as part of a unit of work in an autonomous transaction.

Just to quickly recap how the logger is called, Example 6-3 is an excerpt from an earlier exception block.

Example 6-3. Invoking the logger

```
WHEN NO_DATA_FOUND THEN -- catches all 'no data found' errors
 loggingPackage.LOG_ACTION('Ouch', 'we hit an exception'); ❶
 ROLLBACK;
WHEN OTHERS THEN -- handles all other errors
```

```
err_num := SQLCODE;
err_msg := SUBSTR(SQLERRM, 1, 100);
loggingPackage.LOG_ACTION('We hit a general exception error number - '
|| ' '
|| err_num
|| ' Error message: '
|| err_msg, 'update_employees');
ROLLBACK;
```

❶ The invoker is the call to the LOG_ACTION packaged procedure.

The helper is simply the PL/SQL inside the LOG_ACTION procedure, which commences with INSERT INTO LOGGING in Example 6-2.

One way to think about the interaction between the feature and its helpers is that the feature is the starting mechanism, and the work is then done with the assistance of the helpers. It doesn't get much simpler than that—just one procedure call. But let's imagine that a new requirement arises: the need to record more runtime information during exceptions.

Rather than merely recording the basic information at the point of invoking the logger, let's say we'd like to record some more detail, such as recording where in the code the exception occurs. This requirement can be fulfilled by using the FORMAT_CALL_STACK function from the DBMS_UTILITY package, as shown in Example 6-4.

Example 6-4. Invoking the logger using DBMS_UTILITY.FORMAT_CALL_STACK

```
WHEN NO_DATA_FOUND THEN -- catches all 'no data found' errors
 loggingPackage.LOG_ACTION('Ouch', 'we hit an exception');
 ROLLBACK;
WHEN OTHERS THEN -- handles all other errors
 err_num := SQLCODE;
 err_msg := SUBSTR(SQLERRM, 1, 100);
 callstack_msg := DBMS_UTILITY.FORMAT_CALL_STACK;
 loggingPackage.LOG_ACTION('We hit a general exception error number - ' ❶
 || ' ' ❷
 || err_num
 || ' Error message: '
 || err_msg, 'update_employees'
 || ' Callstack message: '
 || callstack_msg);
 ROLLBACK;
```

❶ Call stack data is added to the error detail. In this way, the helper code has been expanded to meet a new requirement. Clearly, the new code should be tested for issues, such as checking that the string boundary for callstack_msg is not exceeded.

❷ In the second call to LOG_ACTION, the second parameter should not exceed the maximum length of the LOGGING table code_location column.

I hope you get the idea that helpers can be expanded as new requirements arise. Where a change requirement is more extensive, it may be appropriate to add one or more new helpers, at which point the feature structure begins to look more like the item on the left in Figure 6-3.

It's a good idea to keep the helpers as lean as possible. This helps to facilitate testing and the addition of new code as and when the need arises.

Considering the update_employees Procedure as a Feature

Back in Example 6-1, you saw the update_employees procedure described as a feature. Here it is again in Example 6-5.

Example 6-5. Invoking the update_employees procedure

```
CREATE OR REPLACE PROCEDURE update_employees
AS
        err_num NUMBER;
        err_msg VARCHAR2(100);
        CURSOR c_employee IS
                SELECT
                        ename,
                        empno,
                        sal
                FROM
                        emp
                ORDER BY
                        sal DESC;

BEGIN
        FOR r_employee IN c_employee
        LOOP ❶
            updateEmployeeData(
            r_employee.ename, r_employee.empno, r_employee.sal); ❷
        END LOOP;
EXCEPTION
WHEN NO_DATA_FOUND THEN -- catches all 'no data found' errors
        loggingPackage.LOG_ACTION('Ouch', 'we hit an exception');
        ROLLBACK; ❸
WHEN OTHERS THEN -- handles all other errors
        err_num := SQLCODE;
        err_msg := SUBSTR(SQLERRM, 1, 100);
        loggingPackage.LOG_ACTION('We hit a general exception error number - '
        || ' '
```

```
      || err_num
      || ' Error message: '
      || err_msg, 'update_employees');
      -- The callstack code could be added here as part of updating this
      -- procedure.
      ROLLBACK;
END;
```

❶ The call to the `update_employees` procedure is the invocation of the `update_employees` feature.

❷ Once the procedure runs, `updateEmployeeData` (its helper) does most of the heavy lifting.

❸ The other helper in `update_employees` is the packaged `LOG_ACTION` procedure.

By looking at the PL/SQL code in this way, it becomes possible to break it into its constituent feature and helper elements. The clear separation between the elements provides for more ease in understanding the code and the end result should also be more resilient. The latter does of course assume a good score on the scale of resilience.

In the next section, you'll see how to test feature-based PL/SQL code.

Testing Features or Vertical Slices

Earlier in the chapter (in "Vertical Slices and Features" on page 149), I described a feature as a vertical slice of a system. Such a slice is a testable piece of code that more or less has a standalone existence. Because of this standalone characteristic, it then becomes possible for a feature to be fluently discussed by both developers and non-developers. Comparing the following statements provides a simple illustration of this idea:

> The `LOG_ACTION` PL/SQL procedure handles nonspecific exceptions by recording call stack and other details.

> The `LOG_ACTION` *feature* handles exceptions other than `NO_DATA_FOUND` by inserting a row in the `LOGGING` table.

Both statements are essentially saying the same thing, but the second one is couched in the language of features. This means that a nondeveloper can reasonably expect to understand it and maybe even make suggestions about improvements or the addition of new elements to the feature.

In Figure 6-4, there's a full suite of tests to exercise the feature.

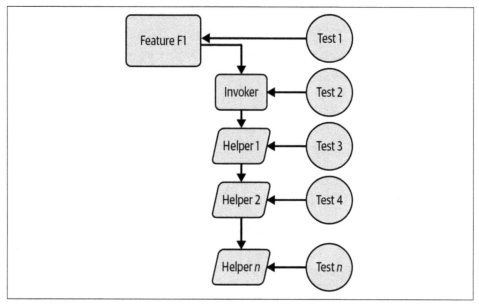

Figure 6-4. Testing a feature

If the full suite of tests passes, then that provides confidence that the feature works as per its specification. The tests aren't a substitute for running the code in a real scenario. But they do give the developer a good indication that the feature works as expected.

In the next section, I present a way to look at the feature code with respect to the suggested depth of testing.

Business-Critical PL/SQL Code

In Figure 6-5, an important set of questions is posed. Actually, it's just one question in relation to the business criticality of the code. The question is applied to all of the feature and helper code in Figure 6-5. The developer's attention is drawn to the importance of testing *critical* code, by which I mean that the code is a key element of the application. It may even be unique to the organization.

If you have to make a choice about which code to produce tests for first, then critical code is a good place to start.

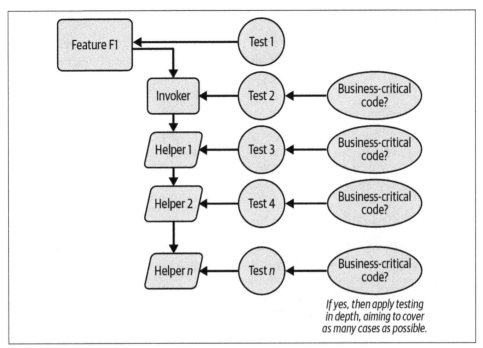

Figure 6-5. Testing a feature

Other Aspects of Features

Can the feature model be used to facilitate checking the health of the system? Isn't system health just another feature? These are good questions that I'll address next.

Features and System Health

Building resilient solutions almost certainly requires us to provide a means of looking at the health status of the system. A given system may be composed of exceptionally well-crafted code, but that system may be far from being resilient.

The health of a system typically comprises a number of metrics concerning:

- Responsiveness
- Liveness
- Correctness
- System resources
- Uptime

Determining the health status can include calls (or endpoints) that provide details about some or all of the metrics in that list.

It is no coincidence that microservices-based systems provide for strong monitoring and health checking. Even further back in the development cycle, we should find first-class automatic tests, which provide the developers with increased assurance about the strength of the solution.

In the context of tests, we can think of the provision of a health check feature in the production system as also being a kind of test. Indeed, a health check can be considered as a shift-right test. That is, the health check exists to boost confidence in the finished/deployed system.

Features Versus Endpoints

In modern software development, one of the foundational mainstream models is loose coupling. In the loose coupling approach, software components are built so that they have as little reliance on other components as possible. Such components are said to have high cohesion and loose coupling. While not being tied to one another at the implementation level, the components collectively interact (loosely) to achieve the business aims.

An important aspect of loose coupling is in relation to state management. This is crucial in applications that support some type of workflow. As the user drives the workflow through its various stages, the underlying state must be managed in some fashion. Various schemes have grown up over the years, including cookies, tokens, and so on. These schemes have the useful benefit of attaching state to the request and response messages. This then has the advantage of freeing up the backend systems from having to handle state.

The microservices model is a good example of loose coupling, where small modules of independent software services run as independent blocks of code. Messages can be passed between such services, but direct interservice calls such as a remote procedure call (RPC), Remote Method Invocation (RMI), and so on are not recommended. This is because such interservice calls introduce coupling, which then starts to move the code toward a monolithic model.

A popular way of creating such loosely coupled, highly cohesive systems of software is by modeling them as a collection of endpoints. An example of a technology in this space is RESTful endpoints. A given microservice can be made up of a bunch of RESTful endpoints (as few as possible). The client then sends an HTTP request to a given endpoint, the service executes the corresponding code, and a result is passed back to the client along with a response code. During its normal operation, such a service might call code that invokes stored procedures, authentication and authorization services, and so on.

In Figure 6-6, the upper-left box depicts a feature and its constituent operations (helpers). The lower-left box depicts traditional RESTful endpoints.

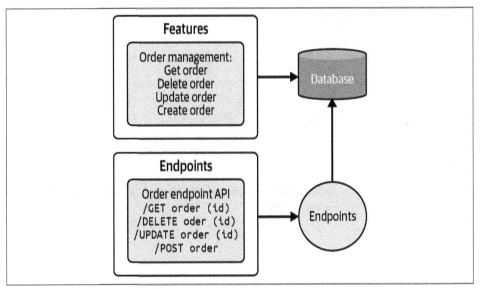

Figure 6-6. Features and endpoints

RESTful is a powerful model because it makes use of a standard transport protocol (HTTP) and the service elements are, as mentioned, loosely coupled. One minor downside of the model is that is can result in a kind of cognitive dissonance for developers. The developers must know and understand the set of endpoints that together constitute a given service. The frontend (or other client system) typically invokes the endpoints in a manner that makes business workflow sense. This means that the frontend is restricted in the endpoints to which it can direct requests.

In other words, the frontend code (e.g., an Angular frontend client) handles the calls to the backend based on the user interactions. The backend then serves the needs of the frontend by calling other systems or services. The end result of the workflow is generally some data or response code being passed back to the frontend.

In this context, features and endpoints are essentially the same thing. But the point of the discussion is to encourage developers to put some thought into the way endpoints are created and documented. The goal is to try to build endpoints that provide a feature-like expression to the client.

Summary

Modern software tools, such as Eclipse, IntelliJ IDEA, and SQL Developer, have all matured in usability. The tools to write code are themselves an invitation to quickly get into coding. Why wait? Well, it's an old adage that the earlier you start to code, the longer your project will take. Indeed, some such projects may never finish.

Using the feature abstraction helps to temporarily push the pause button on the coding phase. By designing PL/SQL code as a set of one or more features and helpers, you give your coding a head start. In other words, the features are initial placeholders for the rest of the code. It's often quite surprising how quickly the code takes shape once the feature scaffolding is is place. You'll see this in the worked example in Part III.

It's useful to keep in mind that features are testable blocks of code—and preferably also vertical slices of system capability.

PART III

Synthesis of the PL/SQL Toolbox and Feature-Driven Development

CHAPTER 7

A Process-Centric, Feature-Based Mini Project

In this chapter, you'll see an overview of all the resilient PL/SQL requirements brought together as part of a solution. The elements include the following:

1. Define the requirements

2. Build a basic invoice outline

3. Create the schema

4. Test the schema

5. Feature description

6. The PL/SQL toolbox elements needed to build a solution

7. Tests

8. Building a resilient PL/SQL solution

9. Verifying the solution by invoking it from a high-level language

Each of these elements is described in the following sections.

A Brief Note on Invoices

Just in case you're not familiar with invoices, note that they are used in businesses to record an amount of money owed to the business, usually for some item or items of work. An invoice is issued to a customer to record the work done and the amount of money owed for that work. Various other items of information are generally included in an invoice, as you'll see later on.

Invoices can be considered a critical business component: they feed into accounting systems and contribute to tax calculations. Another aspect of invoices is that a copy of a given invoice is often sent to a customer. Thus, it's very important that the content of an invoice is both clear and accurate. The vagueness of the second requirement is not a reflection of the low importance of the end result; rather, the author of the requirement is probably assuming the developers have business knowledge that they may or may not have.

Requirement 1: Define the Requirements

Let's imagine we are beginning a new project and have been handed a slightly vague requirement: build an invoice creation feature or tool. In the following sections, I describe requirement 2 in more detail. This elaboration procedure is almost always a good idea because we are delaying the implementation phase as long as possible.

 Remember the old adage: the sooner you start to code, the longer the project will take. Some projects may never get finished.

Rather than coding immediately, I'm instead building a clearer picture of *what* is required before plunging into *how* the code will work.

Requirement 2: Build a Basic Invoice Outline

In the specification we expect to incorporate the following data elements in the finished invoice:

- Customer name
- Project name
- Project code
- Billable hours
- Staff ID or principal contact (for team-based projects)

- Hourly rate or cost to the client
- Revenue calculation
- Tax calculation
- Recipient
- Payment details

Most of these are fairly self-explanatory. The billable hours might come from a staff timesheet system or they might be manually added to the invoice data. The tax calculation will tend to vary based on the location where the work was carried out, e.g., in the United States, different states have different sales tax rates.

Software Systems and the Issue of Modeling

It's always worth remembering that any piece of software is invariably a model of some real-world process. The software aims to mimic the underlying process. As we've seen in the examples up to now, it is essential that the software solution handles errors and exceptions in as graceful a manner as possible. By modeling processes in this way, it becomes possible to create software artifacts that operate in a manner that is as close as possible to the corresponding real-world process.

In this era of digital transformation, a great many processes are now being handled using some sort of digital solution. The mini project under consideration is no exception to this trend.

The essential requirement here is to model an invoice creation procedure. Many businesses have traditionally handled invoice creation in a manual or partly manual manner. For the present case, the invoice creation process will bring together the invoice creation elements as a unified PL/SQL feature project.

Another type of process is that which originates in an automated domain (e.g., ecommerce). This type of process may have never had a nondigital representation. Having said that, it is noteworthy that in general, ecommerce is an online version of what was often originally a brick-and-mortar process.

This idea is illustrated in Figure 7-1, where the top half represents a traditional process that has human and software input. This process is then migrated into an online version where most or all of the operation is automated.

The other type of application, in the bottom half of Figure 7-1, is the variant that started life online, i.e., it was never part of a human-centric process. It was born in the internet. The takeaway is that once a business process moves into the software area, it becomes a model of the original process. This also points to another key skill for modern developers: the cultivation of domain expertise. In a nutshell, the more you know about the domain in which your code runs, the better. Such knowledge can introduce you to various shortcuts and other important elements of the business workflow.

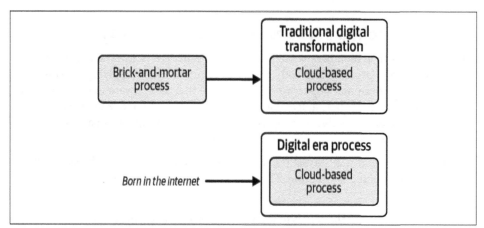

Figure 7-1. Traditional route to the cloud

Once the solution has been created, it must then be introduced into a corresponding process. I call this process *review-repair-rerun,* as shown in Figure 7-2.

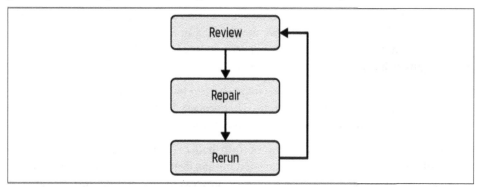

Figure 7-2. The review-repair-rerun cycle

The basic premise of this review-repair-rerun cycle is that if an issue arises in the code, we initiate a review. The review involves the techniques you've seen in the earlier chapters, for example, code review, logfile examination, database table content inspection, and so on. If a change is required to resolve an issue, then a modification or repair is applied, such as a change to the associated PL/SQL code. After redeployment of the corresponding stored procedure, the last step is to rerun it. The cycle is iterative and can be repeated as often as required until a successful resolution is achieved.

Let's now move on to the next requirement, schema creation.

Requirement 3: Create a Schema

Creating a schema is a nontrivial task. It generally involves having a lot of business knowledge. The schema may also represent an aggregation of much data from upstream systems, such as databases, data warehouses, and other systems of record.

In "A Simple Schema" on page 45, I used a really simple, handcrafted schema in order to give us something to look at in the corresponding PL/SQL code examples. Such a basic schema bears no relation to the business schema variants you'll encounter in practice. For this reason, I'll be using a more complex schema from here on.

Rather than defining a new handcrafted schema in this section, I've opted instead to use the Oracle standard HR schema along with the installation steps described in excellent detail in Ben Brumm's Database Star video on YouTube (*https://oreil.ly/v8ueU*).

The first step is to download the four SQL script files from Ben's GitHub repository (*https://oreil.ly/j11ch*), as shown in Figure 7-3.

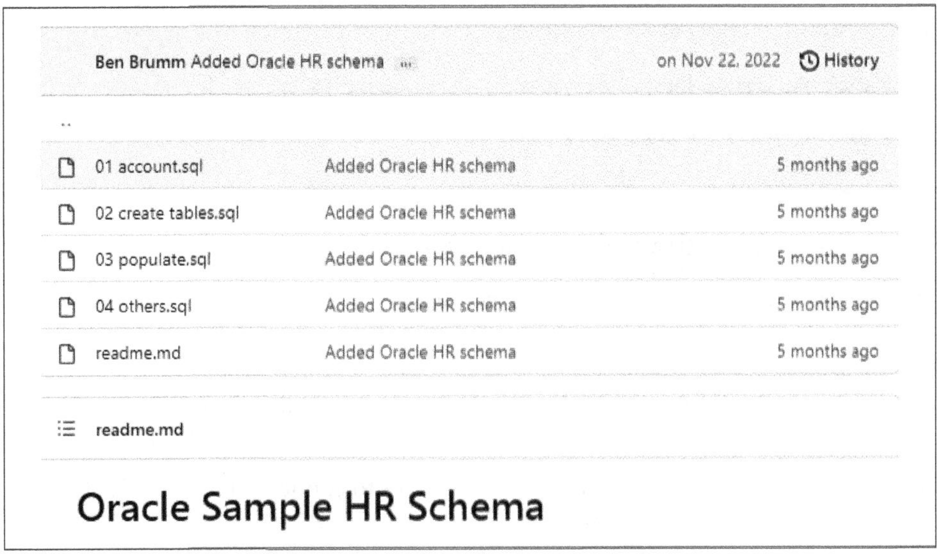

Figure 7-3. The Oracle HR schema installation scripts

The contents of the schema files in Figure 7-3 can be viewed using a text editor. I include the first SQL script file (called *01 account.sql*) here in Example 7-1 for context and reference.

Example 7-1. Creating the HR schema accounts using the 01 account.sql file

```
/*
01 Create Account
Create accounts for HR schema
Run this as either SYS or SYSTEM.
*/

/*
Set the pluggable database if you're running this on Oracle v12 or later.
This can be a different name, depending on the name of your PDB. In the
present case, the name is ORCLPDB1 because that matches the installed PDB.
*/
ALTER SESSION SET CONTAINER = ORCLPDB1;

/*
Drop the HR account and all objects to reset.
Then, create the user and give it the permissions.
*/
DROP USER HR CASCADE;   ❶

CREATE USER HR IDENTIFIED BY hrpass;

ALTER USER HR DEFAULT TABLESPACE users QUOTA UNLIMITED ON users;

ALTER USER HR TEMPORARY TABLESPACE TEMP;

GRANT CONNECT TO HR;

GRANT CREATE SESSION, CREATE VIEW, CREATE TABLE,
ALTER SESSION, CREATE SEQUENCE TO HR;
GRANT CREATE SYNONYM, CREATE DATABASE LINK, RESOURCE, UNLIMITED TABLESPACE TO HR;
```

❶ Drops and re-creates the HR user along with the required privileges. If the HR user is being created for the first time, then the attempt to drop it will just result in a harmless error message.

In order to run the script in Example 7-1, you have to connect to the Oracle Database as the SYS user, as shown in Figure 7-4.

Remember to make sure you use the SYSDBA role during the login, as shown in the drop-down control on the right side of Figure 7-4. The combination of the SYS user and the SYSDBA role provides the required privileges to successfully run the Oracle HR schema accounts creation script.

For the password in Figure 7-4, make sure to use the same password that you entered way back in Example 2-1; I used mySyspwd1.

When you're happy with the updated settings in the menu shown in Figure 7-4, make sure the Save Password control is enabled.

New / Select Database Connection   ✕

Connection Name	Connection Details
Docker19Version	stephen@//localh...
Docker21Version	stephen@//localh...
DockerOracle	SYS@//localhost:...
LISTENER_XE	LISTENER_XE@//...
NewUserConnect...	SYS@//localhost:...
Oracle_Docker	SYS@//localhost:...
OracleDockerNew	HR@//localhost:1...
XE	XE@//192.168.1...
XE1	XE1@//192.168...
XEPDB1	hr@//192.168.1...

Name OracleDockerNew   ⊠ Color

Database Type Oracle ▾

User Info Proxy User

Authentication Type Default ▾

Username SYS   Role SYSDBA ▾

Password ••••••   ☑ Save Password

Connection Type Basic   ▾

Details Advanced

Hostname   localhost
Port   1521
◉ SID   OraDoc
○ Service name

Use the SID entered in the ORACLE_SID parameter in the command line of Example 2-1 ⟶

Status :

Help   Save   Clear   Test   Connect   Cancel

Figure 7-4. The Oracle HR schema installation

Remember to use the Test button in the Oracle HR schema installation to verify that the connection is valid. As you've seen in earlier examples, this Test button is a very handy *feature* of SQL Developer.

If the details in Figure 7-4 are correct, then click Connect to make the connection to the database.

At some point during the schema installation, you may encounter a dialog warning you that your password will expire soon. If this warning appears, make a note of it in order to rectify it at a later time. An appropriate time to fix this issue might be after the schema installation is complete.

To finally run the first SQL script file, select the main File menu followed by Open and then navigate to the folder containing the downloaded scripts. Look for the required file (called *01 account.sql*), as shown in Figure 7-5.

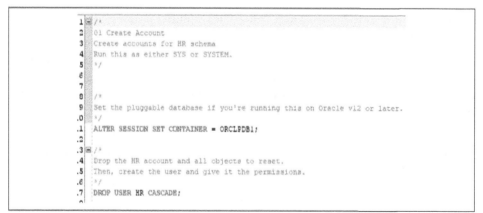

Figure 7-5. Selecting the first HR schema installation script

Double-click the required filename, which will open it in the worksheet, as shown in Figure 7-6.

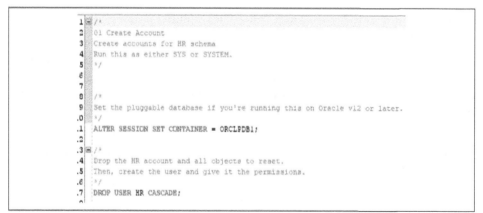

Figure 7-6. Modifying the first schema installation script

In Figure 7-6, I had to make a change in order for the script to work. This is related to the naming of the pluggable database. Once the change is made, you can then click the Run Script button (just to the right of the play button), as shown in Figure 7-6.

The following change is required for the schema creation scripts to work. The script change is to the *01 account.sql* file and consists of changing the ALTER SESSION SET CONTAINER line from ORCLPDB1 to PDB1; i.e.:

```
ALTER SESSION SET CONTAINER = PDB1;
```

Executing the script then creates the HR schema user, which has the password hrpass in the following line:

```
CREATE USER HR IDENTIFIED BY hrpass;
```

The password is case-sensitive. The Oracle Database is mostly case-insensitive; this is one of the exceptions.

Once the HR schema is created, you can then connect to it by once again using the (normal user privilege) combination of the HR account and the default role, as shown in Figure 7-7.

Oracle Database Users and the Principle of Least Privilege

In the discussion preceding Figure 7-7, the connection for the logged-in user (SYS) is retained and a new connection is created for the HR user. Two connections are then present.

This is a good illustration of the principle of least privilege (*https://oreil.ly/fueBX*), which dictates that any given user should only receive sufficient privileges (and no more) to get their job done. It's not to suggest that a legitimate user seeking elevated privileges would have any nefarious intentions, but rather that a bad actor who gets ahold of elevated privileges may well have bad intentions.

It's not uncommon to see this principle being flouted, even in very large organizations. This can take the form of granting software developers (or other nonadmin staff) administrative privileges in some new important system or service.

Initially, it seems like a good idea to let the developers get used to the new system or service and do their thing. However, over time, it often happens that each developer may use the administrative rights in a slightly different way. This in turn can lead to a kind of spaghetti junction of differing configurations, each authored by a different developer. Subsequently unraveling the spaghetti is usually a thankless and laborious task, which in some cases can only be done properly by starting from scratch.

The takeaway from this is to ensure that the principle of least privilege is used and adhered to. In the context of this specific discussion, the principle dictates that the SYS user creates the schema. Then, the SYS user grants appropriate access rights to the HR user and to other users. An example of flouting the principle in this case would be to use only the SYS user for all work (including development).

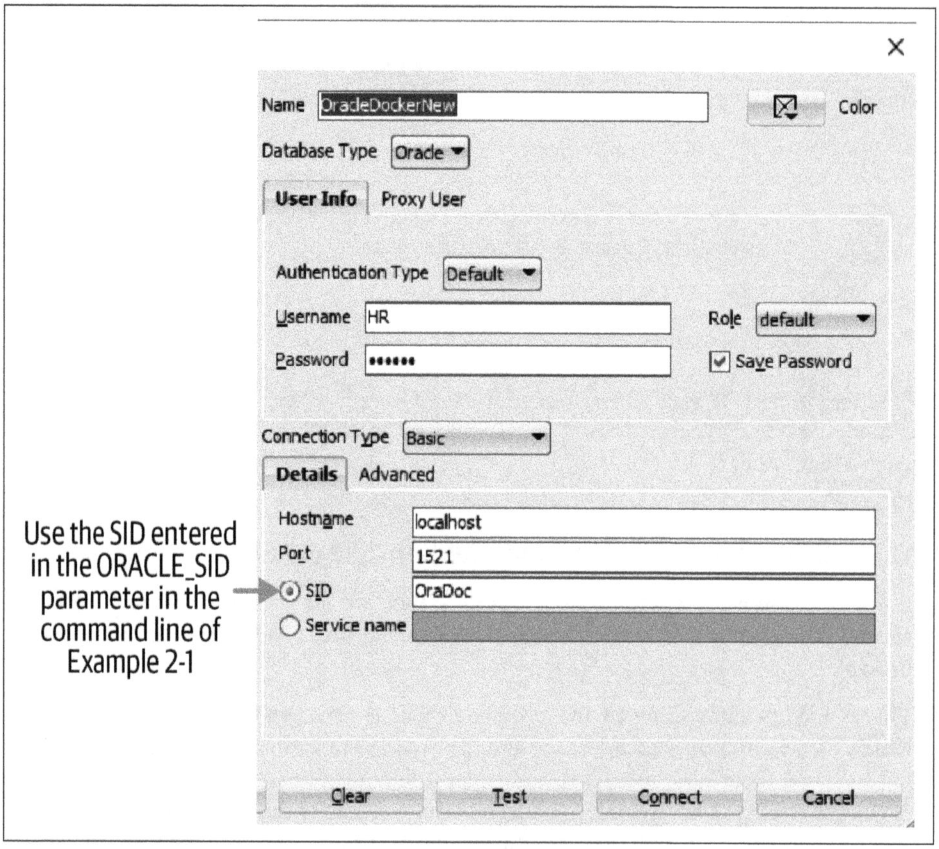

Use the SID entered in the ORACLE_SID parameter in the command line of Example 2-1

Figure 7-7. Connecting to the HR schema to verify installation

If the basic connection works (using our old friend the Test button in Figure 7-7 to verify the connection), then you can now connect to the database using the new HR user with normal privileges by clicking the Connect button. If all is well with the connection, then the remaining installation scripts can be run next.

In Example 7-2, I show an excerpt from the second SQL script file (called *02 create tables.sql*), where the tables are created.

Example 7-2. Creating the HR schema tables (excerpt from the file 02 create tables.sql)

```
/* 02 Create Tables
This script creates the tables needed for the HR schema.
Run this script after script 01, and while you are logged in as the
newly created HR user. */

DROP TABLE job_history CASCADE CONSTRAINTS; ❶
DROP TABLE departments CASCADE CONSTRAINTS;
DROP TABLE employees CASCADE CONSTRAINTS;
DROP TABLE jobs CASCADE CONSTRAINTS;
DROP TABLE locations CASCADE CONSTRAINTS;
DROP TABLE countries CASCADE CONSTRAINTS;
DROP TABLE regions CASCADE CONSTRAINTS;
DROP SEQUENCE locations_seq;
DROP SEQUENCE departments_seq;
DROP SEQUENCE employees_seq;


ALTER SESSION SET NLS_LANGUAGE=American;
ALTER SESSION SET NLS_TERRITORY=America;

/* Regions */

CREATE TABLE regions (
  region_id NUMBER CONSTRAINT regions_id_nn NOT NULL,
  region_name VARCHAR2(25)
);

CREATE UNIQUE INDEX reg_id_pk
ON regions (region_id);

ALTER TABLE regions
ADD CONSTRAINT reg_id_pk
PRIMARY KEY (region_id);

/* Countries */

CREATE TABLE countries (
  country_id CHAR(2) CONSTRAINT  country_id_nn NOT NULL,
  country_name VARCHAR2(40),
  region_id NUMBER,
  CONSTRAINT country_c_id_pk PRIMARY KEY (country_id)
)
ORGANIZATION INDEX;

ALTER TABLE countries
ADD CONSTRAINT countr_reg_fk
FOREIGN KEY (region_id)
REFERENCES regions(region_id);
...
```

❶ The first step is to DROP existing tables and any associated constraints. This is the normal use of SQL scripts of this nature, because it allows you to run the operation multiple times if required.

In fact, this usage model is very similar to the earlier PL/SQL examples where something like the following line is used:

```
CREATE OR REPLACE PROCEDURE update_employees IS
```

In this case, the REPLACE in effect drops or deletes the existing resource. The REPLACE statement means that there is no need to explicitly delete the old version. Follow the next few steps and you'll be finished:

1. Run *script02.sql* to create the tables.

2. Run *script03.sql* to populate the tables.

3. Run *script04.sql* to create the last remaining objects that are required in the schema, i.e., creating indexes, stored procedures, triggers, and so on.

If no unexpected error messages were seen, then the schema installation is now complete and can be tested.

Requirement 4: Test the Schema

The schema installation is complete and it is also populated with some data. I'll be extending the schema in the next chapter in order to accommodate the invoice solution. For the moment, there is a need to verify the schema is operational, and for this it is sufficient to run a query against one of the new schema tables.

Run this query to retrieve some data:

```
select * from countries;
```

This should produce output similar to that shown in Figure 7-8. Notice the columns relating to country-specific data. In the next chapter, I'll be revisiting the schema during the solution creation.

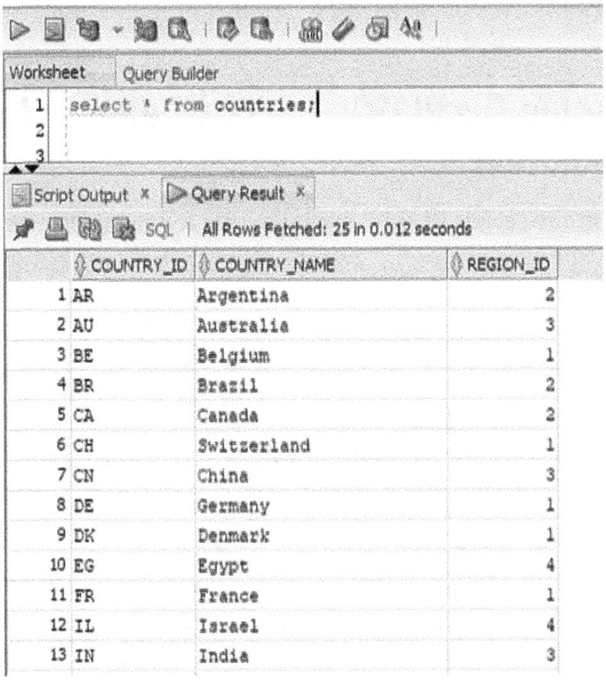

Figure 7-8. Selecting the countries

Now that the Oracle HR schema is created and populated, the required feature can be specified.

Requirement 5: Feature Description

A simple feature description is enough to get the ball rolling. Clearly, the feature can be arbitrarily complex with full invoice CRUD semantics incorporated into a business workflow.

In the context of creating a resilient PL/SQL solution, it's more instructive to start small. To do this, I'll just specify that for each invoice, we want to be able to simply create it from the project and customer data tables as per the following:

- Define the invoice creation feature.
- Define the invoice creation feature helpers.
- Define the invoice creation test code.
- Create the Java code to invoke the invoice creation feature.

In the feature description, the perspective taken is to look at the feature as a whole and enumerate the components.

Requirement 6: The PL/SQL Toolbox Elements Needed to Build a Solution

As you've seen in the earlier PL/SQL examples, the following elements are routinely employed:

- Procedures
- Cursors
- Loops
- Transactions
- Logging
- Packages

In the next chapter, the PL/SQL code will be constructed using some or all of these elements.

Requirement 7: Tests

Tests form an essential part of the feature because they allow us to verify the operation and results. Changes made to ancillary code (such as PL/SQL code in support packages) may have unexpected effects on our feature. Well-constructed and well-conceived tests can help in pointing to such issues. On the other hand, not having decent tests can mean that impaired PL/SQL and feature code gets pushed out to production. End users are rarely the most sympathetic testers of nonfunctional code.

The tests specified include a combination of PL/SQL (utPLSQL) tests and feature-level tests. You read a detailed description of utPLSQL tests earlier in "Installing utPLSQL" on page 106. The focus for this part will be on feature-level tests using Java. This provides more of an end-to-end test experience and has the additional merit of extending the PL/SQL toolbox with the addition of an extra skill set.

Requirement 8: Building a Resilient PL/SQL Solution

Since the overall purpose is to build a resilient PL/SQL solution, this section is something of a placeholder. The main tools used for the construction will include SQL Developer and IntelliJ IDEA (*https://www.jetbrains.com/idea/*).

SQL Developer will be used to create, deploy, and run the required artifacts consisting of SQL scripts and PL/SQL code.

IntelliJ will be used to create a basic Java project that invokes and helps to test the PL/SQL feature.

Requirement 9: Verifying the Solution by Invoking It from a High-Level Language

As per Requirement 8, the Java language is chosen for the high-level invocation of the stored procedure. This was seen in "Setting Up a Simple Java Application" on page 138 where a Java application was used to invoke a stored procedure.

Verification at the level of Java code will then take the form of some simple manual tests.

Summary

Building a resilient PL/SQL solution consists of joining the techniques introduced in Parts I and II. This comprises a number of steps, starting with defining the requirements. Requirements definition is a highly skilled activity, and the most effective requirements are generally created by people with detailed knowledge of the domain and existing tools.

The next step consists of creating a basic outline of the invoice solution output. In the present case, this is a business invoice that contains a small range of data items. Most of the latter are acquired from existing table data and one item (tax) is derived.

The required schema is defined next and it is prudent to test the schema just to ensure that the data is valid and that any required constraints are in place. A minor addition to the schema is required for the solution and this will be done in the next chapter. A short feature description is useful to reinforce the developer's understanding of the domain. It may also be useful to enumerate some or all of the PL/SQL toolbox elements needed to build the solution.

No project should be considered complete without extensive testing. The tests can include in-database unit tests as you saw in Chapter 4. In the next chapter, I'll use a different type of test, namely Java-based tests. This has the merit of illustrating two different types of tests (utPLSQL and Java) and indicating the role each of them plays in building and verifying the solution.

CHAPTER 8

From What to How: Building Feature Components from the Specification

In Chapter 7, you saw the specification for the invoice creation feature. In this chapter and the next, the coding of the specification commences. It is important to note that the translation of requirements into working code is a creative and iterative process.

Any creative process tends to have a finite range of possible pathways to a correct outcome. In other words, the way I go about it might be different from the route you might take. The end result in both cases should be a solution that produces the same output for the same input with equivalent resilience and performance in both cases.

This flexible approach is not a bad thing; I'm following a method that aims to produce a testable feature and its constituent helpers. The adoption of a solution approach provides a convenient framework for articulating the major deliverable artifacts of the development process, namely descriptions of the following:

1. Simple requirements

2. Schema

3. Features

4. Helpers

5. Tests

In a nutshell, the following should be seen as a set of guidelines and not a prescriptive procedure. If you see a better way to implement one of the steps, then don't be afraid to go for it.

The Requirements

The desired end result for the mini project is as shown in Figure 8-1.

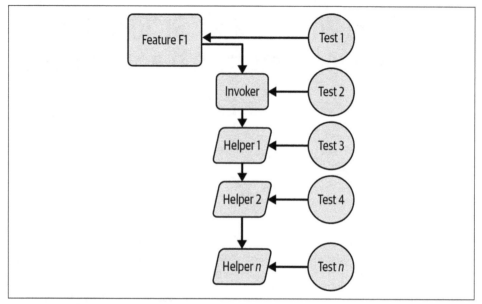

Figure 8-1. The elements of a feature: helpers and tests

The helpers in Figure 8-1 exist purely to assist the main feature code. So, looking at Figure 8-1, the Feature F1 can use (via the Invoker) Helper 1, Helper 2, and so on. in any order. In other words, there's no layering of the code in Figure 8-1. F1 may turn out to be a single line of Java code or it might be a user interface button. From the end user perspective, F1 *is* the feature, whereas from the developer perspective, the feature *is everything in* Figure 8-1.

The plan in this chapter is to describe in detail the main components of Figure 8-1 and sketch the outlines of the code. Then, in the next chapter, I'll do the detailed coding and integration.

The following are the main data requirements for the invoice creation:

- Customer name
- Project name
- Project code
- Billable hours
- Staff ID or principal contact (for team-based projects)

- Hourly rate or cost to the client
- Revenue calculation
- Tax calculation
- Recipient
- Payment details

In the current solution domain, the invoice is a business artifact. An invoice is just a financial record of work done for a given client on a specific project. The invoice might be sent to the client by email or on some other channel, such as a secure web service. By building the code using a feature orientation, it should be possible to integrate the invoice into any desired delivery mechanism by just changing the appropriate helper.

In tabular form, the invoice description might look something like Table 8-1.

Table 8-1. The invoice columns (so far)

Customer	Project	Code	Hours	Contact	Rate	Revenue	Tax	Recipient	Payment
ACME	DEV1	DEV1_A	40	Josh@development.com	100	4000	400	sam@acme.com	4400

So, how does one go about translating these rather vague requirements into working code? Remember that the requirements represent the *what* and the working code represents the *how* of the finished solution.

As you'll see in this chapter, a critical element of the translation to code is having a clear understanding of the requirements. Flexibility is an important part of this and in Table 8-1, you can see that the set of columns listed is referred to as "The invoice columns (so far)." In other words, it is highly likely that there will be changes to the columns as we progress through the coding.

Change Requests and the Need for Mental Toughness

How you react to the need for requirement changes is largely a personal decision. In business environments, change is generally inevitable. My own preference is to try not to expend energy in getting annoyed about customers changing their minds. In a way, such change requests can be seen as a useful test of the robustness of your development process.

A fairly typical change request might require the modification of some database column names and the corresponding report display items. As this type of item is tackled, make sure to verify the changes and to also update any database reconstruction SQL scripts. This way, your procedures easily handle the requirement.

Aside from functional requirement changes, there is a more troublesome type of change request: those that reduce the already agreed-upon time allowed for a given deliverable. I've seen this happen on complex integration project work. One effective way to handle this is to aim to have, as soon as the development starts, a clear list of deliverables and a solid plan for realizing them. Then, if one project item is required in a hurry, you will have already given its realization some thought. Breaking each deliverable down into discrete steps helps visualize the work required. I'll try to demonstrate this in the current chapter.

I'll use the feature-based approach that was described in Chapter 7. Here again (in Figure 8-2) is the basic feature element description, which contains the artifacts necessary to create the feature.

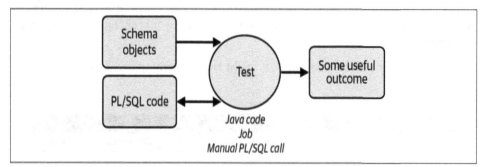

Figure 8-2. The elements of a feature

In order to create the solution, I follow the main steps described in Chapter 7, namely:

1. Define the requirements

2. Build a basic invoice outline

3. Create the schema

4. Test the schema

5. Feature workflow description

6. The PL/SQL toolbox elements needed to build a solution

7. Tests

8. Build a basic invoice creation tool

9. Verifying the solution by invoking it from a high-level language

Let's now walk through these basic steps bearing in mind that one or two of them have already been partially or fully completed in Chapter 7. In this context, I'm using the steps as a kind of development checklist.

Just before doing this, let's take a tiny detour to discuss the issue of iteration and repetition.

Development Checklists, Repetition, and Iteration

The procedure I'm using might appear a little repetitive. This is intentional. Any repetition is purely intended to remind the developer of each deliverable. It's all too easy to forget a required step. This is even more true nowadays with the widespread use of complex configurable frameworks. I'm sure you have your own stories of critical steps that were missed in projects. One case springs to mind as I write this.

Years ago, an organization I was working with developed a completely new ancillary product. It was anticipated that the new product would be an important addition to the existing product suite. Also, the associated development project was the organization's first foray into the Java language. After many adventures, a basic offering was produced.

It was the old days (the '90s), before Agile delivery had been widely adopted, and unfortunately, the project specification was a little on the lightweight side. The testers felt that there was something missing from the new product.

After a while, someone realized that the product didn't have any facility to allow the user to modify the application configuration. You might say it was a case of one size fits all. Given that the product was intended to work in companies of various sizes, it was crucial that the configuration be modifiable.

Removing the configuration immutability was both embarrassing for the developers and technically quite difficult. A simple checklist would almost certainly have prevented this type of outcome. Also, adopting a method such as shift-left (as described back in "Shift-Left in Operation" on page 65) wouldn't have hurt. Though, in fairness, I don't think anybody was talking about shift-left in those days.

Let's get back to the requirements.

Define the Requirements

It is, of course, always important to be flexible about the nine requirements we've been using since Chapter 7—they do have a tendency to change. For example, in our invoice project, changes to the data columns would be typical. There might be changes made to the columns that are included in the invoice, such as adding new columns to the table.

Any such changes should require a schema modification and, ideally, a corresponding update to just one of the helper functions. I say *ideally* because, in this model, the changes are limited to as small a number of solution components as possible. This should have the additional merit that only a small amount of testing is required to verify the change.

While a small change requires just a limited amount of testing to verify it works correctly, it should be noted that the overall amount of testing increases with every change in the product. This is because not just the new feature but all the previous features must be tested to verify that they still work.

Build a Basic Invoice Outline

As for the requirements definition, we've got a basic outline for the invoice, as you saw in Table 8-1 and as is repeated here in Table 8-2.

Table 8-2. The invoice columns

Customer	Project	Code	Hours	Contact	Rate	Revenue	Tax	Recipient	Payment
ACME	DEV1	DEV1_A	40	Josh@development.com	100	4000	400	sam@acme.com	4400

Notice in Table 8-2 that the column names are quite short (e.g., Payment has a row with the value 4400). This reflects the fact that the solution domain typically has its own shorthand. In other words, any person handling an invoice knows that the payment reflects an incoming payment for the organization. So, there's no need for long descriptions of columns.

Likewise, the Code column has a row with a value DEV1_A, which undoubtedly makes sense to a finance team. It might be an accounting code or something like that. The Code data is unlikely to mean much to a developer. But as more development experience is gained in the business domain, the arcane terminology will become less intimidating. Often, the end users can be very forthcoming in explaining the details of their domain.

Regarding the requirements definition, we can now tick the box for this item (build a basic invoice outline). The next step is the schema creation.

The Importance of PL/SQL Skills

Don't forget the unfortunate experience of the rookie PL/SQL developers way back in "A Cautionary Tale" on page 11. The developers in that case had two problems:

- Weak business domain knowledge
- Weak PL/SQL skills

Weak business domain knowledge is not generally a critical weakness for developers because domain knowledge can be acquired over time with some help from sympathetic business users. The same is *not* true for weak PL/SQL skills. Disappointing outcomes are likely to occur when trying to build resilient PL/SQL solutions without the required PL/SQL skills.

It's not so easy to rapidly acquire complex development skills, particularly when delivery deadlines are looming. Also, new skills, such as resilient PL/SQL solution development, tend to require learning at least some relevant process knowledge. It's hard to do this effectively during a single project.

Create the Schema

The schema creation is largely complete from Chapter 7. Given that the Oracle HR schema is what was installed in Chapter 7, I'll continue to use this schema. However, a minor addition is required here in order to fulfill the requirements of this particular project.

Schema Evolution Antipattern and Resilience

Adding new elements to a schema is an important part of schema evolution. Powerful tools, such as SQL Developer, enable you to make sweeping changes to the database schema. One difficulty with this approach is that you might forget (or not opt to have) a corresponding SQL script for those changes.

As new columns are added to the database and a range of other modifications are applied, it can get to the point where the database is the only source of truth in relation to the schema contents. This is an antipattern. It's always prudent to consider how you would recover if the entire database and its host and backup instances suddenly disappeared.

If the tools you use, such as SQL Developer, allow you to generate a script that corresponds to a schema change, then it is strongly advisable to do just that. The script should then be added to the disaster recovery script set as described back in "Version Control for Database Scripts, PL/SQL, and Other Artifacts" on page 73.

The required schema addition (for the moment) is a single table called INVOICES. The INVOICES table will be used to tie together the work done by a given employee on the client project in question and also the other invoice-related data. You'll often encounter the need to modify a schema in your development work. Such changes are an integral part of schema evolution.

It's now time to create the new INVOICES table. To do this, right-click Tables just under the connection name and click New Table. Type in the name of the new table. Type in the name for the first column (PROJECT_ID) and select the NUMBER type from the Data Type drop-down control. Repeat this procedure for each of the columns in the INVOICES table. The new INVOICES table is shown in Figure 8-3.

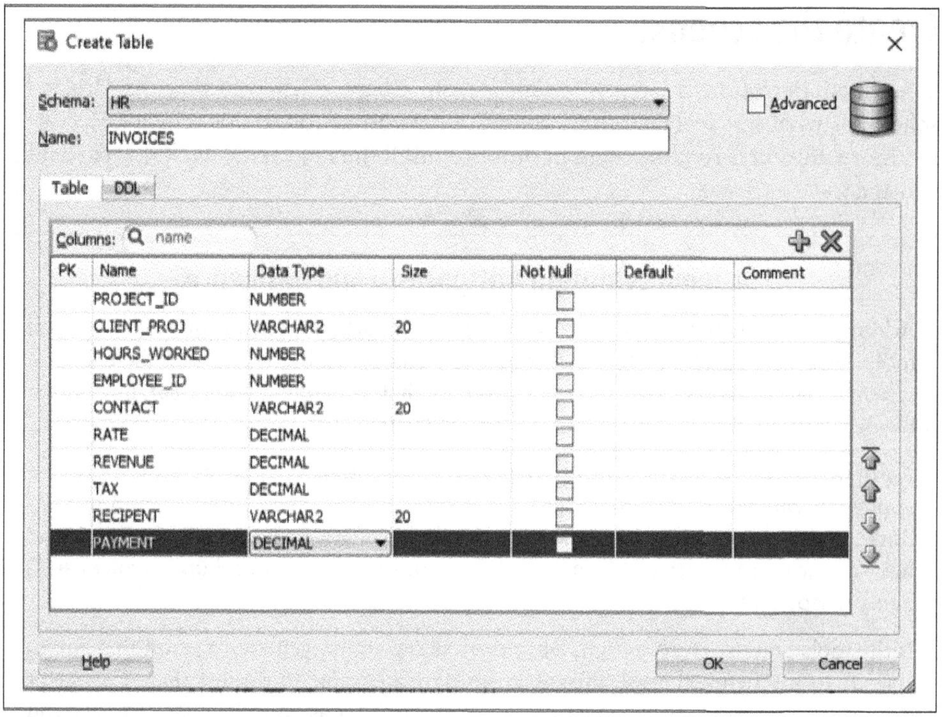

Figure 8-3. Adding an INVOICES table to the schema

Populate the new INVOICES table columns as shown in Figure 8-3 and click OK when you're done. The column names in Figure 8-3 and Table 8-3 can be compared in order to be sure no columns are left out and that the correct column data types are used.

Table 8-3. The invoice column types

Column name	Column data type
PROJECT_ID	NUMBER
CLIENT_PROJ	VARCHAR2(20)
HOURS_WORKED	NUMBER
EMPLOYEE_ID	NUMBER
CONTACT	VARCHAR2(100)
RATE	DECIMAL(19,4)
REVENUE	DECIMAL(19,4)
TAX	DECIMAL(19,4)
RECIPIENT	VARCHAR2(100)
PAYMENT	DECIMAL(19,4)

One point to note about Table 8-3 is the choice of NUMBER format for the new EMPLOYEE_ID column. This is just so that the format of this column is compatible with the corresponding primary key in the EMPLOYEES table. You'll see why this is important when the foreign key constraint is created.

Also required is a foreign key in the INVOICES table to the EMPLOYEE_ID column of the EMPLOYEES table. To add this constraint to the INVOICES table, click into the Columns view and select the Actions drop-down item. Click the option under Constraint to Enable Related Foreign Keys. Click Apply followed by OK. Then, select Constraint and Add Foreign Key, at which point you should see the dialog shown in Figure 8-4.

In Figure 8-4, I've populated the following fields with these values:

- Constraint Name: FK_EMPLOYEE_ID
- Column Name: EMPLOYEE_ID
- References Table Name: EMPLOYEES
- Referencing Column: EMPLOYEE_ID

Click Apply in Figure 8-4 if you're happy with the changes and, if all is well, your new constraint will be created.

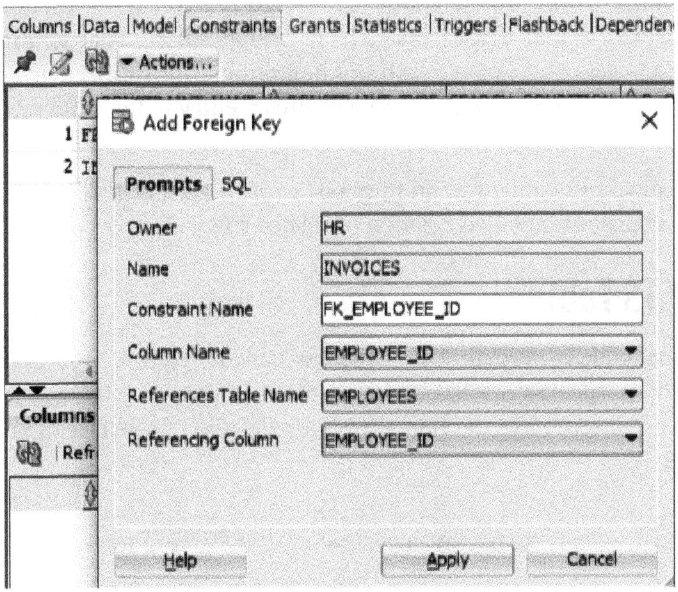

Figure 8-4. Adding a foreign key to the INVOICES table

You might make a mistake when adding a new column—I've gotten it wrong myself often enough. Getting rid of a column is easy; just supply a valid name for the placeholders <ERRONEOUS_TABLE_NAME> and <ERRONEOUS_COLUMN_NAME>:

```
ALTER TABLE <ERRONEOUS_TABLE_NAME>
DROP COLUMN <ERRONEOUS_COLUMN_NAME>;
```

A foreign key is a method for enforcing logical referential integrity within the Oracle Database. A foreign key represents a constraint that values in one table must also appear in another table. The referenced table in the constraint relationship is called the parent table while the table with the foreign key is called the child table. The foreign key in the child table will generally reference a primary key in the parent table.

A foreign key can be defined either in a `CREATE TABLE` statement or as part of an `ALTER TABLE` statement, or by using SQL Developer.

The next step is to test the updated schema. This step becomes optional once you become more experienced with schema management. But I'll describe a simple test in "Test the Schema" on page 196 to verify that we have correctly configured the foreign key constraint.

A minor technical point to note about the foreign key constraint used in the parent table (`EMPLOYEES`) is that it uses the default configuration. That is, there is no `ON DELETE CASCADE` specified in the constraint definition. This means that we will not be allowed to delete a row in the parent table where an entry in the child table references that row.

The default constraint configuration might be considered a little restrictive, but it will help protect against unintended deletion of related rows.

A PROJECTS Table

One additional table is needed next. This new table is required in order to store the customer project–specific details. When invoices are being generated, the `PROJECTS` table will be used to retrieve the relevant billing details. The `PROJECTS` table is shown in Example 8-1.

Example 8-1. Customer-specific project details in the PROJECTS table

```
CREATE TABLE
    "HR"."PROJECTS"
    (
        "PROJECT_ID"   NUMBER          ,
        "CLIENT_PROJ"  VARCHAR2(20 BYTE) ,
```

```
     "HOURS_WORKED"  NUMBER              ,
     "EMPLOYEE_ID"   NUMBER              ,
     "CONTACT"       VARCHAR2(100 BYTE),
     "RATE"          NUMBER(19,4)        ,
     "REVENUE"       NUMBER(19,4)        ,
     "TAX"           NUMBER(19,4)        ,
     "RECIPIENT"     VARCHAR2(100 BYTE),
      CONSTRAINT "FK_EMPLOYEE_ID1"
      FOREIGN KEY ("EMPLOYEE_ID") REFERENCES "HR"."EMPLOYEES"
      ("EMPLOYEE_ID") ENABLE
 );
```

 Note that SQL Developer can be used to generate scripts with double quotes around all the identifiers. This has the effect of making the script case-sensitive. If you accidentally changed PROJECTS to PRoJEcTS, you would end up with a table called PRoJEcTS in your schema, with all the problems that brings.

When an invoice is required, the PROJECTS table will be used for part of the data generation task. Notice in Example 8-1 that, as in the INVOICES table in Figure 8-4, there is also a foreign key constraint—called FK_EMPLOYEE_ID1—in the PROJECTS table. This foreign key references the EMPLOYEE_ID column of the EMPLOYEES table. One other use case for Example 8-1 is that when a new project commences, the project provider inserts a row in the PROJECTS table. You'll see this when the integrated solution is being tested.

The purpose of inserting a new row in the PROJECTS table is for the storage of customer-specific billing details as the project unfolds. One simplification used in Example 8-1 is the assumption that just one employee works on a given customer project. It is entirely likely that there might be a team of employees working on the project, but for our purposes, we have just one employee doing all the work on this customer project.

A quick example of inserting a new row on the PROJECTS table is shown in Example 8-2.

Example 8-2. Inserting a row into the PROJECTS table for testing

```
INSERT INTO PROJECTS(PROJECT_ID, CLIENT_PROJ, HOURS_WORKED, EMPLOYEE_ID,
CONTACT, RATE, REVENUE, TAX, RECIPIENT)
VALUES(1, 'Project', 10, 107, 'mark@provider.com', 100.00,
1000, 0.15, 'mary@acme.com');
```

Now that the schema is more complete, we can run some simple tests to verify that all is in order before moving on to the PL/SQL code.

Test the Schema

The following aspects of the schema are tested in the following sections:

- Executing an insert into the EMPLOYEES table
- Executing an insert into the PROJECTS table
- Executing an insert into the INVOICES table
- Constraint verification

Insert Some Data and Verify the Constraints

First, select all of the EMPLOYEES from the EMPLOYEES table. Pick out one of the rows and use its EMPLOYEE_ID to insert a single row into the new PROJECTS and INVOICES tables, as shown in Example 8-3.

Example 8-3. Testing the integrity constraint

```
Insert into HR.EMPLOYEES (
EMPLOYEE_ID,FIRST_NAME,LAST_NAME,EMAIL,PHONE_NUMBER,HIRE_DATE, ❶
JOB_ID,SALARY,COMMISSION_PCT,MANAGER_ID,DEPARTMENT_ID)
values
(207,'Kimberely','Murphy','KMURPHY','011.44.1644.429263',
to_date('24-MAY-07','DD-MON-RR'),'SA_REP',7000,0.15,149,null);

INSERT INTO PROJECTS(PROJECT_ID, CLIENT_PROJ, HOURS_WORKED, EMPLOYEE_ID,
CONTACT, RATE, REVENUE, TAX, RECIPIENT) ❷
                VALUES(1, 'Project', 10, 207, 'mark@provider.com', 100.00,
                1000, 0.15, 'mary@acme.com');

UPDATE projects SET project_id=1 where employee_id = 207;

delete from HR.employees where employee_id = 207;

INSERT INTO INVOICES(PROJECT_ID, CLIENT_PROJ, HOURS_WORKED, EMPLOYEE_ID, ❸
CONTACT, RATE, REVENUE, TAX, RECIPIENT, PAYMENT)
                VALUES(1, 'Project', 10, 207, 'mark@provider.com', 100.00,
                1000, 0.15, 'mary@acme.com', 1150);

UPDATE INVOICES SET project_id=1 where employee_id = 207;

-- delete from HR.PROJECTS where employee_id = 207;

-- delete from HR.employees where employee_id = 207;
```

---

❶ Create a row in the EMPLOYEES table with EMPLOYEE_ID set equal to 207. We use value 207 because the largest value of this column in the table is 206. Therefore, I know I have a new row in the EMPLOYEES table if I use the value 207.

❷ Add a row to the PROJECTS table also with EMPLOYEE_ID set to 207.

❸ Add a row to the INVOICES table also with EMPLOYEE_ID set to 207.

Notice the two attempts in Example 8-3 to delete the newly added row (with EMPLOYEE_ID set to 207) from the HR.EMPLOYEES table. The deletion is commented out to save you the trouble of having to redo the insert into the PROJECTS table. Because we have a foreign key constraint in both the INVOICES table and the PROJECTS table, the deletion will be disallowed and the result should be as shown in Example 8-4.

Example 8-4. Verifying the integrity constraint violation

```
Error starting at line : 14 in command -

delete from HR.employees where employee_id = 207
Error report -
ORA-02292: integrity constraint (HR.FK_EMPLOYEE_ID) violated - child record found
```

You can see in Example 8-4 that the constraint name (HR.FK_EMPLOYEE_ID) matches the one defined back in Figure 8-4. The response message in Example 8-4 verifies that the constraint has been created successfully in the PROJECTS table and that the rows are correctly related to the counterpart rows in the EMPLOYEES table.

In Example 8-3, you can see the same foreign key constraint test applied this time to the INVOICES table. Again, the attempted deletion of the parent table (EMPLOYEES) row should be disallowed.

Verify That an Insert into the PROJECTS Table Works as Expected

The data resulting from the population of the PROJECTS table will in due course be handled by PL/SQL code. In the meantime, it can be useful just to verify that the table looks OK. So, as you saw in Example 8-3, a simple INSERT can be used, as shown in Example 8-5.

Example 8-5. Insert into the PROJECTS table for testing the workflow

```
INSERT INTO PROJECTS(PROJECT_ID, CLIENT_PROJ, HOURS_WORKED, EMPLOYEE_ID,
CONTACT, RATE, REVENUE, TAX, RECIPIENT)
VALUES(1, 'Project', 10, 207, 'mark@provider.com', 100.00,
1000, 0.15, 'mary@acme.com');
```

After running the SQL in Example 8-5, the PROJECTS table should look like that shown in Figure 8-5.

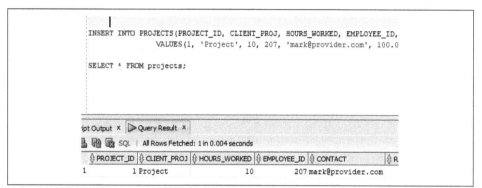

```
INSERT INTO PROJECTS(PROJECT_ID, CLIENT_PROJ, HOURS_WORKED, EMPLOYEE_ID,
                VALUES(1, 'Project', 10, 207, 'mark@provider.com', 100.0

SELECT * FROM projects;
```

	PROJECT_ID	CLIENT_PROJ	HOURS_WORKED	EMPLOYEE_ID	CONTACT	R
1	1	Project	10	207	mark@provider.com	

Figure 8-5. After inserting into the PROJECTS table

The PROJECTS table row shown in Figure 8-5 can be considered as the starting point in the overall invoice workflow. I'll return to this shortly.

The schema is now in place and I can review the basic solution workflow.

Feature Workflow Description

The feature workflow is as follows:

1. Create a project invoice data set.
2. Invoke the feature from Java code.
3. Invoke the PL/SQL procedure passing the required data.
4. Retrieve the relevant invoice data.
5. Send the data to the destination.

As this is the final step in translating the requirements into working code, let's now carefully and briefly describe what happens in each of these steps.

Create a Project Invoice Data Set

The PROJECTS table data can be seen as the driver for the invoice creation workflow. Once this data exists in the PROJECTS table, it can then be used to create an invoice using PL/SQL code.

The invoice data produced by the PL/SQL code can then later be retrieved by the main feature code (i.e., the Java application that calls the main PL/SQL invoker code). In Figure 8-1, the Java code is the item called "Feature F1."

Invoke the Feature from Java Code

The Java code required to invoke the feature can optionally be deferred for a short time. This is because SQL Developer provides a facility to call the PL/SQL code directly. This was described in detail in Chapter 5.

However, calling a stored procedure from Java code is quite straightforward and typically consists of something like Example 8-6 (with no exception handling included, to reduce clutter).

Example 8-6. Calling PL/SQL from Java

```
connection = DBConnection.getConnection();
statement = connection.prepareCall("{call PACKAGE1.PLSQL_CODE(?, ?)}");
statement.setString("action_message", action_message);
statement.setString("code_location", code_location);
statement.executeUpdate();
System.out.println("Successful call");
```

Example 8-6 has a Java call to the PL/SQL procedure called PACKAGE1.PLSQL_CODE. So we can go straight into creating the Java code to invoke the PL/SQL code or we can use the SQL Developer option to get the ball rolling. Which option to use is at the discretion of the developer.

Invoke the PL/SQL Procedure Passing the Required Data

The PL/SQL code invocation is handled by Java code broadly similar to that seen in Example 8-6. The main additions are:

- A call to the new invoice creation PL/SQL procedure
- Including the parameter PROJECT_ID
- Facilitating some means of retrieving the invoice data at the Java caller

I'll look at these in the next sections.

Insert a Call to the New Invoice Creation PL/SQL Procedure

A new PL/SQL procedure is required to generate the invoice data. The PROJECTS table data is used for this purpose and the calling Java code must supply the relevant PROJECT_ID value. The PROJECTS table data is then used to add a new entry to the INVOICES table.

The following steps can be used:

1. Get the details from the PROJECTS table for the specific PROJECT_ID.

2. Add a new row to the INVOICES table with the relevant billing data.

For step 1, a PL/SQL cursor can be used to retrieve the details from the PROJECTS table. As a first draft, I create a PL/SQL procedure similar to that shown in Example 8-7.

Example 8-7. Retrieving data from the PROJECTS table

```
CREATE OR REPLACE PROCEDURE process_project_data (
    project_id_in   IN hr.projects.project_id%TYPE)
IS
    CURSOR proj_cur
    IS
        SELECT PROJECT_ID, client_proj, hours_worked, employee_id, contact,
        rate, revenue, recipient
        FROM hr.projects
        WHERE project_id = project_id_in;

    proj_rec    proj_cur%ROWTYPE;
BEGIN
    OPEN proj_cur;

    FETCH proj_cur INTO proj_rec;
    DBMS_OUTPUT.put_line (
        'Project ID: ' || proj_rec.PROJECT_ID
    || '-'
    || ' CLIENT_PROJ: '
    || proj_rec.CLIENT_PROJ);

    CLOSE proj_cur;
END;
```

In the SELECT statement in Example 8-7, I could instead use a table alias to make the code easier to understand:

```
SELECT p.project_id, p.client_proj, p.hours_worked,
p.employee_id, p.contact, p.rate, p.revenue, p.recipient
FROM hr.projects p
WHERE p.project_id = project_id_in;
```

The use of table aliases (*https://oreil.ly/QqHG3*) can help to make code more readable. The alias exists only for the duration of the query.

In Example 8-7, the first draft is the raw PL/SQL with no exception handling. Once the basic code works, the other resilience items can be added later. Before invoking it from Java, the PL/SQL code in Example 8-7 is first compiled and then run in SQL Developer.

Run the Draft PL/SQL Code First in SQL Developer

To run the new PL/SQL in Example 8-7, it's just a matter of pasting the code into SQL Developer, as shown in Figure 8-6, where I've completed the following steps:

1. Highlighted the entire PL/SQL procedure
2. Clicked the Run button to compile the procedure
3. Verified that the procedure is stored under the Procedures container
4. Right-clicked the procedure name and selected Run
5. Enabled DBMS output

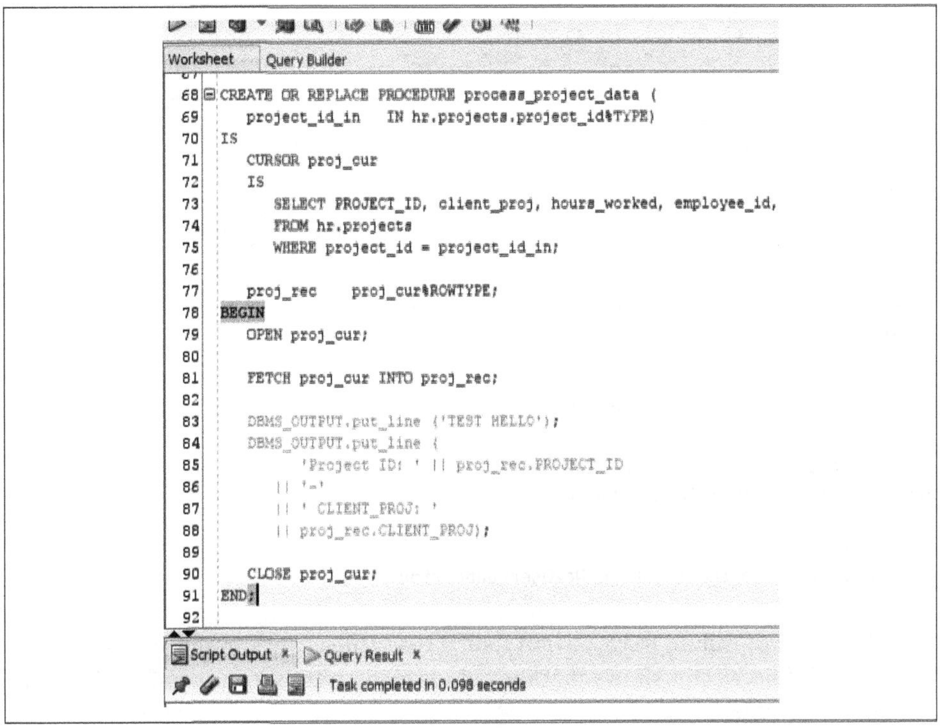

Figure 8-6. Compiling and running the first-draft PL/SQL procedure

On selecting the Run option for the stored procedure in Figure 8-6, you should see the Run PL/SQL dialog appear, as shown in Figure 8-7. Type a value of **1** for the parameter PROJECT_ID_IN and then click OK to finally run the procedure.

Another step that might cause difficulty is that of enabling DBMS output. To do this, click the View menu followed by selecting the DBMS Output option. If all is well, when the procedure is run you should see SQL Developer screen output similar to that shown in Example 8-8.

Figure 8-7. Using the Run dialog with the PL/SQL procedure

Example 8-8. Retrieving data from the PROJECTS table

```
Connecting to the database NewUserConnection.
Project ID: 1- CLIENT_PROJ: Project ❶

Process exited.
Disconnecting from the database NewUserConnection.
```

❶ The result of calling DBMS_OUTPUT.put_line. This is very useful information at this point because it shows that the data is being retrieved successfully from the PROJECTS table.

So far, I've successfully gotten the PROJECTS data. The next step is inserting a corresponding row in the INVOICES table.

Insert a Row in the INVOICES Table

Inserting a row in the INVOICES table is straightforward and consists of the following actions:

1. Calculating the revenue figure

2. Calculating the payment figure

3. Executing an INSERT into the INVOICES table

The only difference between the revenue figure and the payment figure is that the latter is inclusive of tax.

The updated PL/SQL code is shown in Example 8-9.

Example 8-9. Retrieving data from the PROJECTS table and inserting into INVOICES

```
CREATE OR REPLACE PROCEDURE process_project_data (
project_id_in IN hr.projects.project_id%TYPE)
IS
   CURSOR proj_cur   IS
     SELECT
        PROJECT_ID, client_proj, hours_worked, employee_id, contact,
        rate, revenue, tax, recipient
     FROM
        hr.projects
     WHERE
        project_id = project_id_in;

   proj_rec proj_cur%ROWTYPE;
   revenue hr.invoices.revenue%TYPE;
   payment hr.invoices.payment%TYPE;
BEGIN
   OPEN proj_cur;
     FETCH proj_cur
     INTO proj_rec;

     DBMS_OUTPUT.put_line ('Project ID: '
        || proj_rec.PROJECT_ID
        || '-'
        || ' CLIENT_PROJ: '
        || proj_rec.CLIENT_PROJ);
     revenue := proj_rec.hours_worked * proj_rec.rate; ❶
     payment := revenue +
        proj_rec.hours_worked*proj_rec.rate * proj_rec.tax;
     INSERT INTO
        INVOICES
        (
           PROJECT_ID, CLIENT_PROJ,  HOURS_WORKED,
           EMPLOYEE_ID, CONTACT, RATE, REVENUE, TAX,
           RECIPIENT, PAYMENT)
           VALUES(
              proj_rec.project_id  ,
              proj_rec.client_proj ,
              proj_rec.hours_worked,
              proj_rec.employee_id ,
              proj_rec.contact     ,
```

```
            proj_rec.rate        ,
            revenue              ,
            proj_rec.tax         ,
            proj_rec.recipient   ,
            payment
        );

    CLOSE proj_cur;
END;
```

❶ Notice how the cursor record is used for the data written into the row of the INVOICES table.

Again, I have not yet added any exception handling. This will be done in the next chapter. Also, notice the way the values for revenue and payment are calculated inside the procedure body. These calculations, though quite simple, are candidates for being created using helpers. To illustrate how to use helpers, let's now implement two of them for deriving revenue and payment.

Add Two Helpers

Moving the financial calculations in Example 8-9 into helpers is no more difficult than creating two PL/SQL functions. It could also be done using a single procedure. If the financial calculations were very complex (which they're not in this case), then this would also be a good case for implementing two separate functions. The guideline I always use is to check if the end result is hard to understand. If it's complicated, then now is a good time to make it simpler and implement it as two functions. Divide and conquer can be a useful approach.

In Example 8-10, you can see the very first helper (a function called get_revenue), which is simply a function to calculate the revenue figure.

Example 8-10. First helper to calculate revenue

```
CREATE OR REPLACE FUNCTION get_revenue(
in_hours_worked hr.invoices.hours_worked%TYPE, in_rate hr.invoices.rate%TYPE)
RETURN hr.invoices.payment%TYPE
IS
BEGIN
    RETURN in_hours_worked * in_rate;
END;
```

Notice how the function uses anchored declarations for the two input parameters as well as the return value. This has the advantage of tying the parameters and the return type to the underlying database column types.

The updated main PL/SQL procedure now resembles the code shown in Example 8-11.

Example 8-11. The main procedure using the first helper to calculate revenue

```
CREATE OR REPLACE PROCEDURE process_project_data (
project_id_in IN hr.projects.project_id%TYPE)
IS
        CURSOR proj_cur   IS
                SELECT
                        PROJECT_ID ,
                        client_proj ,
                        hours_worked,
                        employee_id ,
                        contact    ,
                        rate       ,
                        revenue    ,
                        tax        ,
                        recipient
                FROM
                        hr.projects
                WHERE
                        project_id = project_id_in;

        proj_rec proj_cur%ROWTYPE;
        payment hr.invoices.payment%TYPE;
BEGIN
        OPEN proj_cur;
        FETCH
                proj_cur
        INTO
                proj_rec;

        DBMS_OUTPUT.put_line ('Project ID: '
        || proj_rec.PROJECT_ID
        || '-'
        || ' CLIENT_PROJ: '
        || proj_rec.CLIENT_PROJ
        || '-'
        || ' hours_worked '
        || proj_rec.hours_worked);
        payment := get_revenue(proj_rec.hours_worked, proj_rec.rate) +
        proj_rec.hours_worked*proj_rec.rate*proj_rec.tax; ❶
        INSERT INTO
                INVOICES
                (
                        PROJECT_ID ,
                        CLIENT_PROJ ,
                        HOURS_WORKED,
                        EMPLOYEE_ID ,
                        CONTACT    ,
```

```
                        RATE          ,
                        REVENUE       ,
                        TAX           ,
                        RECIPIENT     ,
                        PAYMENT
            )
            VALUES
            (
                        proj_rec.project_id                                ,
                        proj_rec.client_proj                               ,
                        proj_rec.hours_worked                              ,
                        proj_rec.employee_id                               ,
                        proj_rec.contact                                   ,
                        proj_rec.rate                                      ,
                        get_revenue(proj_rec.hours_worked, proj_rec.rate), ❷
                        proj_rec.tax                                       ,
                        proj_rec.recipient                                 ,
                        payment
            );

        CLOSE proj_cur;
END;
```

There are two calls to the get_revenue() helper function. One call is just before the
INSERT statement and the other is in the VALUES clause:

❶ Adds an additional helper to offload the payment calculation into a separate
function

❷ Follows exactly the same pattern used for the first helper and is shown in
Example 8-12.

Example 8-12. Second helper to calculate payment

```
CREATE OR REPLACE FUNCTION get_payment(
    in_revenue hr.invoices.revenue%TYPE,
    in_hours_worked hr.invoices.hours_worked%TYPE,
    in_rate hr.invoices.rate%TYPE,
    in_tax hr.invoices.tax%TYPE)
RETURN hr.invoices.payment%TYPE
IS
BEGIN
    RETURN in_revenue + in_hours_worked * in_rate * in_tax;
END;
```

Applying the second helper (get_payment) from Example 8-12 to the main procedure
produces the code shown in Example 8-13.

Example 8-13. The main procedure using the two helpers

```
CREATE OR REPLACE FUNCTION get_payment(in_revenue hr.invoices.revenue%TYPE,
                                       in_hours_worked
                                       hr.invoices.hours_worked%TYPE,
                                       in_rate hr.invoices.rate%TYPE,
                                       in_tax hr.invoices.tax%TYPE)
        RETURN hr.invoices.payment%TYPE
IS
BEGIN
        RETURN in_revenue + in_hours_worked * in_rate * in_tax;
END;

CREATE OR REPLACE PROCEDURE process_project_data (
        project_id_in IN hr.projects.project_id%TYPE)
IS
        CURSOR proj_cur    IS
                SELECT
                        PROJECT_ID  ,
                        client_proj ,
                        hours_worked,
                        employee_id ,
                        contact     ,
                        rate        ,
                        revenue     ,
                        tax         ,
                        recipient
                FROM
                        hr.projects
                WHERE
                        project_id = project_id_in;

        proj_rec proj_cur%ROWTYPE;
BEGIN
        OPEN proj_cur;
        FETCH
                proj_cur
        INTO
                proj_rec;

        DBMS_OUTPUT.put_line ( 'Project ID: '
        || proj_rec.PROJECT_ID
        || '-'
        || ' CLIENT_PROJ: '
        || proj_rec.CLIENT_PROJ
        || '-'
        || ' hours_worked '
        || proj_rec.hours_worked);
        INSERT INTO
                INVOICES
                (
                        PROJECT_ID  ,
```

```
                          CLIENT_PROJ ,
                          HOURS_WORKED,
                          EMPLOYEE_ID ,
                          CONTACT     ,
                          RATE        ,
                          REVENUE     ,
                          TAX         ,
                          RECIPIENT   ,
                          PAYMENT
              )
              VALUES
              (
                          proj_rec.project_id                                 ,
                          proj_rec.client_proj                                ,
                          proj_rec.hours_worked                               ,
                          proj_rec.employee_id                                ,
                          proj_rec.contact                                    ,
                          proj_rec.rate                                       ,
                          get_revenue(proj_rec.hours_worked, proj_rec.rate), ❶
                          proj_rec.tax                                        ,
                          proj_rec.recipient                                  ,
                          get_payment(get_revenue(proj_rec.hours_worked    , ❶
                          proj_rec.rate)                                      ,
                          proj_rec.hours_worked, proj_rec.rate, proj_rec.tax)
              );

      CLOSE proj_cur;
END;
```

 Two helpers are pressed into service in the VALUES clause of the INSERT statement.

The PL/SQL in Example 8-13 is still quite chunky. Can it be reduced somewhat?

A further refactoring of Example 8-13 would be to write another helper (called handle_insert) that contains the INSERT statement. The result of such a refactoring would produce the much simpler procedure shown in Example 8-14.

Example 8-14. The main procedure using the two helpers and a new helper

```
CREATE OR REPLACE PROCEDURE process_project_data (
      project_id_in IN hr.projects.project_id%TYPE)
IS
      CURSOR proj_cur   IS
            SELECT
                      PROJECT_ID  ,
                      client_proj ,
                      hours_worked,
                      employee_id ,
                      contact     ,
                      rate        ,
```

```
                        revenue      ,
                        tax          ,
                        recipient
              FROM
                        hr.projects
              WHERE
                        project_id = project_id_in;

      proj_rec proj_cur%ROWTYPE;
BEGIN
      OPEN proj_cur;
      FETCH
              proj_cur
      INTO
              proj_rec;

      DBMS_OUTPUT.put_line ( 'Project ID: '
      || proj_rec.PROJECT_ID || '-' || ' CLIENT_PROJ: '
      || proj_rec.CLIENT_PROJ || '-' || ' hours_worked '
      || proj_rec.hours_worked);

      -- THE ADDITIONAL HELPER
      handle_insert(proj_rec.project_id, proj_rec.client_proj, ❶
  proj_rec.hours_worked, proj_rec.employee_id, proj_rec.contact,
  proj_rec.rate, hr.projects.tax, hr.projects.recipient);

      CLOSE proj_cur;
END;
```

 The third helper (`handle_insert`) is provided to handle the INSERT and the calls to the two earlier helpers.

The merit of adding another helper like this is to substantially reduce the size of the main procedure (`process_project_data`). Writing the third helper (`handle_insert`) is quite straightforward (Example 8-15).

Example 8-15. The new helper that handles the database INSERT

```
create or replace PROCEDURE handle_insert (
   PROJECT_ID_IN IN hr.projects.project_id%TYPE,
   CLIENT_PROJ_IN IN hr.projects.client_proj%TYPE,
   HOURS_WORKED_IN IN hr.projects.hours_worked%TYPE,
   EMPLOYEE_ID_IN IN hr.projects.employee_id%TYPE,
   CONTACT_IN IN hr.projects.contact%TYPE,
   RATE_IN IN hr.projects.rate%TYPE,
   TAX_IN IN hr.projects.tax%TYPE,
   RECIPIENT_IN IN hr.projects.recipient%TYPE)
IS
BEGIN
      INSERT INTO
```

```
      INVOICES
      (
        PROJECT_ID  ,
        CLIENT_PROJ ,
        HOURS_WORKED,
        EMPLOYEE_ID ,
        CONTACT     ,
        RATE        ,
        REVENUE     ,
        TAX         ,
        RECIPIENT   ,
        PAYMENT
      )
      VALUES
      (
        PROJECT_ID_IN                            ,
        CLIENT_PROJ_IN                           ,
        HOURS_WORKED_IN                          ,
        EMPLOYEE_ID_IN                           ,
        CONTACT_IN                               ,
        RATE_IN                                  ,
        get_revenue(HOURS_WORKED_IN, RATE_IN),
        TAX_IN                                   ,
        RECIPIENT_IN                             ,
        get_payment(get_revenue(HOURS_WORKED_IN, RATE_IN),
          HOURS_WORKED_IN, RATE_IN, TAX_IN));
END;
```

To verify the new code in Examples 8-14 and 8-15, just follow the usual steps in SQL Developer:

1. Delete the contents of the INVOICES table.

2. Paste the new PL/SQL code into a worksheet.

3. Select all in the main window.

4. Click Run to replace the older code.

5. Run the Java code as per Figure 8-7.

6. Verify the contents of the INVOICES table.

The new code is significantly more compact than was the case even in Example 8-13.

In step 4, remember the create or replace in the PL/SQL procedure definitions. This declaration ensures that the new code replaces its older counterpart. It's not a bad idea to also visually verify that the new PL/SQL code is in place. The takeaway from Example 8-14 is that smaller procedures are easier to understand.

Performance Note: PL/SQL Versus SQL

In the preceding examples, there are two calls to PL/SQL helper functions from within the SQL INSERT statement, namely get_revenue and get_payment.

Each such call results in a context switch inside the Oracle Database from SQL to PL/SQL and back again to SQL. For reasons of performance, this may or may not be of concern; it depends on the use case. However, for completeness, please note that for improved performance, it is best to present parameters (rather than PL/SQL function calls) when running SQL. In other words, call the helpers in PL/SQL, assign the results to parameters, and then use the latter in the SQL INSERT statement, as shown in Example 8-16.

Example 8-16. Improving the performance of the new handle_insert helper

```
create or replace PROCEDURE handle_insert (
   PROJECT_ID_IN IN hr.projects.project_id%TYPE,
   CLIENT_PROJ_IN IN hr.projects.client_proj%TYPE,
   HOURS_WORKED_IN IN hr.projects.hours_worked%TYPE,
   EMPLOYEE_ID_IN IN hr.projects.employee_id%TYPE,
   CONTACT_IN IN hr.projects.contact%TYPE,
   RATE_IN IN hr.projects.rate%TYPE,
   TAX_IN IN hr.projects.tax%TYPE,
   RECIPIENT_IN IN hr.projects.recipient%TYPE)
IS
   revenue hr.invoices.revenue%TYPE := get_revenue(HOURS_WORKED_IN, RATE_IN);
   payment hr.invoices.payment%TYPE := get_payment(
       get_revenue(HOURS_WORKED_IN, RATE_IN),
                     HOURS_WORKED_IN, RATE_IN, TAX_IN); ❶
BEGIN
       INSERT INTO
         INVOICES
         (
           PROJECT_ID  ,
           CLIENT_PROJ ,
           HOURS_WORKED,
           EMPLOYEE_ID ,
           CONTACT     ,
           RATE        ,
           REVENUE     ,
           TAX         ,
           RECIPIENT   ,
           PAYMENT
         )
         VALUES
         (
           PROJECT_ID_IN  ,
           CLIENT_PROJ_IN ,
           HOURS_WORKED_IN,
           EMPLOYEE_ID_IN ,
```

```
               CONTACT_IN    ,
               RATE_IN       ,
               revenue       ,
               TAX_IN        ,
               RECIPIENT_IN  ,
               payment);
END;
```

 Two variables (revenue and payment) are calculated in PL/SQL and then passed into the SQL INSERT statement.

In the next section, I'll do a brief status report on how far we are into the feature development.

Quick Project Status Report

An important part of any development project is its status, or its proximity to completion. In feature-oriented development, the status reporting can be a little less opaque. What do I mean by this? Well, given that the new helpers have been added, let's now have a look at Figure 8-8, which is a slightly decorated version of Figure 8-1.

In Figure 8-8, the darker sections reflect the coding done up to the previous block of work (i.e., the basic PL/SQL is complete without yet having implemented the exception handling). I've also indicated that all of the test placeholders on the right side are business-critical. This means that the constituent code inside the darker sections is critically important to the organization. Therefore, tests must be written to exercise this code. The bottom section of the figure is now used for the third helper (i.e., the handle_insert procedure).

Now, imagine that it is required (as a simple proof of concept or as some sort of reassurance to the project manager) to provide an interim feature that executes the full happy path, i.e., run the not-yet-written Feature F1 item in Figure 8-8 and let it call the invoker, which in turn calls the helpers. Can this be done? Can we quickly provide a basic implementation of Feature F1?

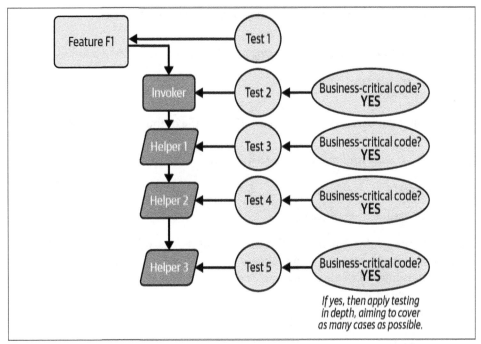

Figure 8-8. Feature status so far with three helpers

Adding an outline feature such as this amounts to some Java code. The Java code makes a call to the `process_project_data` stored procedure. This brings to mind the Java code back in Example 8-6. In order to bring the code in Example 8-6 up to date, I've changed two lines; the updated Java code is shown in Example 8-17.

Example 8-17. Calling the PL/SQL invoker from Java

```
connection = DBConnection.getConnection();
statement = connection.prepareCall("{call HR.PROCESS_PROJECT_DATA(?)}");
statement.setInt("project_id_in", 1);
statement.executeUpdate();
System.out.println("Successful call");
```

In Example 8-17, a call is made from the Java code to the stored procedure: PROCESS_PROJECT_DATA, our so-called invoker from Figures 8-1 and 8-8. The purpose of this invoker is to set in progress the required database updates. How do I now verify that the Java call to PROCESS_PROJECT_DATA in Example 8-17 has in fact updated the INVOICES table? Easy; it's just a matter of doing a SELECT on the INVOICES table.

Before doing that, I delete the entries in the INVOICES table and only then run the Java code. This way, the call to the stored procedure PROCESS_PROJECT_DATA is running against an empty INVOICES table.

The two required SQL statements are shown in Example 8-18.

Example 8-18. Checking and then clearing the INVOICES table before the Java is run

```
select * from INVOICES;
delete from INVOICES;
```

Now, running the Java code in Example 8-17, I get the output in Example 8-19.

Example 8-19. Successful call from the Java feature

```
Successful calls

Process finished with exit code 0
```

There is not much information in this output, but it does at least tell us that the Java code didn't throw any exceptions. This is useful information—it indicates that the happy path is intact. I then run the single SQL statement in Example 8-20.

Example 8-20. Select from INVOICES table

```
select * from INVOICES;
```

The statement in Example 8-20 should then produce the result shown in Figure 8-9.

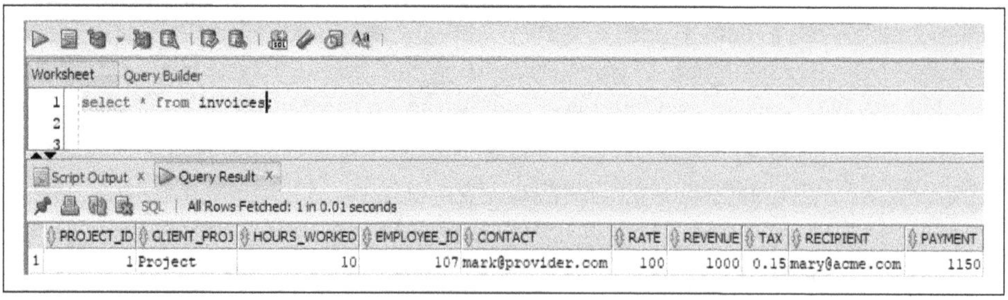

Figure 8-9. New row in the INVOICES table

You can see in Figure 8-9 that a new invoice row has been successfully created. This means that the Java call to the PROCESS_PROJECT_DATA stored procedure was successful, which is a fulfillment of the happy path (no errors or exception has occurred).

Where does this leave us in relation to delivering the overall project feature?

Project Feature Status Report Revisited

The data creation result verified with reference to Figure 8-9 also means that we can now, with confidence, augment the decoration of the feature status report that was shown in Figure 8-8. This report now looks like that shown in Figure 8-10.

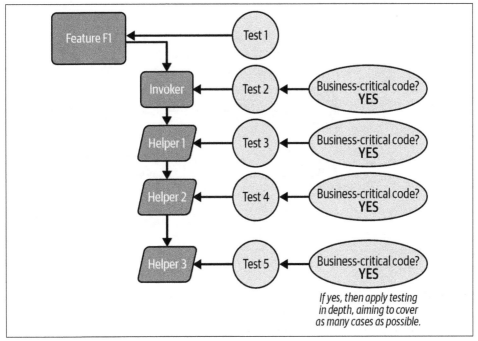

Figure 8-10. Feature status so far

From the upper-left box in Figure 8-10, you can see that we now have a basic feature in place. Still no exception handling or any of the other major resilience elements (such as tests, packaging, modularity, etc.), but this is good progress.

Regarding tests at the feature level—i.e., the topmost part of Figure 8-10—there is in fact already a visual test. This is because we have verified that the correct data has been created in the INVOICES table in Figure 8-9.

This also means that there has already been a small amount of end-to-end (or feature-level) testing done, which has a further positive effect on the project status in Figure 8-10, as shown in Figure 8-11.

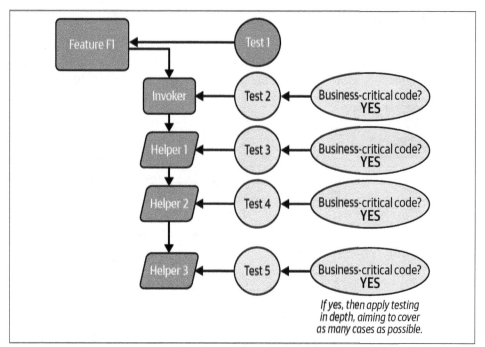

Figure 8-11. Feature status including basic manual testing

Notice that in Figure 8-11, Feature F1 has a basic test implemented. This iterative approach is one of the benefits of feature-oriented development. The project work proceeds in a manner that is informed at the level of the major feature under development.

The test item at the feature level in Figure 8-11 also exercises all of the subordinate code. This means that the existing code has already been tested to a small extent. There is, of course, a need for more extensive testing, as you saw with the use of utPLSQL in Chapter 4, where multiple tests are added to exercise the individual units of code.

A Feature Is a Macroscopic Deliverable

The feature can be considered a macroscopic deliverable, and its fulfillment helps to inform decisions made regarding its constituent microscopic deliverables. The latter includes the components of code, such as the invoker, the helpers, test code, and so on. By referring to the feature, there is far less cognitive dissonance or cognitive disconnection when building the component elements. This can help avoid the situation in which the wrong system is created. Building the wrong system is more common than you might think.

I'll revisit the issue of the testing content in Figure 8-11, but for the moment we can have some confidence in the code written so far.

A Cautionary Tale: Building the Wrong System

A colleague once described to me a case of a recruitment organization building the wrong system. It concerned a familiar enough project category, that of replacing a legacy system with one built using more modern technologies. The legacy system had been in use for years and had served the organization well. It was one of those bedrock systems that many people had worked on over the years. Many users and developers of the system had come and gone, though a core of key individuals remained and this group collectively had expert knowledge of its workflows as well as its various vagaries.

Regarding the new system, the decision was made to *do it right* and call in an external consultancy. The consultancy sold itself well; its concept was to adopt some sort of Agile approach that involved minimal contact with the aforementioned experts. It seems the consultancy felt that its own internal consultants were well up to the job of figuring out the old system.

A few months into the project, some of the monthly demonstrations of the new system started to raise a few eyebrows, as in feature X is missing, feature Y is incomplete, and feature Z is plain wrong. Eventually, the delivery day arrived and the new system was revealed to the company. The expert users descended on the final demonstration and it then finally came to light that the new system was merely a more modern, reasonably faithful copy of about 50% of the legacy system.

It doesn't take an expert to predict that the blame game started, but the company was stuck with the new "50% system," as it became known. Being halfway there was little consolation when the end result was a discount of 10% on the original price. The consultancy had not so much built the *wrong* system as it had built only half of the *right* system. All of which, of course, amounted to building the wrong system.

Summary

Traditionally, navigating the transition from requirements to code is quite tricky. This is because it moves us from the domain of the *what* into the domain of the *how*. Much care is needed in managing this domain shift.

In this chapter, the solution has been further elaborated. The next chapter will produce the working solution code. All the discussions so far about the invoice solution might seem somewhat repetitive. This is as intended; it provides for cross-checks to avoid forgetting important details. An important point to note is that any supporting documentation for the feature-oriented elaboration need not be voluminous in nature. A short document of fewer than 10 pages should be sufficient unless the feature is very complex.

The ultimate deliverable for the project is a customer invoice. It is entirely possible that the developer may not have extensive knowledge of the business domain. This is another reason why the iterative nature of the process can be helpful. The developer is reminded not to leave anything out.

The schema is a foundational aspect of the solution and schema updates such as adding any required tables, columns, and constraints should be verified if necessary. Schema changes should also generate disaster recovery scripts for those unlikely scenarios in which both the main and backup databases for some reason cease to exist. An extensive natural disaster could be sufficient to destroy the databases, so it is essential to have a path to recovery.

Some basic feature data is required and this can be created by hand or from real data. The latter might need to be anonymized. The code for the invoice solution will be finalized in the next chapter.

The judicious introduction of helper code has simplified the main stored procedure. This took the form of two functions for calculating financial data and an additional helper procedure was then used to handle the SQL INSERT statement. By moving this type of code into helpers, the main flow is much simplified, which helps both the current developers and also the downstream DevOps developers. A further merit of helpers is that they can be written in a technology-specific manner. For example, the handle_insert helper could be written to execute just SQL. In other words, the handle_insert helper could add two new parameters: one for payment and the other for revenue. The latter change would make the handle_insert helper purely SQL-oriented. This is of course an optional step, left to the discretion of the developer.

CHAPTER 9

Building the Complete Feature: Final Project Integration

This chapter can be considered the final project integration phase for the resilient invoice generation solution. To get started, I'll review the current scale of resilience for the project.

Revisiting the Scale of Resilience

Way back in Chapter 1, you saw the major nonfunctional resilience requirements introduced in "Requirements for Resilience: What Versus How" on page 6. The resilience requirements (and the current resilience scores) are shown in Table 9-1.

Table 9-1. The resilience requirements

Resilience requirement	Status	Resilience score
Capture all errors and exceptions	NOT DONE YET	0
Recoverability	NOT DONE YET	0
Observability	NOT DONE YET	0
Modifiability	NOT DONE YET	0
Modularity	NOT DONE YET	0
Simplicity	NOT DONE YET	0
Coding conventions	NOT DONE YET	0
Reusability	NOT DONE YET	0
Repeatable testing	NOT DONE YET	0
Avoiding common antipatterns	NOT DONE YET	0
Schema evolution	NOT DONE YET	0

One or two of the items in Table 9-1 are at least started (e.g., Simplicity), but for the moment, I've marked them all as "NOT DONE YET."

In the following sections, I'll be applying the Table 9-1 requirements to the existing code from Chapter 8. The code is currently composed of:

- The PL/SQL driver/invoker procedure
- Three PL/SQL helpers
- Some Java code to call the PL/SQL driver/invoker procedure

I'll start with the PL/SQL code and then briefly move on to the Java code. As mentioned, the PL/SQL code currently consists of a main procedure and three helpers. The main procedure is shown in Example 9-1.

Example 9-1. The main procedure using the three helpers

```
CREATE OR REPLACE PROCEDURE process_project_data (
        project_id_in IN hr.projects.project_id%TYPE)
IS
        CURSOR proj_cur   IS
                SELECT
                        PROJECT_ID  ,
                        client_proj ,
                        hours_worked,
                        employee_id ,
                        contact     ,
                        rate        ,
                        revenue     ,
                        tax         ,
                        recipient
                FROM
                        hr.projects
                WHERE
                        project_id = project_id_in;

        proj_rec proj_cur%ROWTYPE;
BEGIN
        OPEN proj_cur;
        FETCH
                proj_cur
        INTO
                proj_rec;

        DBMS_OUTPUT.put_line ( 'Project ID: '
        || proj_rec.PROJECT_ID || '-' || ' CLIENT_PROJ: '
        || proj_rec.CLIENT_PROJ || '-' || ' hours_worked '
        || proj_rec.hours_worked);

        -- THE ADDITIONAL HELPER
```

```
        handle_insert(proj_rec.project_id, proj_rec.client_proj,
    proj_rec.hours_worked, proj_rec.employee_id, proj_rec.contact,
    proj_rec.rate, hr.projects.tax, hr.projects.recipient);

        CLOSE proj_cur;
END;
```

As you've seen in the earlier chapters, robust error and exception management is a key part of resilient coding.

Just before looking at the area of exceptions, the schema additions from the previous chapter need to be reviewed. With a view to expanding our PL/SQL toolbox, I'll use the SQL Developer model facility for the review.

Revisiting the Schema with Reference to the Model

In the PROJECTS and INVOICES tables, there is currently no primary key field. This is shown for the INVOICES table in Figure 9-1 where you can see that the HR.INVOICES table has a foreign key called FK_EMPLOYEE_ID, but no primary key.

I'll fix this missing primary key (in Figure 9-1) momentarily. If you want to view the model details for the INVOICES table shown in Figure 9-1, just click the table name under Connections. Then click the Model tab on the right side of the screen.

The problem with having no primary key is that we can keep adding duplicate rows to these tables. It's better to have only a single copy of the row in our use case. So, for the PROJECTS table, the required relational model should look like Figure 9-2.

It's easy to add a primary key to both of these tables: add a new constraint to the INVOICES and PROJECTS tables. Click the Constraints tab, select Add > Actions > Constraint, and Add Primary Key. This is similar to adding the foreign key to the INVOICES table (see Figure 8-4).

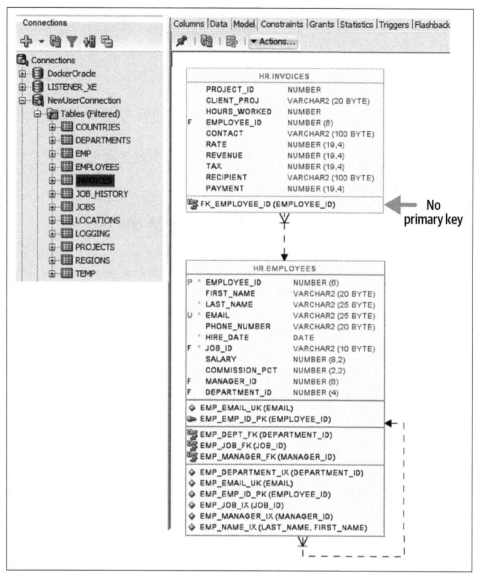

Figure 9-1. No primary key in the INVOICES table

Notice that there is a primary key in the PROJECTS table, called PROJECTS_PK, in the box labeled HR.PROJECTS at the upper-right corner of Figure 9-2.

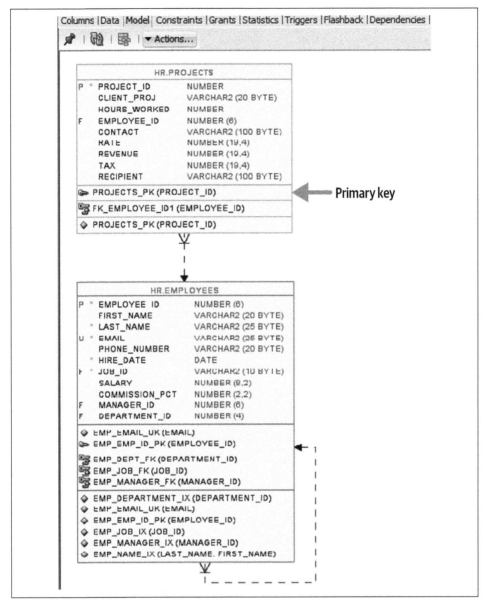

Figure 9-2. After adding a primary key to the PROJECTS table

After adding the primary key to the INVOICES tables, the model should look like Figure 9-3.

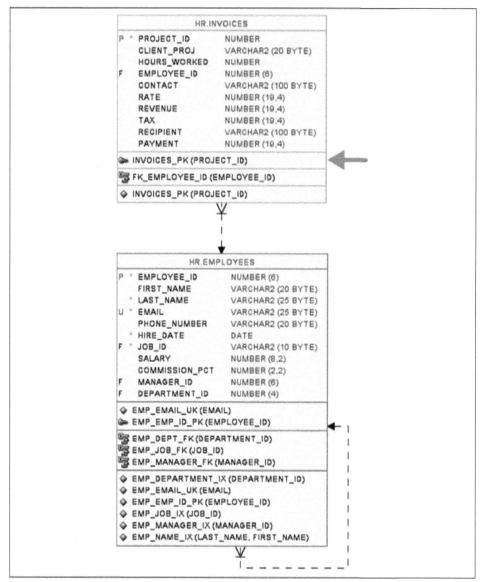

Figure 9-3. After adding a primary key to the INVOICES table

Notice in Figure 9-3 the arrow indicating that the HR.INVOICES table now includes a primary key constraint called INVOICES.PK. To test the model change, just try do the same insert twice into the INVOICES table and you should see the error message shown at the end of Example 9-2.

Example 9-2. Primary key violation on duplicate row insertion into the INVOICES table

```
-- RUN THIS INSERT TWICE TO CHECK THAT THE PRIMARY KEY WORKS
--************************************************************
INSERT INTO INVOICES(PROJECT_ID, CLIENT_PROJ, HOURS_WORKED, EMPLOYEE_ID,
CONTACT, RATE, REVENUE, TAX, RECIPIENT, PAYMENT)
 VALUES(1, 'Project', 10, 207, 'mark@provider.com', 100.00,
 1000, 0.15, 'mary@acme.com', 1150);


Error report -
ORA-00001: unique constraint (HR.INVOICES_PK) violated
```

A similar test can be done for the PROJECTS table. The primary key constraints in the INVOICES and PROJECTS tables will have an important bearing on the associated PL/SQL (e.g., in the exception handling). As always, make sure to generate a script for each modified table and add it to the set of disaster recovery scripts.

One easy way to acquire a SQL creation script for a table is to open the table in SQL Developer. Then, click on the SQL tab at the upper right of the worksheet. This results in the creation of a DDL script, which can be used in the creation of a recovery script.

For completeness, on Oracle version 12 onward, the primary key in both tables can be configured to auto-increment starting with the value 1. The SQL script to achieve this might look something like the following:

```
CREATE SEQUENCE project_seq START WITH 1;

CREATE TABLE projects (
  PROJECT_ID NUMBER(10)
  DEFAULT project_seq.nextval NOT NULL,
  etc.
```

Back to Error and Exception Management

In Example 9-1, the major operations from the context of possible errors and exceptions are shown in Table 9-2.

Potential issues that might arise from the actions on the left of the table include possible exceptions and logical conditions (e.g., "Is this cursor open?"). The possible exceptions can be handled in an EXCEPTION block. The logical conditions point to inline code changes such as cursor state ("Is the cursor open before attempting to use it?"). Both items are shown in the updated PL/SQL in Example 9-3.

Table 9-2. The potential errors and exceptions table

Operation	Associated errors or exceptions
`CURSOR proj_cur creation`	`NONE`
`OPEN proj_cur`	`IF NOT (proj_cur%ISOPEN) THEN`
`FETCH proj_cur INTO proj_rec`	`IF (proj_cur%FOUND) THEN`
`INSERT INTO INVOICES`	`DUP_VAL_ON_INDEX`
Calls to the helpers	`NONE`
`CLOSE proj_cur`	`IF (proj_cur%ISOPEN) THEN`

> Additional facilities allow for deep examination of the interaction between your code and the Oracle Database platform. For an example, see the `DBMS_APPLICATION_INFO` package (*https://oreil.ly/ZNCML*).
>
> One of the procedures in the `DBMS_APPLICATION_INFO` package is called `SET_SESSION_LONGOPS`, which is used to set a row in the `V$SESSION_LONGOPS` view. This allows for an improvement in observability by monitoring the ongoing progress of a long-running operation.
>
> Appendix B contains some details concerning logging facilities.

Just before proceeding with Example 9-3, please note that in this example (and throughout the book) I use what is called *positional* rather than *named* notation. Positional notation is more concise but it does require that the developer knows what each parameter represents when invoking a given subprogram.

Example 9-3. Driver procedure including error and exception handling

```
create or replace PROCEDURE process_project_data (
   project_id_in   IN hr.projects.project_id%TYPE)
IS
   CURSOR proj_cur
   IS
      SELECT PROJECT_ID, client_proj, hours_worked, employee_id, contact,
      rate, revenue, tax, recipient
      FROM hr.projects
      WHERE project_id = project_id_in;

   proj_rec     proj_cur%ROWTYPE;
   err_num NUMBER;
   err_msg VARCHAR2(100);
   callstack_msg VARCHAR2(32767);
BEGIN
   IF NOT (proj_cur%ISOPEN) THEN ❶
     OPEN proj_cur;
```

```
    FETCH proj_cur INTO proj_rec;

    IF (proj_cur%rowcount = 0) THEN  -- (proj_cur%notfound) can also be used ❷
      LOGGINGPACKAGE.LOG_ACTION('process_project_data',
      'NO DATA FOUND IN CURSOR');
    -- The ELSIF below is for illustration only, ELSE would work fine
    ELSIF (proj_cur%rowcount > 0) THEN
      DBMS_OUTPUT.put_line ('Project ID: ' || proj_rec.PROJECT_ID || '-'
      || ' CLIENT_PROJ: ' || proj_rec.CLIENT_PROJ || '-' || ' hours_worked '
      || proj_rec.hours_worked);
      handle_insert(proj_rec.project_id, proj_rec.client_proj,
        proj_rec.hours_worked, proj_rec.employee_id, proj_rec.contact,
        proj_rec.rate, proj_rec.tax, proj_rec.recipient);
      COMMIT;
    END IF;

    IF (proj_cur%ISOPEN) THEN ❸
      CLOSE proj_cur;
    END IF;
  END IF;

EXCEPTION
  WHEN INVALID_CURSOR
  THEN
    LOGGINGPACKAGE.LOG_ACTION('process_project_data', 'INVALID_CURSOR');
    ROLLBACK;
  WHEN OTHERS
  THEN
    err_num := SQLCODE; ❹
    err_msg := SUBSTR(SQLERRM, 1, 100);
    callstack_msg := DBMS_UTILITY.FORMAT_CALL_STACK;
    loggingPackage.LOG_ACTION('We hit a general exception error number -
    '|| ' ' || err_num || ' Error message: ' || err_msg,
    'process_project_data' || ' Callstack message: ' || callstack_msg);
    ROLLBACK;
END;
```

In Example 9-3, I've incorporated the contents of the anticipated errors and exceptions listed in Table 9-2. The main changes are:

❶ Check if the cursor is open before opening it.

❷ If you get zero rows returned from the cursor, log that. If you get zero rows returned from the cursor, skip the INSERT.

❸ Check if the cursor is open before closing it. Add an exception block.

❹ Inside the exception block, attempt to capture the error details. Add a COMMIT in the call to handle_insert.

A note on the cursor checks (items 1 and 3) is that this check really only applies to shared cursors, such as cursors that reside in shared packages. In the case of Example 9-3 it is clear that these cursor checks aren't really required. I leave them in just as a reminder that there are cases where such checks are strongly recommended.

The "zero rows returned" checks (items 2 and 3) enable the skipping of unnecessary calls to insert nonexistent data. The exception block currently handles the case of INVALID_CURSOR. This can occur if a cursor operation is attempted on a closed cursor. In the exception block, the WHEN OTHERS clause is the usual location for catching all other exceptions. To verify that this pathway is correct, I can simulate an exception with the changed code in Example 9-4.

 The hardcoded values in Example 9-4 (such as cause_an_error := '12345678901') should really be represented as constants. An example of such a constant in the declaration section in Example 9-4 could be as follows:

```
cause_an_error_str CONSTANT VARCHAR2 := '12345678901';
```

Using a constant in this case would have an additional merit because it would result in a compile-time error rather than a run-time error. This is more in keeping with the shift-left development approach, which you saw in "Shift-Left in Operation" on page 65.

Example 9-4. Driver procedure with a known exception (see variable cause_an_error)

```
create or replace PROCEDURE process_project_data (
   project_id_in    IN hr.projects.project_id%TYPE)
IS
   CURSOR proj_cur
   IS
      SELECT PROJECT_ID, client_proj, hours_worked, employee_id, contact,
      rate, revenue, tax, recipient
      FROM hr.projects
      WHERE project_id = project_id_in;

   proj_rec    proj_cur%ROWTYPE;
   err_num NUMBER;
   err_msg VARCHAR2(100);
   callstack_msg VARCHAR2(32767);
   cause_an_error VARCHAR2(10);
BEGIN
   cause_an_error := '12345678901';

   IF NOT (proj_cur%ISOPEN) THEN
      OPEN proj_cur;
      FETCH proj_cur INTO proj_rec;

      IF (proj_cur%rowcount = 0) THEN
```

```
      LOGGINGPACKAGE.LOG_ACTION('process_project_data',
        'NO DATA FOUND IN CURSOR');
    ELSIF (proj_cur%rowcount > 0) THEN
      DBMS_OUTPUT.put_line (
        'Project ID: ' || proj_rec.PROJECT_ID || '-'  || ' CLIENT_PROJ: '
        || proj_rec.CLIENT_PROJ || '-' || ' hours_worked ' ||
        proj_rec.hours_worked);
      handle_insert(proj_rec.project_id, proj_rec.client_proj,
        proj_rec.hours_worked, proj_rec.employee_id, proj_rec.contact,
        proj_rec.rate, proj_rec.tax, proj_rec.recipient);
      COMMIT;
    END IF;

    IF (proj_cur%ISOPEN) THEN
      CLOSE proj_cur;
    END IF;
  END IF;

EXCEPTION
  WHEN INVALID_CURSOR
  THEN
    LOGGINGPACKAGE.LOG_ACTION('process_project_data', 'INVALID_CURSOR');
    ROLLBACK;
  WHEN OTHERS
  THEN
    err_num := SQLCODE;
    err_msg := SUBSTR(SQLERRM, 1, 100);
    callstack_msg := DBMS_UTILITY.FORMAT_CALL_STACK;
    loggingPackage.LOG_ACTION('We hit a general exception error number -
    '|| ' ' || err_num || ' Error message: ' || err_msg,
    'process_project_data' || ' Callstack message: ' || callstack_msg);
    ROLLBACK;
END;
```

In Example 9-4, I've deliberately inserted a line that causes a general exception. Can you spot it? It's around the main BEGIN statement and consists of the snippet in Example 9-5.

Example 9-5. Driver procedure exception-causing code

```
  cause_an_error VARCHAR2(10);
BEGIN
  cause_an_error := '12345678901';
```

The string variable cause_an_error in Example 9-5 is too small for the assignment of an 11-character string and this causes an exception to occur. After running this code, the LOGGING table will have a row with the CODE_LOCATION column that contains the message shown in Example 9-6.

Example 9-6. Exception message

```
We hit a general exception error number -
        -6502 Error message: ORA-06502: PL/SQL: numeric or value error:
        character string buffer too small
```

In Example 9-6, the string buffer error is captured. By confirming that the WHEN OTHERS exception pathway is called, we can now be confident that the overall procedure is working as expected. Remember to delete the code shown in Example 9-5 and then recompile the procedure process_project_data.

I'd like to take a short detour into the area of exceptions in general and look at a possible strategy for the issue of what to do if the underlying database platform becomes unstable (e.g., low disk space, out of memory, etc.).

Back in Example 6-4, you saw the code repeated here in Example 9-7. This code attempted to handle a WHEN OTHERS exception in one of the callers of the logging facility.

Example 9-7. Invoking the expanded logger using FORMAT_CALL_STACK

```
WHEN NO_DATA_FOUND THEN -- catches all 'no data found' errors
  loggingPackage.LOG_ACTION(('Ouch', 'we hit an exception'));
  ROLLBACK;
WHEN OTHERS THEN -- handles all other errors
  err_num := SQLCODE;
  err_msg := SUBSTR(SQLERRM, 1, 100);
  callstack_msg := DBMS_UTILITY.FORMAT_CALL_STACK;
  loggingPackage.LOG_ACTION('We hit a general exception error number - '
     || ' ' || err_num || ' Error message: ' || err_msg, 'update_employees'
     || ' Callstack message: ' || callstack_msg);
  ROLLBACK;
```

One issue with having a WHEN OTHERS clause in general and back in Example 9-3 is that we are not allowing any exceptions to propagate up the chain. In many cases, this is OK. As long as the LOGGING table is under DevOps monitoring, this will cover most cases.

There is, however, a more difficult case. What should you do when the database itself is failing? Some sort of horrible out-of-memory error might occur, or the platform might run out of disk space, or the database might become corrupted. Basically, a catastrophic error occurs. For cases like these, it might be crucial to try to get some sort of relevant indication to the DevOps team.

One way to address this is to simply write an emergency text file to a directory on an external, monitored drive. Once the designated file appears in that location, it is then up to the DevOps team to investigate the matter, possibly even making contact with the DBAs.

An example of this is shown in Example 9-8. Please note that this applies to the Docker platform.

Example 9-8. The resilience requirement for platform emergencies

```
CREATE OR REPLACE DIRECTORY EXT_DIR AS '/emergency_dir';

CREATE OR REPLACE PROCEDURE EMERGENCY_OUTPUT(err_num IN NUMBER,
err_msg IN VARCHAR2, call_stack IN VARCHAR2)
AS
  output_file UTL_FILE.FILE_TYPE;
BEGIN
  output_file := UTL_FILE.FOPEN('EXT_DIR', 'emergency.txt' , 'A');

  IF UTL_FILE.IS_OPEN(output_file) THEN
    UTL_FILE.PUT_LINE(output_file, SYSTIMESTAMP || ' A platform issue may
    have occurred - error number -  ' || err_num || ' Error message: ' ||
    err_msg || ' Callstack message: ' || call_stack);
  END IF;
  IF UTL_FILE.IS_OPEN(output_file) THEN
    UTL_FILE.FCLOSE(output_file);
  END IF;
END;
```

Where might be an appropriate location for the code in Example 9-8? Does it belong in the logging code or in one of the callers of the logging code? This is a design question and it might also feed into issues such as service level agreements between DevOps, database administration, and possibly even end users.

Let's say, for example, I added the code in Example 9-8 as part of the logging procedure. The augmented logger might then look something like the code in Example 9-9.

Example 9-9. The exception-aware code we want to call to record log events

```
create or replace PROCEDURE LOG_ACTION ❶
        (action_message IN logging.action_message%TYPE,
        code_location  IN logging.code_location%TYPE)
IS
    PRAGMA AUTONOMOUS_TRANSACTION;

    err_num NUMBER;
    err_msg VARCHAR2(100);
BEGIN
    INSERT INTO LOGGING
            (EVENT_DATE
                , action_message
```

```
                , code_location
            )
            VALUES
            (SYSDATE
                , action_message
                , code_location
            );
        COMMIT;

    EXCEPTION
        WHEN OTHERS THEN
            err_num := SQLCODE;
            err_msg := SUBSTR(SQLERRM, 1, 100);
            EMERGENCY_OUTPUT(err_num, err_msg, DBMS_UTILITY.FORMAT_CALL_STACK);
            ROLLBACK;
END;
```

❶ The LOG_ACTION procedure acts as a kind of last-resort information provider. That is, if an error occurs in the logging code (which is just attempting a table INSERT), the tacit assumption is that this may be pointing to a more serious issue. The issue might not be so serious, but at least there is some level of detail provided in the emergency output file.

To test the updated logger in Example 9-9, I make a temporary code change in Example 9-10. This is the same deliberate exception producer you saw in Example 9-4.

Example 9-10. Inserting a known error to cause an exception in logging

```
create or replace PROCEDURE LOG_ACTION
        (action_message IN logging.action_message%TYPE,
         code_location  IN logging.code_location%TYPE)
IS
    PRAGMA AUTONOMOUS_TRANSACTION;

    err_num NUMBER;
    err_msg VARCHAR2(100);
    cause_an_error VARCHAR2(10); ❶
BEGIN
    cause_an_error := '12345678901'; ❶

    INSERT INTO LOGGING
            (EVENT_DATE, action_message, code_location);

    COMMIT;

    EXCEPTION
        WHEN OTHERS THEN
            err_num := SQLCODE;
            err_msg := SUBSTR(SQLERRM, 1, 100);
```

```
        EMERGENCY_OUTPUT(err_num, err_msg, DBMS_UTILITY.FORMAT_CALL_STACK);
END;
```

❶ Temporary changes to text the updated logger in Example 9-9

Running the code in Example 9-10 produces the external emergency file (Example 9-11).

Example 9-11. A possible emergency issue occurs in logging

```
[root@9b6af7c0e426 emergency_dir]# cat emergency.txt
03-DEC-22 17:54:47.816631000 +00:00 A platform issue may have occurred - error number
- 6502 Error message: ORA-06502: PL/SQL: numeric or value error: character string
buffer too small
Callstack message: ----- PL/SQL Call Stack -----
  object       line     object
  handle     number     name
0xfd7de290        31     procedure HR.LOG_ACTION
0xfd207558         8     anonymous block

[root@9b6af7c0e426 emergency_dir]#
```

Once the emergency file has been created in the designated emergency directory, it then becomes a process issue where someone in DevOps has to take stock of the situation and determine if the problem is critical or not. In such a context, it can be seen that the logging facility really is a feature doing useful work, as shown way back in Figure 8-2.

In Examples 9-8 and 9-9, I'm attempting to connect the worlds of platform administration, DevOps, and PL/SQL solution development. Example 9-8 is written as a procedure with these three parameters:

- err_num IN NUMBER

- err_msg IN VARCHAR2

- call_stack IN VARCHAR2

By providing these three parameters in the calling procedure, the context is then correct for recording the error as close as possible to the point it occurs. Let's break it down.

The line CREATE OR REPLACE DIRECTORY EXT_DIR AS '/emergency_dir'; is used to create a directory object, which is an alias for a directory on the Oracle Database server filesystem.

Because the underlying directory (called *emergency_dir*) is an operating system object, you must explicitly grant ownership of it. In this case, access to the directory must be granted to the oracle user. Why the oracle user? Because the oracle user is the one that will access the emergency directory in question and update the contained file.

In Figure 9-4, you can see the steps required, starting with opening a bash session in the Docker container.

```
[root@9b6af7c0e426 /]# ls -l
total 88
lrwxrwxrwx    1 root     root          7 May 30  2017 bin -> usr/bin
dr-xr-xr-x    2 root     root       4096 Aug 30  2016 boot
drwxr-xr-x    5 root     root        340 Dec 21 11:55 dev
drwxr-xr-x    2 root     root       4096 Dec  1 19:26 emergency_dir  ⬅
drwxr-xr-x    1 root     root       4096 Nov 17 14:57 etc
drwxr-xr-x    1 root     root       4096 Dec  1 12:53 home
lrwxrwxrwx    1 root     root          7 May 30  2017 lib -> usr/lib
lrwxrwxrwx    1 root     root          9 May 30  2017 lib64 -> usr/lib64
drwxr-xr-x    2 root     root       4096 Aug 30  2016 media
drwxr-xr-x    2 root     root       4096 Aug 30  2016 mnt
drwxr-xr-x    2 root     root       4096 Aug 30  2016 opt
dr-xr-xr-x  266 root     root          0 Dec 21 11:55 proc
dr-xr-x---    1 root     root       4096 Dec  5 13:15 root
drwxr-xr-x   12 root     root       4096 May 30  2017 run
lrwxrwxrwx    1 root     root          8 May 30  2017 sbin -> usr/sbin
drwxr-xr-x    2 root     root       4096 Aug 30  2016 srv
dr-xr-xr-x   11 root     root          0 Dec 21 11:55 sys
drwxrwxrwt    1 root     root       4096 Dec 21 11:55 tmp
drwxr-xr-x    3 oracle   oinstall   4096 Nov 17 14:54 u01
drwxr-xr-x    3 oracle   oinstall   4096 Nov 17 14:56 u02
drwxr-xr-x    3 oracle   oinstall   4096 Nov 17 14:56 u03
drwxr-xr-x    3 oracle   oinstall   4096 Nov 17 14:54 u04
drwxr-xr-x    1 root     root       4096 May 30  2017 usr
drwxr-xr-x    1 root     root       4096 May 30  2017 var
[root@9b6af7c0e426 /]#
```

Figure 9-4. Opening a bash session in the container and creating the emergency directory

In Figure 9-4, to begin with, you can see the result of this command to open a bash shell in the Docker container:

```
docker exec -it 9b6af7c0e426 bash
```

Once the bash shell is open, I list the directories and then create a new directory with the following command:

```
mkdir emergency_dir
```

Notice that a verbose directory listing (using the command ls -l) in Figure 9-4 indicates that the new directory *emergency_dir* is owned by the root user. This is because I'm logged in as root and the call to mkdir is applied with root user privileges.

Doing administrative tasks as the root user is generally not recommended. As root, you have the maximum possible set of privileges and this makes it easy to inadvertently damage the system. It is a better practice to log in as a normal user and to then request privileged access (e.g., with sudo) as and when it is needed. Then, when done, revert again to a lower privilege level. Please refer to "Oracle Database Users and the Principle of Least Privilege" on page 177 for more on this issue.

In order for PL/SQL code to be able to write to a file in the *emergency_dir* directory, the directory ownership has to change from root. One way to do this is shown in Figure 9-5, where the oracle user is assigned as the new owner of *emergency_dir*.

```
[root@9b6af7c0e426 /]# ls -l
total 88
lrwxrwxrwx  1 root    root       7 May 30  2017 bin -> usr/bin
dr-xr-xr-x  2 root    root    4096 Aug 30  2016 boot
drwxr-xr-x  5 root    root     340 Dec 21 11:55 dev
drwxr-xr-x  2 oracle  root    4096 Dec  1 19:26 emergency_dir
drwxr-xr-x  1 root    root    4096 Nov 17 14:57 etc
drwxr-xr-x  1 root    root    4096 Dec  1 12:53 home
```

Figure 9-5. After changing ownership of the emergency_dir directory

Notice in Figure 9-5 that the oracle user is now listed as the owner of *emergency_dir*. With these changes in place, I can now run the PL/SQL code in Example 9-8. Just before running the PL/SQL code, notice in Example 9-12 that the file is empty; no emergencies have occurred yet.

Example 9-12. An empty emergency file

```
[root@9b6af7c0e426 emergency_dir]# cat emergency.txt
[root@9b6af7c0e426 emergency_dir]#
```

Now, I can run the (intentionally erroneous) PL/SQL code in Example 9-10 and then check the contents of the file *emergency.txt*, as shown in Example 9-12.

Notice in Example 9-11 that there is content related to the emergency situation indicating where it occurred in the PL/SQL code. The code in Example 9-9 is a candidate for what to do if an exception occurs in the logging code.

If the *emergency.txt* file suddenly appears in a DevOps-monitored folder, then the DevOps team has at least some indication that the database is experiencing what may be very serious platform issues. This might be preferable to waiting for a complete runtime failure, where the root cause information may be quite limited.

Resilience Requirements Checklist

Now that errors and exceptions have been handled in Example 9-3, the requirements table looks like Table 9-3. I've awarded a score of 8 out of 10 for the errors and exceptions code. Recoverability and observability in Table 9-3 are also filled in (the details are covered in the next sections).

Table 9-3. The resilience requirements updated

Resilience requirement	Status	Resilience score
Capture all errors and exceptions	DONE	8
Recoverability	DONE	8
Observability	DONE	8
Modifiability	NOT DONE YET	0
Modularity	NOT DONE YET	0
Simplicity	NOT DONE YET	0
Coding conventions	NOT DONE YET	0
Reusability	NOT DONE YET	0
Repeatable testing	NOT DONE YET	0
Avoiding common antipatterns	NOT DONE YET	0
Schema evolution	NOT DONE YET	0

Before moving on, we shouldn't forget the issue of errors and exceptions in Java client code. The Java code can also be a source of exceptions, as you saw back in Chapter 5. For this reason, the Java code (or any other high-level language client) requires an appropriate strategy for handling exceptions. Fortunately, the issue of Java exception handling is relatively straightforward and was described in detail back in "Who Owns the Java Error?" on page 143.

Recoverability

Recoverability is closely related to having good error and exception handling in place. Similar considerations apply to the current discussion as you saw way back in "Scale of Resilience Requirement 2: Recoverability" on page 79.

As the PROJECTS and INVOICES tables now have primary keys, there's no issue of being able to insert duplicate rows. So, the PL/SQL procedure that creates the INVOICES row can be run multiple times without side effects.

The logging of issues is also in place; in "Back to Error and Exception Management" on page 225 you saw a candidate solution for those knotty situations where the logging mechanism fails. With this in mind, I updated the resilience score for recoverability in Table 9-3.

Observability

Observability reflects the ability to *look into* the code and have a reasonable idea of the pathways being taken. The logging facility gives us the ability to broadly understand the code pathways. Logging and the absence of exceptions in the LOGGING table explain the observability score in Table 9-3.

Modifiability

The modifiability of the PL/SQL in Example 9-3 is reasonable. Adding another helper call to the procedure process_project_data would require just a single line of code. It looks like the code is modifiable without itself needing any substantial refactoring. I'll award myself a score of 9 for modifiability, as shown in Table 9-4.

Table 9-4. The resilience requirements updated up to and including modifiability

Resilience requirement	Status	Resilience score
Capture all errors and exceptions	DONE	8
Recoverability	DONE	8
Observability	DONE	8
Modifiability	DONE	9
Modularity	DONE	7
Simplicity	NOT DONE YET	0
Coding conventions	NOT DONE YET	0
Reusability	NOT DONE YET	0
Repeatable testing	NOT DONE YET	0
Avoiding common antipatterns	NOT DONE YET	0
Schema evolution	NOT DONE YET	0

In Table 9-4, I've applied a slightly lower score of 7 for modularity and this is explained in the next section.

Modularity

Up to now, I've been referring to the PL/SQL procedure process_project_data as a driver procedure or the backend invoker. In terms of modularity, it might make sense to provide a very thin PL/SQL procedure that itself calls process_project_data, somewhat like the procedure shown in Example 9-13.

Example 9-13. A new invoker procedure for external calls, e.g., from Java

```
create or replace PROCEDURE process_project_invoker (
    project_id_in    IN hr.projects.project_id%TYPE)
IS
BEGIN
    process_project_data(project_id_in);
END;
```

The procedure in Example 9-13 is itself called by the feature back in Figure 8-2. The invoker then calls the (now backend) procedure process_project_data, as shown in Example 9-14. Adding the process_project_invoker procedure is an optional refactoring step that essentially makes the procedure process_project_data into a helper.

Example 9-14. The backend procedure that is called by the invoker

```
create or replace PROCEDURE process_project_data (
    project_id_in    IN hr.projects.project_id%TYPE)
IS
    CURSOR proj_cur
    IS
        SELECT PROJECT_ID, client_proj, hours_worked, employee_id, contact,
        rate, revenue, tax, recipient
        FROM hr.projects
        WHERE project_id = project_id_in;

    proj_rec      proj_cur%ROWTYPE;
    err_num NUMBER;
    err_msg VARCHAR2(100);
    callstack_msg VARCHAR2(32767);
    smaller_callstack hr.logging.code_location%TYPE;
BEGIN
    IF NOT (proj_cur%ISOPEN) THEN
        OPEN proj_cur;
        DBMS_OUTPUT.put_line ('Opened CURSOR');
        FETCH proj_cur INTO proj_rec;
        DBMS_OUTPUT.put_line (
            'Project ID: ' || proj_rec.PROJECT_ID
        || '-'  || ' CLIENT_PROJ: ' || proj_rec.CLIENT_PROJ || '-'
        || ' hours_worked ' || proj_rec.hours_worked);

        IF (proj_cur%rowcount = 0) THEN
            LOGGINGPACKAGE.LOG_ACTION('process_project_data',
            'NO DATA FOUND IN CURSOR');
        ELSIF (proj_cur%rowcount > 0) THEN
            DBMS_OUTPUT.put_line ('Calling handle_insert');
            handle_insert(proj_rec.project_id, proj_rec.client_proj,
                proj_rec.hours_worked, proj_rec.employee_id, proj_rec.contact,
                proj_rec.rate, proj_rec.tax, proj_rec.recipient);
            COMMIT;
```

```
      END IF;

    IF (proj_cur%ISOPEN) THEN
      DBMS_OUTPUT.put_line ('Closing CURSOR');
      CLOSE proj_cur;
    END IF;
  END IF;

EXCEPTION
  WHEN INVALID_CURSOR
  THEN
    LOGGINGPACKAGE.LOG_ACTION('process_project_data', 'INVALID_CURSOR');
    ROLLBACK;
  WHEN OTHERS
  THEN
    err_num := SQLCODE;
    err_msg := SUBSTR(SQLERRM, 1, 100);
    callstack_msg := DBMS_UTILITY.FORMAT_CALL_STACK;
    smaller_callstack := SUBSTR(callstack_msg, 1, 200);
    loggingPackage.LOG_ACTION('We hit a general exception error number -
    '|| ' ' || err_num || ' Error message: ' || err_msg,
    'process_project_data' || ' Callstack message: ' || smaller_callstack);
    ROLLBACK;
END;
```

There are further modularity-related changes that could be applied to Example 9-14, such as moving the cursor into a helper function. Also, the exception handling could be moved into the new invoker procedure process_project_invoker. You can see that these types of changes all have one thing in common: they reduce the code size of the PL/SQL in Example 9-14. This has merits, including making that code easier to understand, which can help downstream DevOps developers.

Safety and Resilience Code Change

Reading code written by others is an important skill to acquire. It also applies to code you write. Why is it important? Well, the examples discussed in Part I all illustrate that even simple PL/SQL code can contain egregious errors and antipatterns. With this in mind, it's always useful to have an effective capability to visually scan existing code for such issues. In Example 9-14, I've made a pragmatic fix to the exception code.

This fix is applied to avoid exceeding the boundary of the CODE_LOCATION column in the LOGGING table. The code change resides in the WHEN OTHERS clause and is simply to take a substring of the incoming parameter callstack_msg:

```
smaller_callstack := SUBSTR(callstack_msg, 1, 200);
```

Why bother with this code change? Well, one reason is that the incoming call stack string is not bounded by the preceding code. In many cases, this will not present a

---

problem, but what if a very long string is presented? Long in this context relates to the size of the relevant column in the LOGGING table, which as can be seen in Example 9-15 is CODE_LOCATION. This column has the type VARCHAR(255).

Example 9-15. The logging table columns (run describe LOGGING to get this information)

```
Name            Null?    Type
-------------   -------- -------------
LOGGING_ID      NOT NULL NUMBER
EVENT_DATE      NOT NULL TIMESTAMP(6)
ACTION_MESSAGE           VARCHAR2(255)
CODE_LOCATION           VARCHAR2(255)
```

The CODE_LOCATION column in Example 9-15 is quite small, so it's a good idea to limit the size of the string that is to be written to it. This last code change then protects against exceeding the boundary of the LOGGING table CODE_LOCATION column. I could of course make a schema change, but this option might be disallowed—close to the end of the project, the schema might be frozen. One further point is that it might make more sense to apply this fix to the logging procedure itself. The decision is at the discretion of the developer.

It's always a good idea to be on the lookout for this type of issue, particularly if someone says it can't happen.

Another change required for modularity is putting the PL/SQL code into a package. This is a good practice and is recommended by Oracle. The new package specification structure is shown in Example 9-16.

Example 9-16. Packaging the PL/SQL code

```
CREATE OR REPLACE
PACKAGE MAIN_CODE_PACKAGE AS

PROCEDURE process_project_data (
   project_id_in   IN hr.projects.project_id%TYPE);

  PROCEDURE process_project_invoker (
   project_id_in   IN hr.projects.project_id%TYPE);

   PROCEDURE handle_insert (PROJECT_ID_IN   IN hr.projects.project_id%TYPE,
CLIENT_PROJ_IN IN hr.projects.client_proj%TYPE,
HOURS_WORKED_IN IN hr.projects.hours_worked%TYPE,
EMPLOYEE_ID_IN IN hr.projects.employee_id%TYPE,
CONTACT_IN IN hr.projects.contact%TYPE,
RATE_IN IN hr.projects.rate%TYPE,
TAX_IN IN hr.projects.tax%TYPE,
RECIPIENT_IN IN hr.projects.recipient%TYPE);
```

```
PROCEDURE EMERGENCY_OUTPUT(
  err_num IN NUMBER, err_msg IN VARCHAR2, call_stack IN VARCHAR2
);
```

```
END MAIN_CODE_PACKAGE;
```

Example 9-16 is the package header, which needs an associated package body. Revisit "Creating a Logging Package" on page 95 for a description of how to create the package body; it's the same. The end result with the populated package should look something like that shown in Figure 9-6.

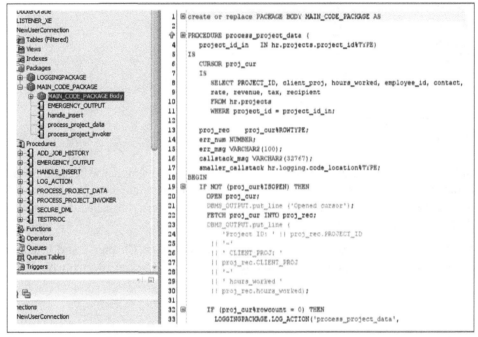

Figure 9-6. A populated package

Once the new package in Figure 9-6 is created, it can be invoked from PL/SQL or from Java, as shown in Example 9-17.

Example 9-17. Calling the newly packaged PL/SQL code

```
CALL main_code_package.process_project_invoker(1);
```

Or from Java:

```
statement = connection.prepareCall(
"{call MAIN_CODE_PACKAGE.PROCESS_PROJECT_INVOKER(?)}");
```

If all is well, either of the calls to the newly modularized PL/SQL code shown in Example 9-17 should result in a new row in the INVOICES table. Let's have a look at the resilience scores in Table 9-5.

Table 9-5. The resilience requirements updated up to and including reusability

Resilience requirement	Status	Resilience score
Capture all errors and exceptions	DONE	8
Recoverability	DONE	8
Observability	DONE	8
Modifiability	DONE	9
Modularity	DONE	7
Simplicity	DONE	8
Coding conventions	DONE	8
Reusability	DONE	8
Repeatable testing	NOT DONE YET	0
Avoiding common antipatterns	NOT DONE YET	0
Schema evolution	NOT DONE YET	0

In Table 9-5, I've awarded a score of 8 out of 10 for code simplicity. Because of the effort put into reworking the modularity, there is a single line invoker called MAIN_CODE_PACKAGE.PROCESS_PROJECT_INVOKER, which can be called from either PL/SQL or Java code. It doesn't get much simpler than that.

I've followed the informal coding conventions described in Chapter 4 and listed in "Scale of Resilience Requirement 7: Coding Conventions" on page 102, namely:

- Good comments
- Consistent variable names
- Clear formatting
- Exception handling
- Testing
- Avoiding excessive complexity

Given this, a coding conventions score of 8 seems reasonable.

For reusability, there's now a packaged PL/SQL solution with a single-line invoker. This means that another development team could potentially use the logging code. In regard to logging, there is also scope for reusing the platform emergency mechanism, although doing so would probably necessitate some detailed discussions to make sure it is incorporated correctly.

As you've seen, the integration of the PL/SQL code with a Java client is straightforward. All these considerations suggest that a reusability score of 8 is reasonable.

 If you're repeatedly running the Java code and then clearing down the LOGGING and INVOICES tables, it is a good idea to commit the latter changes. This has the effect of restoring the tables to a known state.

Tests

The tests in this case should be a combination of utPLSQL tests and any other feature-level tests. As I noted in Figure 8-11, an end-to-end test was already confirmed using SQL Developer and the Java client code. While the combination of testing with SQL Developer and Java code is useful, that is not a unit test. Unit tests allow for running tests on a more repeatable basis than is generally possible using development tools.

One use case for unit tests is when it is required to verify unit operation in an automated context. A Jenkins build pipeline or some other continuous integration scenario is a good example of this. Tackling this requirement can be done using a tool such as utPLSQL.

For detailed directions on installing and using utPLSQL, please see "Installing utPLSQL" on page 106. In this section, I'll demonstrate a unit test to exercise the invoker PL/SQL code (process_project_invoker). The unit test is shown in Example 9-18.

Example 9-18. A utPLSQL unit test for the process_project_invoker procedure

```
procedure process_project_invoker is
   l_actual   integer := 0;
   l_expected integer := 2;
begin
   -- arrange
   -- Not required, DB state should be known in advance
   -- delete from INVOICES;

   -- act
   main_code_package.process_project_invoker(1);

   -- assert
   select count(*) into l_actual from INVOICES;
   ut.expect(l_actual).to_equal(l_expected);

   --%rollback(auto)
end process_project_invoker;
```

Based on the discussion in "Installing utPLSQL" on page 106, can you figure out what the unit test in Example 9-18 is doing? Let's break it down. The code is testing just one procedure, `main_code_package.process_project_invoker`, into which it passes a single parameter, a project ID with the value 1.

The result of calling `process_project_invoker` is the creation of a row in the `INVOICES` table. The test code verifies this by updating the value of `l_actual`, which is then compared to the expected value. If they match, the test passes. The test in Example 9-18, while being a unit test, actually performs a functional end-to-end test. This is because the test calls the main invoker.

 The addition of this latest test allows a further change to Figure 8-11, i.e., the box for Test 2 (the invoker) can now be filled in.

Adding more tests to Example 9-18 would be the correct thing to do in order to verify the PL/SQL code in a more granular fashion. With utPLSQL, as you saw in "Installing utPLSQL" on page 106, it's quite easy to add a new test, as shown in Figure 9-7.

```
TEST_MAIN_CODE_PACKAGE                1  create or replace package test_main_code_package is
 TEST_MAIN_CODE_PACKAGE Body          2
 emergency_output                     3      -- generated by utPLSQL for SQL Developer on 2022-12-05 14:36:32
 handle_insert                        4
 process_project_data                 5      --%suite(test_main_code_package)
 process_project_invoker              6      --%suitepath(alltests)
TEST_PACKAGE1                         7
 TEST_PACKAGE1 Body                   8      --%test
   log_action                         9      procedure process_project_data;
 log_action                          10
edures                               11      --%test
:tions                               12      procedure process_project_invoker;
rators                               13
ues                                  14      --%test
ues Tables                          15      procedure handle_insert;
jers                                 16
ts                                   17      --%test
iences                              18      procedure emergency_output;
rialized Views                      19
rialized View Logs                  20  end test_main_code_package;
```

Figure 9-7. A new utPLSQL test

In Figure 9-7, you can uncomment and modify the call to this line by adding the required parameters:

```
-- main_code_package.handle_insert;
```

That will produce something like this:

```
main_code_package.handle_insert(
1, 'CLIENT_PROJ_IN', 10, 207, 'barney', 100, 0.15, 'Wilma');
```

Then, when the new code is run, we get a failure, as shown in Figure 9-8.

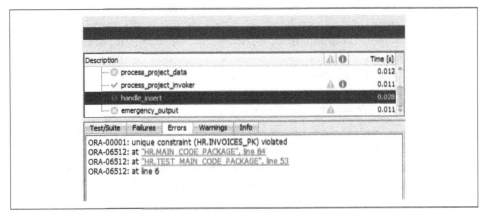

Figure 9-8. A new (failing) utPLSQL test

You can see in Figure 9-8 that the test is more granular because it exercises the associated database constraint. The reason for the primary key violation is because the test is attempting to add a new row into the INVOICES table using an existing key. To get the test to work, the affected row in the table can be deleted, or we can move to using auto-generated primary key values or whatever else is deemed to be a solution.

The important takeaway is that the unit tests provide assistance in producing an improved solution. While the tests are not complete, it's not a difficult task to produce an acceptable suite of tests. One point to note is that utPLSQL tests can also be packaged for invocation by command-line tools such as automated build systems. With this in mind, I'll award myself a score of 7 out of 10 for testing (see Table 9-6).

Table 9-6. The completed resilience requirements

Resilience requirement	Status	Resilience score
Capture all errors and exceptions	DONE	8
Recoverability	DONE	8
Observability	DONE	8
Modifiability	DONE	9
Modularity	DONE	7
Simplicity	DONE	8
Coding conventions	DONE	8
Reusability	DONE	8
Repeatable testing	DONE	7
Avoiding common antipatterns	DONE	8
Schema evolution	DONE	8

In Table 9-6, I've scored an 8 both for avoiding common antipatterns and for schema evolution. Perhaps the most important antipattern I've avoided is the big block of SQL with no error or exception handling. The code in its current form handles its cursors in a disciplined fashion. In a similar way, the small amount of file handling is tightly managed. An attempted solution has been provided for the case where something bad happens to the underlying database platform. The solution also can perhaps be extended to avoid having to propagate exceptions up to the main application invoker, which is undesirable in most cases.

The schema has evolved over the course of the coding exercises. Starting with the Oracle HR schema as a good foundation, I've added tables as part of the solution. An important part of schema evolution is the maintenance of a full set of scripts to facilitate database reconstruction in the event of a catastrophic destruction.

Build a Basic Invoice Creation Tool

Creating an invoice data set starts with a SQL INSERT statement into the PROJECTS table. The purpose of this is to keep things relatively simple. In a commercial environment, it is likely that invoice creation would happen as a result of aggregating the requisite data from a range of sources, such as employee timesheets and project-specific tables. These data sources could in turn come from databases, data warehouses, HR systems, consolidated views, and so on.

For completeness, the following section describes the procedure for adding logging into the Oracle HR schema.

Add Logging

As we're now working with the Oracle HR schema, it's important that we have access to logging facilities. Given that the logging PL/SQL and SQL from Chapter 4 is relatively simple, I'll add this logging infrastructure to the HR schema.

To do this, connect to the Docker container for your Oracle image and run the SQL script shown in Example 9-19.

 The SQL script in Example 9-19 should also be placed under source control as described back in "Schema Evolution Antipattern and Resilience" on page 191. It's always important to be able to rebuild your database in its entirety should the need arise.

Example 9-19. Creating the LOGGING table

```
CREATE TABLE LOGGING (
 Logging_ID NUMBER GENERATED ALWAYS AS IDENTITY,
```

```
EVENT_DATE TIMESTAMP NOT NULL,
ACTION_MESSAGE VARCHAR2(255),
CODE_LOCATION VARCHAR2(255)
);
```

```
COMMIT;
```

After adding the LOGGING table to the HR schema, remember to follow the steps from "Creating a Logging Package" on page 95 to create and compile the logging procedure. To avoid excessive repetition, the detailed steps are not included here.

If the installation of logging is successful, your setup should look somewhat like Figure 9-9.

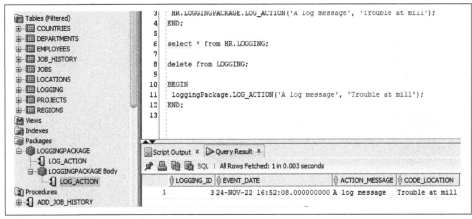

Figure 9-9. After setting up LOGGING in SQL Developer

Notice the new LOGGING table and the new LOGGING package and its implementation on the left side of Figure 9-9. On the right side, I have some code to verify the configuration. The salient items are shown in Example 9-20.

Example 9-20. Exercising the logging code

```
BEGIN
 HR.LOGGINGPACKAGE.LOG_ACTION('A log message', 'Trouble at mill');
END;

select * from HR.LOGGING;

delete from LOGGING;
```

In Example 9-20, I add a row to the LOGGING table using an anonymous PL/SQL block. Then, I select the contents from the LOGGING table for verification followed by deleting the test row.

With the logging infrastructure now configured in the HR schema, we now need a basic driving procedure in the PL/SQL code. This is handled next.

Call the Logging PL/SQL Procedure from Java Code

Back in Chapter 5, I made a Java call to the PL/SQL logging code. Since that chapter, we're now using the Oracle HR schema. The details of the connection are slightly different from Chapter 5 and include the following:

- The username is now HR.

- The password is now hrpass.

- The connection now uses a SID rather than a Service name.

You can see these differences in Figure 9-10.

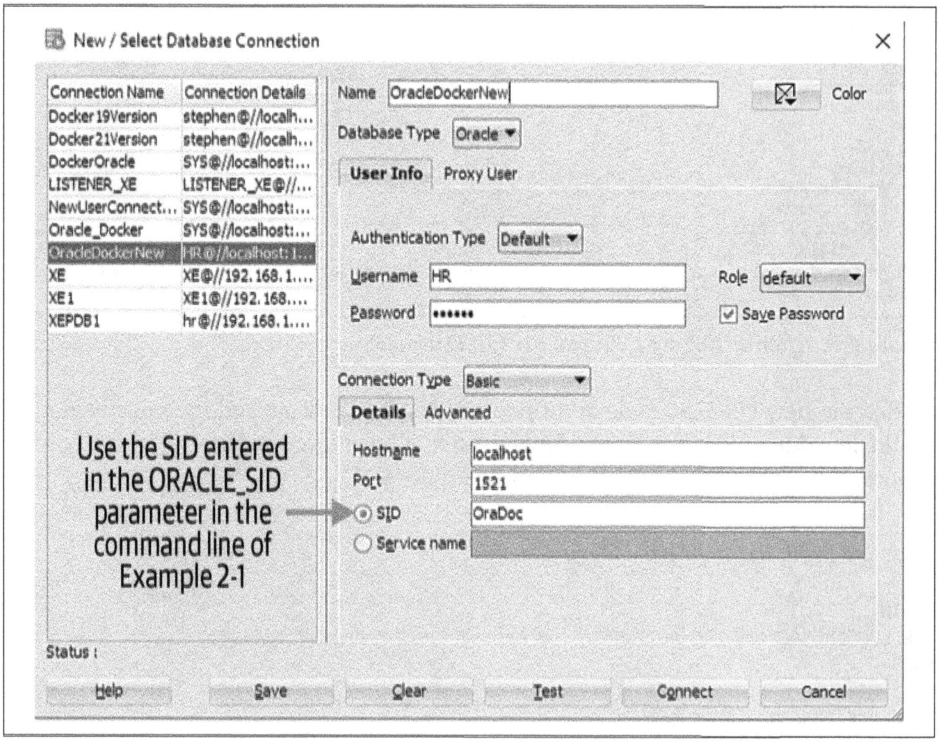

Figure 9-10. The new connection details

To accommodate the changes in Figure 9-10, the Java code that handles the Oracle Database connection is modified as shown in Example 9-21.

Example 9-21. Java changes required for connecting to the Oracle Database with a SID

```java
public class DBConnection {

    private static final String DB_DRIVER_CLASS = "oracle.jdbc.driver.OracleDriver";
    private static final String DB_USERNAME = "HR";
    private static final String DB_PASSWORD = "hrpass";

    public static Connection getConnection() {
        Connection connection = null;
        try {
            // Load the Driver Class
            Class.forName(DB_DRIVER_CLASS);
            // Create the connection
            connection = DriverManager.getConnection(
                // Connect to Oracle using a SID
                "jdbc:oracle:thin:@localhost:1521:OraDoc",
                DB_USERNAME, DB_PASSWORD); ❶
                // Connect to Oracle using a service name
                // "jdbc:oracle:thin:@localhost:1521/ORCLCDB.localdomain", ❶
                // DB_USERNAME, DB_PASSWORD);
        } catch (ClassNotFoundException e) {
            e.printStackTrace();
        } catch (SQLException e) {
            e.printStackTrace();
        }
        return connection;
    }
}
```

For the sake of comparison, I've left in the original (service name) connection code; it is commented out. The callouts illustrate the difference with connecting to a SID:

❶   The SID is appended following a colon rather than a forward slash character.

Then, to call the PL/SQL logging code, the other part of the Java code requires just one change in the package, as follows:

```java
statement = connection.prepareCall("{call HR.LOGGINGPACKAGE.LOG_ACTION(?, ?)}");
```

The new Java code is shown (without exception handling), along with invoice retrieval, in Example 9-22.

Example 9-22. Java code to call the PL/SQL logging code and get invoice data

```java
connection = DBConnection.getConnection();
statement = connection.prepareCall("{call
  HR.LOGGINGPACKAGE.LOG_ACTION(?, ?)}");
statement.setString("action_message", action_message);
statement.setString("code_location", code_location);
statement.executeUpdate();
```

```
// Get all invoices
 OracleResultSet rs = (OracleResultSet)
    statement.executeQuery("select * from invoices");

 while(rs.next())
 {
    BigDecimal projectId = (BigDecimal) rs.getObject(1);
    System.out.println("projectId: " + projectId);
    String clientProjectId = (String) rs.getObject(2);
    System.out.println("clientProjectId: " + clientProjectId);
    BigDecimal hoursWorked = (BigDecimal) rs.getObject(3);
    System.out.println("hoursWorked: " + hoursWorked);
    BigDecimal employeeId = (BigDecimal) rs.getObject(4);
    System.out.println("employeeId: " + employeeId);
    BigDecimal payment = (BigDecimal) rs.getObject("payment");
    System.out.println("payment: " + payment);
 }
 System.out.println("Successful call");
```

When I run the updated Java code, the following is the console output in IntelliJ IDEA. Notice the invoice data:

```
projectId: 1
clientProjectId: Project
hoursWorked: 10
employeeId: 107
payment: 1150
Successful calls
```

To verify that the LOGGING call has worked, just use the query shown in Figure 9-11.

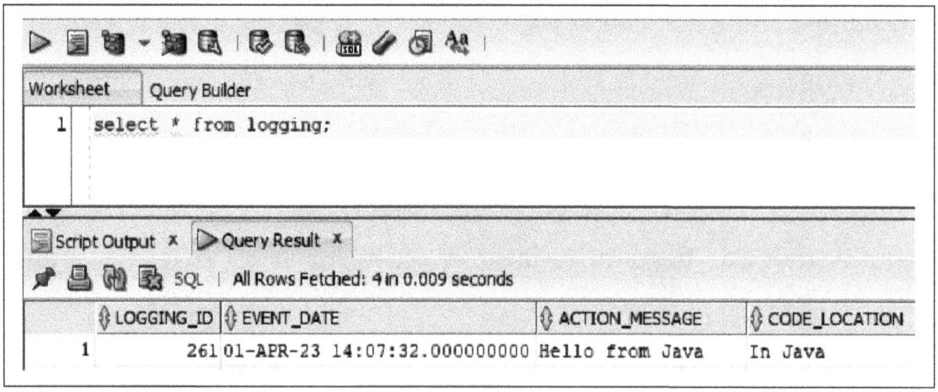

Figure 9-11. The LOGGING output from Java

As you can see in Figure 9-11, we have a new row in the LOGGING table. This is purely for illustrating the fact that the PL/SQL code can be called from an external Java application. The PL/SQL logging code should really only be used exclusively from within PL/SQL and not from a high-level language.

Summary

Solution integration is hard work. However, a disciplined approach coupled with good tools, such as SQL Developer, can make life easier. Table modifications such as adding primary keys and other constraints can be easily achieved using the SQL Developer model.

Error and exception management are another key area of resilient solution development. This can range from closing a cursor to checking that a file handle is open before attempting to update the file. Special consideration may be required in the case where it appears that the database itself is getting into difficulties. Examples of the latter are out-of-memory errors and shortage of disk space. Early detection of such issues may help in resolving the underlying problem. Indeed, early detection may be mandatory because a runtime failure may not provide sufficient data for meaningful root cause analysis. Strategic use of logging can help in understanding code pathways in both normal workflows and when things go wrong.

When your code has applied a data change, it may be crucial to commit that change early in the workflow. It's not uncommon for a data change to occur and then the developer forgets to do a commit. This can result in unnecessary downstream complications.

Following the resilience requirements checklist is a convenient approach to implementing functionally tight, compact solutions. This is further facilitated by the judicious use of a range of testing techniques, including manual developer tests, client tests (e.g., calls from Java code), and of course, unit testing. The test cases should always include test artifacts (such as utPLSQL tests) that can be extended as needed as the code matures.

CHAPTER 10

Conclusion

In this chapter, we'll draw together the main strands discussed throughout the book. Is it feasible to learn a new language and at the same time deliver resilient solutions? I think so, but it requires a disciplined approach. An important element is having a simple process. Rather than using complex documents at each stage of the development journey, it is possible to have a simple, 11-item checklist. Each of the resilience requirements introduced in "Requirements for Resilience: What Versus How" on page 6 guides the developer in ensuring that the code delivered is compliant.

Is the code easy to understand? Is it modular? Does it capture all errors and exceptions? The checklist keeps these questions at the front of the developer's mind as the project progresses. In this way, a simple process aids the developer and acts as a constant reminder that for code to be resilient it also has to survive a combination of new author additions and new requirements.

By structuring the resilient code as a testable feature, it has a macroscopic identity that subsumes the microscopic elements of which it is comprised. By using a feature orientation, it also becomes possible to open projects up in a meaningful way to other stakeholders, including more junior developers.

In Part III, the idea of a feature-oriented project is demonstrated with a simple invoice generator feature. The invoice starts life once a project is created (one row in a PROJECTS table) and then it becomes possible to generate an invoice from a simple Java client or by a direct call to the PL/SQL invoker code.

The resilience requirements checklist guides the development during any refactoring or restructuring. In the invoice project, the end result was a one-line PL/SQL invoker procedure and a small collection of clearly defined helpers. This follows the Linux philosophy of writing simple utilities that *do one thing well.*

The structure shown in Figure 8-1 is the basic feature, which includes these elements:

- The feature and its user interface
- The main invoker
- The various helpers
- End-to-end functional tests
- Unit tests
- Business-criticality indication

The framework I used for the example invoice project is pretty much all incorporated in the combination of Figure 8-1 and in this itemized scale of resilience:

1. Capture all errors and exceptions
2. Recoverability
3. Observability
4. Modifiability
5. Modularity
6. Simplicity
7. Coding conventions
8. Reusability
9. Repeatable testing
10. Avoiding common antipatterns
11. Schema evolution

It's a small and simple framework that aims to keep reminding developers of the macroscopic requirements that help to produce a more resilient solution.

As you saw in the previous three chapters, the feature is first sketched out in broad terms and then elaborated. Then, the happy path code is produced followed by breaking this down into an invoker and helpers. Then, tests can be added, followed by integration into a packaged, modular, and simple solution.

New requirements can be accommodated by changing one or more of the helpers or adding new helpers. In this way, the basic feature becomes enriched with additional capability in line with stakeholder needs. This incremental approach is preferable to a more forklift-based approach where everything changes when new requirements arise or for the special case of new staff joining up.

Is a Big Rewrite Actually Needed?

Over the years, I've heard stories about developers leaving organizations and being replaced by new entrants. The new developers sometimes remark when looking at the existing code that "This will all have to be rewritten." Sometimes this is a reflection of a developer's disinclination to work with legacy code and products. Sometimes it's because the code really does need to be rewritten.

Worse still is what I call the *serial-rewrite* organization. Years ago, I saw this occur in a small but thriving organization that had difficulty retaining developers. Each year a new entrant was recruited and, with depressing regularity, would announce that all of the code would have to be rewritten. No extra features, just new code. The management seemed to have little choice but to accede to the latest demand. The rewrite would commence and at the end of the year, as the code was nearing completion, the developer would depart for pastures new. You can see the cycle as the same thing then happened again and again.

At other times, a developer may make a strong case for a rewrite after spotting an opportunity to work on a new or emerging technology, such as microservices. There may in fact be no business benefit other than the developer getting that skill set on their resume. On the other hand, if the code has been written as a suite of features, it is much less likely that a new developer would be able to make a strong business and technical case for dumping all the code and starting again. The entire staff of stakeholders may well have an investment in the existing features and their interactions with the business workflows. It is knowledge of the latter that can inform stakeholders of the risks and possible benefits of large rewrites of existing code.

Some Takeaways

Learning is the key to PL/SQL development career longevity. Just as every journey begins with a single step, a motivation to learn can become a daily commitment. Indeed, the attainment of expertise in a language such as PL/SQL can be achieved over a relatively short period of time.

Rather than struggling to rapidly acquire fluency, it may be more achievable to get a basic grounding in the language and then try to learn one new thing each day. My own PL/SQL story started more than 10 years ago when I was on contract to a financial services organization. I was asked to edit some stored procedure code for Microsoft SQL Server. It seemed a bit daunting at first, but I gained confidence as I started to get used to the tools and the environment. After a few days, I was struck by my new-found ability to at least do basic things with the language.

Fast-forward a few years and my first PL/SQL project proper came along. I had the advantage of working in parallel on another subproject, so I could incrementally implement the PL/SQL code while doing the main coding in C#. The project was structured so that the database heavy lifting took place in PL/SQL, which was carefully orchestrated from C#. The examples in this book follow a similar approach using PL/SQL and Java. By "database heavy lifting," I mean database-centric actions, such as merging tables.

The incremental approach to the PL/SQL work gave me the idea for this book. By breaking the coding up into testable chunks, it was possible to learn the language at the same time. Adding the PL/SQL chunks together during integration then provided the idea of a feature-driven method. Features can be written to be resilient if a scale of resilience is created.

The scale of resilience provides a process template and the simple deliverables help in avoiding common antipatterns. Examples of the latter include:

- Excessively large code blocks
- Weak error/exception management
- Overly complex code
- Lack of testing

By following the scale of resilience, the team is reminded of the need to deliver the required artifacts, such as unit tests, modular code, simplicity, etc. As you saw in Part III, the scale of resilience enables you to step back from the code and look at it from a macroscopic perspective.

There will be days when there doesn't appear to be any time for learning. It is crucial to also try to learn on these days. This way, your language skills will grow. It's similar to learning a spoken language in which a basic proficiency is achieved—many learners will stop at this level and not advance any further. This is also true of pretty much any discipline.

With PL/SQL, you can add to your knowledge in easy-to-digest chunks. So, rather than trying to emulate the character Neo in *The Matrix*, who was rather amusingly able to learn jiujitsu in a few seconds via a neural download, it is more practical to do your PL/SQL learning slowly and steadily.

Take notes and document your PL/SQL code, making sure to follow an established coding standard. A 200-line PL/SQL procedure that is crystal-clear to you today will, most likely, be forgotten in a few months time. Good documentation can also get you and others out of difficulties in the future. The need for documentation diminishes if your code is written in a layered fashion (see Chapters 7, 8, and 9).

Daily note taking can also be an invaluable aid when you are asked how some of your code works or why certain decisions were taken. I always work off a daily list of work items and find this useful in DevOps work.

Avoiding Egregious Antipatterns

One of the most important antipatterns to avoid is the big block of SQL shown in Figure 1-1. You saw this in Chapter 1, and while there might be a temptation to produce this type of work, it tends to be brittle and unreliable. This type of code will often come back to haunt you until such time as it is properly refactored. The problem is that you may only get one chance to write the code well. After that, it's often just one firefighting episode after another as you try to retrofit a more robust structure. If the code is in production and in wide use, then it may be too late to convince your management of the need to refactor it.

If you have a choice between a process-oriented approach and a quick outcome, then experience teaches that it's best to inform outcomes by following process. It's not uncommon for some organizations to try to reverse this in an ill-advised effort to be Agile. One of the signs of this approach is what I've come to refer as *archive-only artifacts*, which are typically long documents that are required as project deliverables but are then never referred to again unless required for internal audits.

The creation of archive-only artifacts may even take place after coding is complete, essentially taking the place of design documents. This is a process antipattern that should be avoided; it's a waste of time and it may be inimical to the growing need for resilient solutions.

For creating resilient solutions, you can use the 11-item scale of resilience list and try to ensure that your code addresses these requirements:

- Capture all errors and exceptions
- Recoverability
- Observability
- Modifiability
- Modularity
- Simplicity
- Coding conventions
- Reusability
- Repeatable testing
- Avoiding common antipatterns
- Schema evolution

This scale is, I think, preferable to referring to a 500-page coding guide that almost nobody will ever read. A sticky note can accommodate 11 items and then be stuck for reference on your monitor or on the nearest wall.

As illustrated in the worked examples of Part I, it is a better idea to refactor the PL/SQL block in Figure 1-1 into code that is more in line with the scale of resilience. Taking this path helps in avoiding the adventures described in "A Cautionary Tale" on page 11.

PL/SQL is a mature programming language with useful abstractions and constructs that can save you time and energy. Examples include procedures, functions, triggers, cursors, exception handling, and so on. These features can help in writing robust, understandable code.

Docker: A Technology to Learn Oracle Database

The examples from Chapter 2 onward are all based on an installed Oracle Database instance in a Docker container. Docker is a great means of learning both PL/SQL coding and Oracle Database technology. If, when getting started, you happen to dead-lock your database instance, then you don't have to explain yourself to an irate database administrator. It's simply a matter of stopping and restarting the container. Of course, as you get more experienced with fixing issues, you'll find superior ways to solve or (better yet) avoid these kinds of problems.

Container technology is also mainstream technology. For this reason, learning it is a good investment for any technical person. Gone are the days where you absolutely need a corporate instance of Oracle Database, at least for learning PL/SQL and resilient solution development. The simple Docker-based development workflow introduced in "Recap of the Basic Docker Workflow" on page 42 is a good place to get started.

Another important area of focus is the development tooling, such as SQL Developer, which is described in detail in "Running SQL Developer" on page 43. Your productivity will improve as you learn more about such tools and their interaction with your environment. SQL Developer also contains features that assist in the area of schema evolution. One example is the model visualization described in "Revisiting the Schema with Reference to the Model" on page 221.

Errors as Teachers and Reading Code

The first rule of chess is to never underestimate your opponent! This also applies to fixing coding errors, some of which can be formidable opponents. Not underestimating your own abilities is also an important attribute. It's a good idea to try to take such (error) opponents on and aim to fix the code issue just as if it were a small project. Don't get impatient. The harder the problem is, the more you will learn. Don't be put off if it seems overly difficult. Each problem you fix will help you in your future work. Remember that when the error is fixed, it may be a good idea to create a test to verify the fix both now and into the future.

Learning to fluently read other people's code is yet another key skill. One powerful use of this technique is when you opt to reuse existing code. By understanding such code, you are then saved the effort of having to write it from scratch. It also helps you in adopting in-house coding conventions.

Legacy Code and the Scale of Resilience

Existing PL/SQL code can be put under the scale of resilience microscope, as you saw in Chapter 4. If no exception management exists in the legacy code, it can be carefully added. The same applies for recoverability and the other areas that contribute to resilience, including observability, modifiability, test code, logging, and so on.

Continuous integration setups for PL/SQL code can incorporate command-line calls to run unit tests. The command-line invocation of unit tests applies in this case to the use of utPLSQL test code and has the merit of allowing the integration of PL/SQL code testing into pipelines based on Jenkins or similar products. This way, PL/SQL code gets tested automatically just like artifacts written in any other programming language, such as Java or C#.

PL/SQL and High-Level Language Integration

PL/SQL code lends itself to a number of invocation mechanisms. In Chapter 5, you saw the invocation of PL/SQL from within SQL Developer and also from within Java code.

Java code invocation necessarily involves translation from the Java virtual machine (JVM) domain into the Oracle domain and vice versa. This can have a significant performance overhead. It's worth bearing this in mind if performance is extremely important for your use case. One example of this might be a complex data aggregation job that ends up taking many hours to complete when run from Java. It is not unknown for nightly batch jobs written in this way to run into the next day's operations, which can be inconvenient. An equivalent PL/SQL implementation *might* have a much improved performance. The best advice is to try it out and see which works best for your use case.

In the example in Chapters 8 and 9, I use a very thin Java layer calling into a very thin PL/SQL invoker. This structure may also help to make it clear where issues occur.

Features as Coarse-Grained Placeholders

Resilient solutions are driven by clearly defined features. As shown in Figure 8-1, features are coarse-grained software elements that achieve useful work by orchestrating an invoker in conjunction with one or more helpers. An important aspect of resilience is the need for careful refinement of the helper code.

When you look at a multifeature, resilient solution, you can view it as a suite of features. This feature suite can then be discussed with nondeveloper stakeholders. In other words, each feature and its associated helpers can be discussed, used, modified, and tested in isolation.

An example of a helper change might be where the helper code calculates the tax due for a sale in a given state or country. Adding a new state to the helper should amount to little more than an additional case statement clause or an extra if statement clause. The new code can then be verified with an additional utPLSQL test case. This approach isolates the effect of adding the new code to no more than a small, localized modification to an existing helper.

Summary

We've covered a lot of ground together in the book. I hope that the various elements of PL/SQL, Oracle Database, SQL Developer, and Docker are now seen more as inter-related tools than as complex islands of technology. I wish you the very best in your resilient solution development journey.

Troubleshooting a Native Oracle Installation

This appendix is included to assist readers who have a native Oracle Database installation rather than one installed as a Docker container.

As I began to write the book, I opted for a native installation of Oracle Database on Windows 10. After a while, I had the usual Windows updates applied to the machine. The result was that the Oracle installation started to exhibit errors. So, rather than do battle with Windows, I preferred to move over to a more forgiving environment. This was the reason for hosting the Oracle Database in a Docker container.

I realize not all readers will have the luxury of such an installation and they may have to use a native approach. I hope the following content is of some assistance.

Installation Procedure

As you may be using different platforms, it's probably best to use some of the web-based resources for installing Oracle, such as Oracle Tutorial (*https://oreil.ly/V3ZBi*) or Oracle-Base (*https://oracle-base.com*).

We'll start using the installation shortly. First, let's briefly go over some important Oracle terminology.

Container Versus Pluggable Databases

The notions of container and pluggable databases are very important in coming to grips with Oracle Database technology. A container database is what is called the *ROOT* container. A pluggable database is stored within the container database. A container database can contain one or more pluggable databases.

Let's start up the mighty SQL Developer product and you should see something like Figure A-1, which illustrates a pluggable database called *XEPDB1*. The *XEPDB1* object is indicated by an arrow and it is one of the sample databases that comes with the Oracle Database Express Edition (XE) installation. This saves us the effort of creating and installing our own database and as it's provided by Oracle, it allows us to see how these database products can be set up and used.

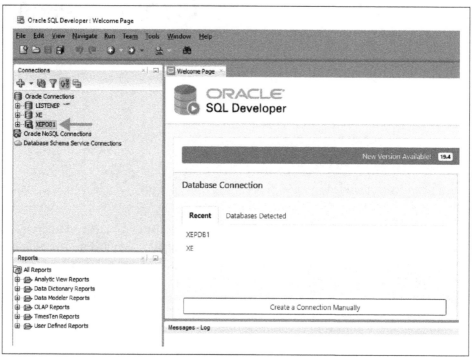

Figure A-1. A pluggable database

Let's now look inside *XEPDB1* by clicking the plus sign to the left of the *XEPDB1* item. This expands the pluggable database and allows us to look at its contents. If all is well with your installation, you should see something similar to Figure A-2. We have a list of elements, starting with Tables (Filtered), Views, Indexes, and so on, all the way down to Public Synonyms. In this book, we'll mostly be looking at the contents of Tables and Procedures. But feel free to have a poke around the other elements as we learn more and more about Oracle Database technology.

Figure A-2. The main structure of the XEPDB1 pluggable database

Database views are an incredibly powerful feature. A view provides an aggregated set of data that can come from a variety of database sources. Views can be used to visualize data that excludes content that might be considered privileged.

An example of such security is where data is built up into a view using a range of tables, such as from HR. In the case of HR, there may be quite sensitive information, such as salary or other financial data. The use of views allows you to extract non-sensitive data and ignore the sensitive content. In other words, when the view is built, any sensitive data is just ignored and is not available to anyone looking at the view.

The emphasis in this book is specifically on PL/SQL. So, the fine details of database design won't be looked at in so much detail. Let's now have a quick look at the tables in the *XEPDB1* database. To do this, click the plus sign to the left of Tables (Filtered) and you'll see the constituent tables in Figure A-3.

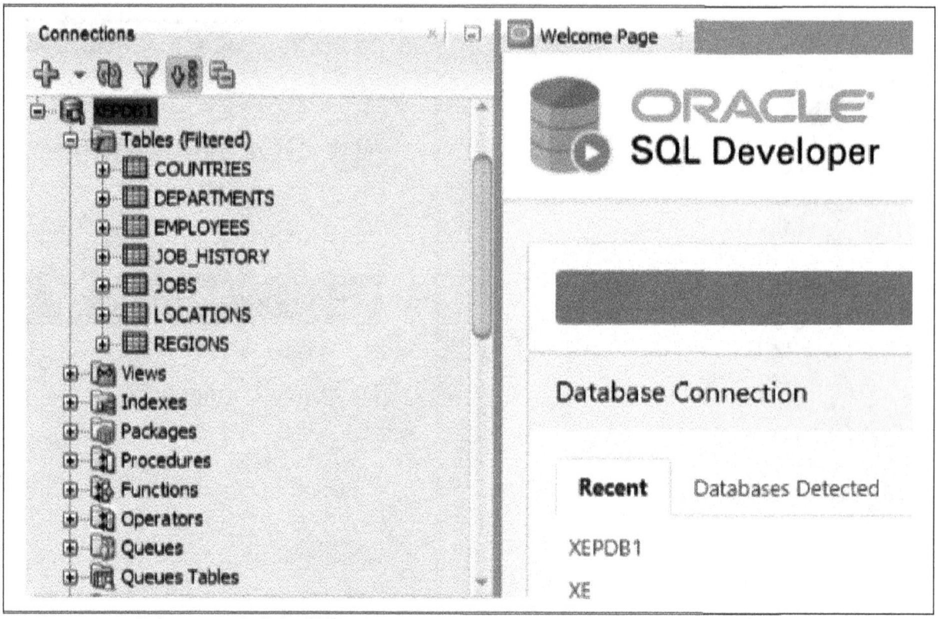

Figure A-3. The tables in XEPDB1

Notice in Figure A-3, we have a total of seven tables in the schema, namely:

- COUNTRIES
- DEPARTMENTS
- EMPLOYEES
- JOB_HISTORY
- JOBS
- LOCATIONS
- REGIONS

Let's have a look at these tables.

Table Structure

To view the structure of a table, we first need a connection to the pluggable database. The previous section more or less assumes that your setup is operational. Let's look a little deeper to make sure it's working correctly.

Is the Oracle Service Running?

Just in case you have problems connecting to your database, let's make sure that the OracleServiceXE service is running. If the service is not running, you'll probably see an Error dialog pop up when you attempt to expand the *XEPDB1* control. To fix this problem on Windows 10, we need to look at the Services menu. Click Start and then type **services**, and this will load the Services application. Scroll down to the Oracle section and look for a service called OracleServiceXE, as shown in Figure A-4.

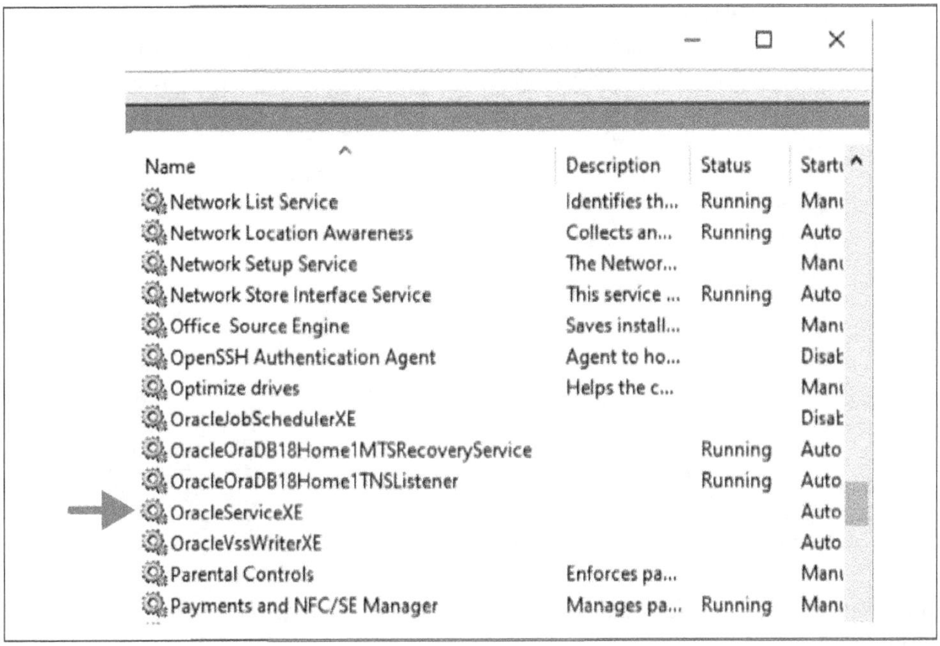

Figure A-4. The OracleServiceXE service

The service status in Figure A-4 is blank, which means that OracleServiceXE isn't running. This is easily fixed: right-click the service name (OracleServiceXE) and then click the Start option, as shown in Figure A-5.

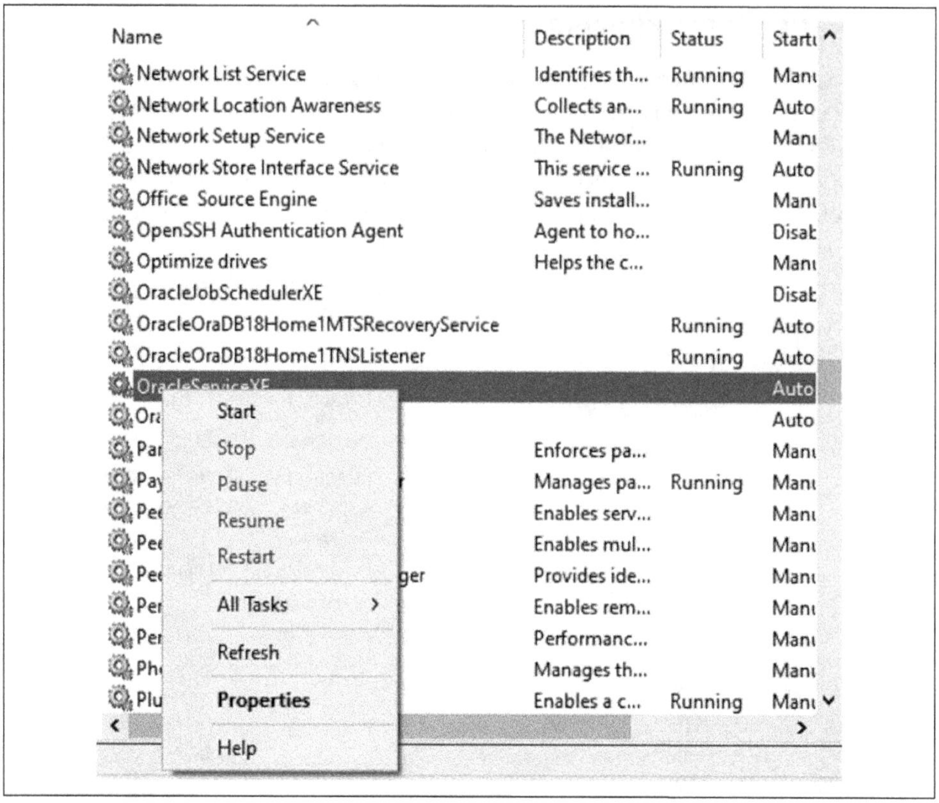

Name	Description	Status	Startu ^
Network List Service	Identifies th...	Running	Manu
Network Location Awareness	Collects an...	Running	Auto
Network Setup Service	The Networ...		Manu
Network Store Interface Service	This service ...	Running	Auto
Office Source Engine	Saves install...		Manu
OpenSSH Authentication Agent	Agent to ho...		Disab
Optimize drives	Helps the c...		Manu
OracleJobSchedulerXE			Disab
OracleOraDB18Home1MTSRecoveryService		Running	Auto
OracleOraDB18Home1TNSListener		Running	Auto
OracleServiceXE			Auto

Or			Auto
Par	Start	Enforces pa...	Manu
Pay	Stop	Manages pa... Running	Manu
Pee	Pause	Enables serv...	Manu
Pee	Resume	Enables mul...	Manu
Pee	Restart	Provides ide...	Manu
Per	All Tasks >	Enables rem...	Manu
Per	Refresh	Performanc...	Manu
Phe		Manages th...	Manu
Plu	Properties	Enables a c... Running	Manu ∨
	Help		

Figure A-5. Starting the OracleServiceXE service

If the service is successfully started, the status should change to reflect that, as shown in Figure A-6.

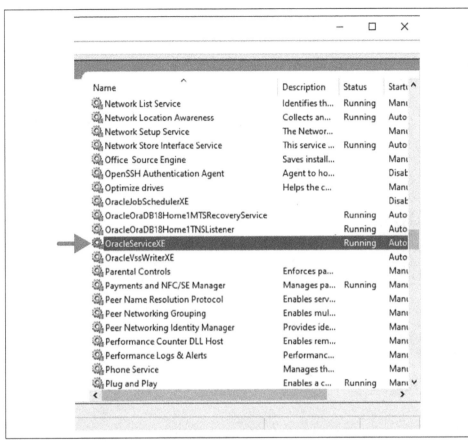

Figure A-6. The OracleServiceXE service is now running

At this point, the attempt to connect to *XEPDB1* from SQL Developer should work as described back in Figure A-1: right-click the required database, in this case *XEPDB1*, and you'll see the drop-down menu where the topmost option is Connect, and so on. At this point, you should see a SQL Developer session, as shown in Figure A-7.

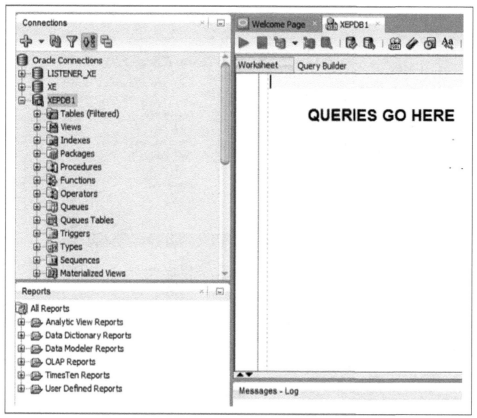

Figure A-7. At last, we're ready to do some work on the database

Let's leave it there for the native setup of the database and SQL Developer.

Additional Options for Oracle Database Logging

This appendix includes some logging alternatives available in Oracle Database.

The sys.dbms_system.ksdwrt Procedure

Developers often use the old but reliable `sys.dbms_system.ksdwrt` procedure to write to trace files, alert logs, or both. This procedure has been widely used, but unfortunately, it is not documented and even has a wrapped declaration:

```
sys.dbms_system.ksdwrt(
    dest in binary_integer,
    tst  in varchar2)
```

dest is one of the following:

- Write to trace file
- Write to alert log
- Write to both

The dbms_adr and dbms_adr_app Packages

Using the `dbms_adr` and `dbms_adr_app` packages is another option. These packages contain procedures for creating alert messages and incidents in the Automatic Diagnostic Repository (ADR); note that *alert.log* is a part of ADR. Although these procedures are not documented, we can still read their declaration section with a short description in the package specification. Some of the procedures include `write_trace`, `write_log`, and `create_incident`.

The Error Stack

Finally, documented trace events can be used to dump an error stack of the current process, which can provide valuable information for debugging. A trace event is a diagnostic feature that allows you to gather additional information about the behavior of your code at runtime. To dump the error stack, you can execute the following command:

```
execute immediate q'[
ALTER SESSION SET EVENTS 'immediate trace name errorstack level 3']';
```

Alternatively, if you only need to write a short message to the trace log, you can execute the following command:

```
execute immediate q'[
alter session set events 'immediate trace(
"Something is wrong here...")']';
```

To learn more, we can run oradebug doc in sqlplus as a sys user; for example, ora debug doc event action errorstack. OraSQL (*https://oreil.ly/-ZuMo*) has more details.

Index

D

data cleaning features, 151

data consolidation features, 151

data extraction features, 151

data modification procedure, 92

data protection, 4

data reconciliation features, 152

data types

  invoice column types, 192

  showing for table columns in SQL Developer, 57

data-centric workflows (complex), avoiding use of high-level languages directly to orchestrate, 9

database constraints (see constraints)

database jobs, running PL/SQL as (see jobs)

database logic, attempting to implement in application development languages, 7

database schemas (see schemas)

database scripts, version control for, 73

databases

  container versus pluggable, 261

  database version–specific features, use by high-level languages, 10

  isolation in development environment, 28

  metadata provided by Java call of PL/SQL, 144

  mixing high-level languages with complex database operations, 8

  recreation from scratch, 73

  runtime system, taking care of, 90

  separation from Java code, 143

dbms_adr and dbms_adr_app packages, 269

DBMS_APPLICATION_INFO package, SET_SESSION_LONGOPS, 226

DBMS_OUTPUT, 70, 201

DBMS_OUTPUT.PUT_LINE, 70, 77, 202

DBMS_UTILITY package, FORMAT_CALL_STACK function, 159

DB_USERNAME and DB_PASSWORD, 139

declarative programming, 90

  scalable PL/SQL and declarative mechanisms, 128

DECLARE statement, 16

defense in depth, 37, 73

DESCRIBE LOGGING, 85

development, 147

  (see also feature-driven PL/SQL development)

checklists, repetition, and iteration, 188

major deliverable artifacts of development process, 185

weak PL/SQL skills, 190

development environment

  isolation of database while learning, 28

  need for PL/SQL learning and development environment, 21

development pipeline, 105

development tooling, 258

DevOps

  bridging gap between platform admin, DevOps, and PL/SQL solution, 233

  shift-left, 65

directories, creating or replacing, 233

disk space requirement for Docker-based Oracle Database installation, 32

divide and conquer strategy, 88

Docker

  CLI use, alternatives to, 50-53

    listing containers with Docker Desktop, 52

    Portainer, 50

  getting started with, 29-35

    downloading and installing Docker, 29

  gotchas, 49

    case sensitivity, 49

    impact on Docker of Windows updates, 50

    patience with Docker container starts, 49

  great means of learning PL/SQL and Oracle Database technology, 258

  installation of utPLSQL on containerized Oracle Database, 106

  key commands to manage Docker container, 129

  opening bash shell in container, 234

  Oracle Database installation based on, 27

  recap on basic workflow, 42-43

docker container ls -a command, 29

docker login container-registry command, 31

docker logs command, 33

docker pull command, 31

docker run command, 32, 34

  docker run -d -p, 50

docker start command, 34

docker stop command, 34

docker volume create portainer_data command, 50

About the Author

Stephen B. Morris (*https://oreil.ly/stephen-morris*) has been writing code professionally since the early '90s. During this time, he has seen the programming model move from monolithic applications all the way to the web and smartphone era. Much has changed during this time. Back in the '90s, there were all kinds of discussions/wars about which programming language was the best. Some thought that C was the best language, while others favored the emerging C++. More forward-looking people figured that Java was going to be the language to end all languages.

Stephen's early technology efforts were in factory automation and process control. Leaning toward manufacturing, these technologies were typically proprietary and specialized, but they were very effective in that domain. While this was an interesting area that subsequently moved toward robotics, the part of the world he lived in moved away from manufacturing and into a service-centric model. So, he moved into the enterprise application space before it was known as that! In the early '90s, this was typically shrink-wrapped application software or proprietary point solutions. Languages at the time ranged from proprietary domain-specific languages (DSLs) to Pascal to C.

Then, the web came along and most of the arguments about the best language began to look a bit quaint. Suddenly, the frontend user interface took center stage and even now, in 2023, there are proponents of JavaScript as the principal enterprise application development language. In an echo of the language wars of the '90s, Python was even considered to be the natural replacement for all previous programming languages.

During this time, there were two inescapable constants: end users and data requirements. Users have increasingly demanded rich, responsive frontends and safe data storage. For this reason, programmers have tended to be divided into two camps: frontend and backend. Stephen has generally been one of the latter, with a smattering of experiences as the former.

Stephen's technology journey has helped inform his writing. His first book was on the area of automated network management. Following that, he moved around various industries including the following as a consultant/contractor:

- Telecommunications
- Financial systems
- Web services
- Audio identification
- Vehicle management systems
- Aircraft software
- International insurance systems
- National insurance systems
- Vehicle leasing
- Medical examination systems

- Single sign-on
- Financial batch systems
- Security for government systems

Stephen has used a wide range of platforms and languages. With the proliferation of web-based technologies, frameworks have been added to the mix, for example, the Spring Framework. Even in 2023, programmers around the world wrestle with this and other frameworks as they go about their daily work.

There is still a demand for integration specialists, the area in which Stephen now tends to work.

Colophon

The animal on the cover of *Resilient Oracle PL/SQL* is a Wallich's owl moth (*Brahmaea wallichii*). It is named after Nathaniel Wallich, a Danish botanist who helped found the Indian Museum of Kolkata in the 19th century by donating specimens from his personal collection. Wallich's owl moth can be found in the north of India, as well as in Nepal, Bhutan, Myanmar, China, Taiwan, and Japan.

Wallich's owl moth has distinguishable eye spots on its front wings that mimic owls, as well as a bold pattern of black and brown stripes. It is one of the largest moths with an average wingspan of 3.5–6.25 inches.

The owl moth feeds on the nectar of plants like lilacs that it can find in the temperate and tropical forests it inhabits. During the day, when they are resting, Wallich's owl moths will lie on the ground or against tree trunks with their characteristic wings stretched out. If disturbed, the moth will shake fiercely rather than fly directly away.

Many of the animals on O'Reilly covers are endangered; all of them are important to the world.

The cover illustration is by Karen Montgomery, based on a black and white engraving from *Histoire Naturelle*. The cover fonts are Gilroy Semibold and Guardian Sans. The text font is Adobe Minion Pro; the heading font is Adobe Myriad Condensed; and the code font is Dalton Maag's Ubuntu Mono.

Printed in the USA
CPSIA information can be obtained
at www.ICGtesting.com
JSHW051652201123
52414JS00010B/86